Infantry

Infantry

A Global History

Jeremy Black

Pen & Sword
MILITARY

First published in Great Britain in 2025 by
Pen & Sword Military
An imprint of
Pen & Sword Books Ltd
Yorkshire – Philadelphia

ISBN 978 1 39905 047 0

A CIP catalogue record for this book is available from the British Library.

Typeset by Mac Style
Printed in the UK by CPI Group (UK) Ltd, Croydon, CR0 4YY.

FSC www.fsc.org
MIX
Paper | Supporting responsible forestry
FSC® C013604

The Publisher's authorised representative in the EU for product safety is Authorised Rep Compliance Ltd., Ground Floor, 71 Lower Baggot Street, Dublin D02 P593, Ireland.
www.arccompliance.com

For a complete list of Pen & Sword titles please contact

PEN & SWORD BOOKS LIMITED
47 Church Street, Barnsley, South Yorkshire, S70 2AS, England
E-mail: enquiries@pen-and-sword.co.uk
Website: www.pen-and-sword.co.uk
or
PEN AND SWORD BOOKS
1950 Lawrence Road, Havertown, PA 19083, USA
E-mail: uspen-and-sword@casematepublishers.com
Website: www.penandswordbooks.com

Contents

Preface

'The brigade moved on across the open field for more than half a mile, receiving, as it came in range, fire of shell, grape, canister and musketry, which rapidly thinned its ranks; still pushed on until the first line of the enemy, strongly posted behind a stone wall, was broken and driven from its position.... By this time the troops on our right and left were broken and driven back, and the brigade exposed to a severe musketry fire from the front and both flanks and an enfilading artillery fire from the rocky hill some distance to the right. No supports coming up, the position was untenable, and we were compelled to retire, leaving more than two-thirds of our bravest and best killed or wounded on the field.'

Colonel William Aylett, Pickett's Charge, subsequently totemic but unsuccessful Confederate assault during battle of Gettysburg, American Civil War, 1863.[1]

'In the forest lay the remaining parts of Infantry Regiment Number Thirty-Four, which had attacked in the first gray morning light and was now mostly demolished ... a first lieutenant with the entire back of his head missing. His field gray uniform was completely spattered with blood and was difficult even to recognise. His eyes which were encrusted with blood, were wide open and his stare looked as though he were still seeing something terrible in front of him.'

Eastern Front, the First World War, 1915, Hans Schiller, German combatant.[2]

'a group of blackshirts, a curious collection of men who looked like brigands and enjoyed looking like it. Their discipline I should say was evil. For field purpose I cannot imagine them being of much use; but I should say that they would prove admirable in a street fight.'

Underlining the problem of defining infantry, J.F.C. Fuller, former British general, reporting on an Italian force attacking Abyssinia (Ethiopia) in 1935.[3]

Before discussing often seemingly abstract issues such as capability and effectiveness, it is necessary to understand that the nature of infantry conflict was grim. This was/is true of combat as a whole, but the possibilities of care for troops and, notably, for the wounded were far lower in the past than is generally the case today. Much conflict involved skirmishes, generally close-in fighting, the consequences of which were frequently brutal and deadly. Nevertheless, battles were particularly harsh, and especially those involving densely packed formations, with troops crushed, hot, thirsty, and standing, often for a long period, on, or by, the dead or wounded. The urine, viscera and blood of the troops and their horses produced a strong smell, and the noise was terrible and incessant. And so from Antiquity to the move to more open formations, in the late nineteenth century, under the threat of casualties from improved weaponry. These formations reduced the crush, but there was still a massing of troops as in the trenches in the First World War.

Moreover, the acceptance of casualties by commanders meant that infantry service could be very hazardous. This was not only true of battles, but also of sieges and, indeed, of campaigning as a whole. A British army administrator wrote accurately of the successful French storming of the major Dutch fortress of Bergen-op-Zoom in 1747: 'It has certainly been carried on with great fury by the enemy, without regard to the loss of men.'[4] Jean Martin de La Colonie, a defender, recalled of the British successful storming (at the cost of about 1,500 killed and 4,000 wounded) under John, Duke of Marlborough, of the Schellenberg Height in Bavaria in 1704:

> 'We were all fighting hand to hand, hurling them back as they clutched at the parapet; men were slaying, or tearing at the muzzles of guns and the bayonets which pierced their entrails; crushing under their feet their own wounded comrades, and even gouging out their opponents' eyes with their nails, when the grip was so close that neither could use their weapons.'[5]

There were many other factors that made service in the infantry grim, contributing to the often-repeated British remark about the 'poor bloody infantry,' one that became axiomatic with repetition. Already hazardous when in combat, and very boring in other circumstances, including repeated drill, much infantry service took place in terrible circumstances. Disease was generally a major problem, as were the consequences of accidents and wounds, while the supply of food, clothing, boots, and equipment could be limited if not grim.

These circumstances deteriorated, as they still do, when the troops were on campaign, not least facing heat and cold. Colonel Francis Ligonier referred in April 1743 to 'the inevitable delays of a cantonment march, the excessive bad weather, and roads,' all greatly delaying the British army's march into Germany.[6] This was a background to a hard-fought victory over the French at Dettingen, a victory, however, that did not bring the anticipated successful consequences later in the campaign.

Lieutenant William Digby of the 53rd, the Shropshire Regiment of Foot, took part in the campaign that rapidly drove the Americans from Canada in 1776, leaving an account of continual difficulties, including the reflection:

> 'The idea of service to those who have not had an opportunity of seeing any, may induce them to believe the only hardship a soldier endures on a campaign is the danger attending an action; but there are many others, perhaps not so dangerous, yet in my opinion, very near as disagreeable: remaining out whole nights under rain and almost frozen with cold with very little covering perhaps without being able to light a fire, fearing the enemies discovering the post, and not knowing the moment of an attack, but always in expectation of one.'

Snakes, heavy rainfall, and cold weather were all major problems for Digby.[7]

Such a situation often contributed to poor morale, as did the repeatedly-harsh nature of discipline and the frequently arbitrary operation of conscription. At best, conscript morale was often poor. All of these factors encouraged desertion which, in turn, accentuated the harshness of discipline. This harshness was intended to be intimidatory and prophylactic, and led to such practices as the wearing of uniforms which, designed to improve unit cohesion, made desertion more difficult.

Circumstances varied in their harshness, but conditions were particularly difficult when operating in already devastated territory, as with the latter stages of the Thirty Years' War in Germany (1618–48) or when garrisons were isolated. This was true for example of the British garrison on the recently-captured Breton island of Belleisle during the Seven Years' War (1756–63):

> 'Letters from Bellisle of the 10th instant mention the great distress of the army, for want of fresh provisions and greens. A sheep sells for upwards of three pounds, and a hog for two, and these seldom to be got. Everything else in proportion. The scurvy and putrid fevers, the consequence of living many weeks on sea provisions, were beginning to prevail.'[8]

Fatigue was also a key element, the sheer hard work of being infantry, not least given the loads that had to be carried. This hard work increased when on campaign. General Sir Henry Clinton of the British army noted of the battle of Monmouth Court House in New Jersey in 1779, when it was around 98° to 100°F: 'the heat of the weather was intense, and our men already suffered severely from fatigue.' So also for his opponents under George Washington. The subsequent battle was indecisive.

At the same time, it is important to understand the degree to which individual responses varied, and such that it is appropriate to use them with great caution. For example, Captain P.L. Wright and Private J.T. Darbyshire of the Oxfordshire and Buckinghamshire Light Infantry left very different accounts, in both tone and content, of the First World War (1914–18):

> 'the condition on the ground was such as to render the chances of a successful attack exceedingly small, if not impossible, but the progress made actually was considerably greater than expected, though casualties were high.' [Wright].

> 'At 4 am we were relieved by the Woster Regt who went "over the lid." We raced like hares along the duck board to try to get away before the barrage opened, but we were caught in it and several of the fellows who had been in England with me met their end, "God rest their souls in Peace", left in the land of desolation.' [Darbyshire].[9]

The sources available for that war from ordinary soldiers, who were generally literate to a hitherto unseen extent, means that it is easier to recreate the stolid sense of duty that was so important then,[10] and, presumably, for all conflict. Nevertheless, there was still much variety. Separately, there is excellent scholarship on the degree to which the perception of battle differed, both at the time and across time.[11]

A sequel to my similar books on air power, cavalry, artillery, naval power, logistics, fortifications and insurgencies, this book has been the most difficult to write because of the range of types and activities summarised by infantry, whether noun or adjective. Indeed, while the definition may appear simple, it is less so than for these subjects, as indeed should be expected for a phenomenon found across time and space, and one, moreover, that requires discussion for earlier than when the word infantry was first used which, in English, is the sixteenth century. The relationship with youth (infant) reflects boy soldiers, too young to be cavalry, and also young enough to cope with the demands of foot soldiering.

A branch of the army that fights on foot might appear to be the obvious definition, but that raises a number of questions, not least how to address modern mechanised infantry that may take moving by vehicle to the extent of fighting from it, as with infantry support vehicles. Separately, in unit designation, there may be infantry in armour units, and tanks in infantry ones. Indeed, earlier, if the functional definition is fighting on foot, then that raises issues across the continuum centred on dragoons and mounted infantry, both of which could fight from horseback but generally dismounted to fight. As a different point, but underlining issues of nomenclature, there was the British 'infantry tank' of the Second World War, a concept, shared by France, of heavily-armoured, slow tanks designed to support infantry.

There are also the questions posed by support weaponry, notably light guns, such as the leather-bound ones of the seventeenth century, trench mortars in the First World War, shoulder-fired surface-to-air missiles in the 1970s, and rocket-propelled grenades today. All are portable artillery that can be seen as infantry or artillery, with definitions in terms of intermediate or heavy portable weapons not terribly helpful.

Nevertheless, how infantry get to the fight is less consequential than the degree to which the definition is fighting on foot, with infantry support weapons there to provide direct support to them. Furthermore, although infantry can be classed as regular, heavy, light, marine, paratroop, special forces, irregular, guerrilla, or in another way, it is the mode of combat that is important. They are all infantrymen. In addition, armour, artillery, and other troops can be deployed in an infantry role, as by Britain in Northern Ireland and America in Iraq.

Moving to another aspect of the description, a 'branch of the army' is an invitation to a definitional minefield, as it 'privileges' the regular military over irregulars and, separately, rebels. Such an approach offers a mistaken account of the past. For example, it is unclear how far the Dutch rebels against Philip 2 in the late sixteenth century should be treated as conventional opponents, and, if so, when. So also with the Confederates in the American Civil War. The current rise of anti-Western narratives also pose a challenge to this approach. Thus, India is now the world's most populous country, and it is a little difficult there to see any rejection of the idea that those who fought the British in 1857–9, in what the latter called the Indian Mutiny, were an army.

If, therefore, organised combatants can be regarded as a *de facto* army, it follows that much infantry, past, present and future, should be discussed in terms of guerrilla warfare and/or aspects of civil conflict. Thus, the rioting gangs in Haiti in early 2024 are infantry; as are the cadres of large Mexican crime forces, many of which, indeed, are heavily armed and have considerable continuity, as individual recruits and in terms of the forces as a whole. This approach would mean that much, in contrast, that is generally understood as the history of infantry should be reconceptualised, instead, as the history of a particular, albeit very important, strand of it, namely that of sovereign states; and, yet, this classification might appear far too narrow.

There is also the place of infantry in progressivist models of military change, usually at the expense of cavalry, and, more generally, with reference to developmental accounts of state formation and re-formation, and social transformation. These accounts have classically focused on European history, but can also be applied more widely.

Thus, in West Africa, the emphasis in the seventeenth century on missile weapons, bows and, later, muskets, interacted with socio-economic changes and, in particular, with the transformation of peasants into militarily effective soldiers, a development that led to the formation of mass infantry armies and to wars that lasted longer. Warfare based on earlier shock tactics had been selective in its manpower requirement, but, on the Gold Coast (coastal modern Ghana) and the Slave Coast (coastal modern Togo and Benin), the replacement of shock by missile tactics was linked to a shift from élite forces relying on individual prowess to larger units. As a reminder, however, of the variety of directions that infantry could take, all males fit to bear arms in the states of Akwamu and Denkyira were eligible for conscription, but, in Dahomey, there was an emphasis on a small standing army. Although very different in content, these military changes were related to the rise of powerful states.

An understanding of variety is necessary due to the impact of visual presentations of infantry and to the general tendency to write in terms of national styles of infantry, whether organisation, formation or capability. However, Lieutenant Gordon writing about the heavy British defeat by a defending American army at the battle of New Orleans in 1815, serves as a reminder that British formations were far from fixed as lines and squares, and that victory at Waterloo six months later did not define British infantry performance:

> 'A most destructive and murderous fire was opened on our column of round [shot], grape [shot], musquetry, rifle and buckshot along the whole course and length of their line, in front, as well as on our left flank.... The officers and men being as it were mowed down by ranks.'

Alongside the misleading tendency to treat infantry in national categories, as if fighting quality was thus determined, came the habit among professionals of disaggregating armies in terms of the characteristics of individual units, whether divisions or with smaller units. This could be in terms of longevity, geographical and social origin, experience, training, or command. Thus, writing from Gallipoli in December 1915, Lieutenant General Sir William Birdwood, who had had extensive experience in India, and was now the commander of the Australian and New Zealand Army Corps, emphasised the problem with new troops:

> 'I have only one regular division, vis the 29th which ... came out here as a most magnificent force of old soldiers from India. I fancy that about 80% of those have disappeared for one reason and another, so it now consists of a vast proportion of young soldiers. With the exception of my own [Anzac] corps, the other divisions are Territorial and New Army, and I am sorry to say that the former

> include certainly one so-called division which is, to all intents and purposes, useless.'[12]

Concerns about the Territorial Force, the British reserve force established in 1908 to absorb both the yeomanry and the (pre-war) volunteers, were more widely expressed, one officer complaining from Gallipoli:

> 'The men fight gallantly enough, but to be honest the Territorials here have not all the soldiery instinct: officers and still more NCOs are diffident in giving *orders*. They ask men to do things.'[13]

There is also the danger of questionable comparisons, and, more particularly, problematic contrasts across time. Thus, in 1985, the historian Arthur Ferrill discussed how the highly successful Macedonian leader Alexander the Great (r. 336–323 BCE), popularly regarded as the greatest general in Antiquity, could have beaten the British at Waterloo in 1815, doing better than Napoleon, an argument that was an ironic commentary on the apparent timelessness of conflict between the two periods. The infantry was seen as the major contrast, and Ferrill conceded that the Classical world lacked firearms, but he argued that the effectiveness of the latter in 1815 was not a quantum leap greater than those of the projectile weapons of the Classical period, namely arrows, javelins and slings.[14] In terms of the repeated fire that the firearms of 1815 could offer during a long day, Ferrill was inaccurate as far as the use of javelins was concerned.

Rethinking the subject has proved both a major challenge and highly stimulating. I have benefited greatly from the excellent work of others, although infantry has attracted fewer overall studies than armour or cavalry. I have also profited from the opportunities to speak in 2022–4 to the Indonesian Defence University as Visiting Professor to the Staff College, and at the Athenaeum Club in London. The comments of Florin Ardelean, Ian Beckett, Ethan Coulson-Haggins, Mark Darnley, John France, Bill Gibson, Edward Gutiérrez, Enrique Garcia Hernán, Constantin Hlihor, John Lynn, Sascha Möbius, Scott Myerly, Murray Pittock, Alexander Querengässer, Paul Rahe, Harold Raugh, Kaushik Roy, Klaus Schmider, Glenn Steppler, Mark Stevens, and Simon Trew on all or part of an earlier draft have been most helpful. They are not responsible for any errors that remain. This book is dedicated to Jim Paugh with thanks for his friendship.

Abbreviations

Add.	Additional Manuscripts
AWM	Canberra, Australian War Memorial
BL	London, British Library, Department of Manuscripts
Bod.	Oxford, Bodleian Library
CO	Colonial Office papers
CRO	County Record Office
FO	Foreign Office papers
HL	Huntington Library, San Marino, California
IO	India Office papers
LH	London, King's College Library, Liddell Hart Library
JMH	*Journal of Military History*
NAS	Edinburgh, National Archives of Scotland.
SP	State Papers

Chapter 1
Introduction

'A great camp kettle of thick chocolate revived us surprisingly, though we devoured it among dead bodies in all directions.'

Journal of Lieutenant John Le Couteur of the British 104th Foot, battle of Lundy's Lane, 1814.[1] He went on to be a post-war militia colonel. 258 men were killed out of the 6,000 troops on both sides who took part, about 1,100 men wounded, and 83 were missing.

The same year, Chippawa, also in the Anglo-American War of 1812 (1812–15), was a battle typical of many, one that can be seen in different lights. Despite their numerical superiority, and the fact that the British had abandoned their defensive position in order to mount an attack that was driven back by firepower, the Americans were unable to inflict a decisive blow. As on other occasions, it proved difficult to convert defensive successes into victorious attacks, in part due to the problems of reconfiguring formations and gaining tempo in the midst of a battle.[2] The battle of Monmouth Court House in 1779 was a larger Anglo-American clash that also led to very differing estimations of success or failure, differences that did not solely arise from national preferences. Such differences can make it difficult to assess combat effectiveness.

More generally, as a correspondent in *The Times* lately returned from Morocco where Spain was at war with native forces, noted in the issue of 20 January 1925, the response to infantry conflict is in large part set by assumptions about combat. Referring back to the First World War (1914–18), he observed:

> 'Four years of warfare in European trenches adjusted the modern mind to the idea of a united front, along which all who fought on the same side could join hands and muster in endless lines without a thought for the safety of their communications and only friends or vanquished behind them.

> In order to understand the present situation in Morocco and the events which have led up to it, it is first of all necessary to blot out this picture of an infinite trench and replace it by that of a front – if such a word is permissible in this case – consisting of a series of islets scattered over a country which may have been conquered, but have not yet been pacified. Some of these were known as base camps or positions, others were called blockhouses … the Moors were at liberty to select both the target and the moment for attacking it.'

As it also remains, the role of assumptions was very significant, whether the response was by contemporaries or subsequent, and, separately, whether it was by combatants or others. Yet even these categories (contemporary and subsequent) are far from fixed, and this helps ensure that there can be no set way to write the history of infantry. In part, there are the problems more generally inherent to history, in particular how much to emphasise the continuity of circumstances and/or the place of existing situations, and how much to stress change; as well as how best to prioritise between periods, and also between parts of the world.

There are, moreover, also the problems of aggregating experience in order to ease an overall account. In practice, there were many differences between and within the constituent parts of larger units, let alone the infantry section of armies as a whole.[3] Furthermore, these differences existed at any one time and also were shown up in events and change across particular periods.

In part, in assessing infantry, there are issues more generally common to military history, namely the respective emphasis on recruitment, capability, motivation,[4] control, and supplies, as well as the weight to be devoted to combined operations. There is also the degree of agency to give to the other side, both the challenge they pose and their actual moves. Thus, tactical success, the prime requirement from infantry units, requires the use of means of combat so as to lessen the challenge posed by opponents,[5] and indeed to disorientate them.[6] This situation is repeated at the operational level.

More specifically, there is also the issue of the widespread tendency today to treat infantry as an also-ran, the sump after the focus on units of greater manoeuvrability, from cavalry to tanks, aircraft and special forces. I have heard unsympathetic (and misleading) reference in the British army to 'bog standard infantry regiments.' Linked to this is the sense that infantry has less relevance unless the focus is on firepower (meaning missile weapons, more particularly gunpowder ones), and, therefore, that much of its history is somehow primitive. That is misleading as infantry effectiveness was not only a matter of firepower but also of the shock of assault, classically as represented by pikemen but also seen from spears to bayonets. Due, however, to the focus on firepower, spears have attracted less attention than bayonets, which reflect the degree to which it is possible to combine firepower with shock.

All of these points are factors that should be understood as implicit in discussion throughout this book, for there is only so much space for explicit discussion. These points also serve to demonstrate the conceptual and methodological significance of this study. Furthermore, it cannot be a mirror to my books on cavalry, tank and artillery warfare, because the criteria for development and, at times, discussion are not parallel. Moreover, infantry is more significant than the other three, however much that might appear to be counter-intuitive in terms of respective lethality. In part, this is because of the greater full-spectrum usage of infantry. This is the case not only in combat but also for other tasks such as the occupation of territory and the politics of the military, not least aid to the civil power. In addition, turning to the past, infantry was still important in areas and armies historically noted for their cavalry, such as those of the African *sahel*; and a parallel point will doubtless be the case in the future for infantry and other arms.

Issues of definition for infantry and over infantry warfare occurred repeatedly, and there are cultural, chronological and geographical variations in questions, discussion and answers. For example, the distinction between infantry and artillery weaponry was one frequently debated. There is no clear definition of artillery that is equally valid across time and space. Thus, alongside the traditional dividing line of calibre, weapons used by infantry, such as portable rocket launchers, recoilless rifles and small mortars, can be classed as infantry weapons, not artillery. Reporting on experiments with machine guns in 1884, Lieutenant General Sir Frederick Roberts, then Commander-in-Chief of the British Madras army, noted:

> 'The accuracy and power of a weapon which when worked by men unskilled in its use, can fire 777 shots in 2 minutes at a range of

> 1,200 yards, and obtain about the same number of hits as fifty first class shots, firing for the same time with Martini-Henri rifles, must be acknowledged by all. It seems clear, therefore, that machine guns must play an important part in future warfare... Great diversity of opinion exists as to the tactical position which should be assigned to machine guns, and this because there has been no practical experience of any value to decide the question.
>
> Personally I am not in favour of machine guns forming part of the equipment of artillery. They appear to me to be essentially an infantry weapon: there is nothing in their manipulation that requires any knowledge of artillery matters, and their fire is but a multiplicity of infantry fire.
>
> In what way machine guns can best be utilised in war can never be satisfactorily settled until some opportunity offers to try them, but I am inclined to think they are better suited for defence than offence.'[7]

Another issue is that of nomenclature, what it might imply, and how far it can help in the establishment of definitions. Thus, in Tudor England, the term used was not infantry but footmen. The problem of definition can be seen in the case of marines. They were/are properly naval infantry, but that understanding is not generally applied. Across time, water-borne vehicles have been a way for infantry to achieve tactical and operational mobility in riverine, lacustrine or coastal environments, as much as, and in some cases more effectively, than cavalry. The Vikings provided a particularly good example of such mobility.

More generally, as is only to be expected, the doctrinal definition and the formal consciousness of infantry have varied both chronologically and geographically. In particular, it is only relatively recently that there has been relevant specialised journal literature. For example, *Infantry Journal* began publication in 1904 as the *Journal of the United States Infantry Association.* There has also been a specialised book literature, albeit a minor one. For example, John English's *A Perspective on Infantry* (1981) was republished in paperback, as *On Infantry*, in 1984, and in a revised edition, co-authored with Bruce Gudmunsson, in 1994. The last was translated into Chinese.

Formal infantry training has also varied greatly, while evidence for it has also been far from consistent. In part, such training, which became more prominent in the nineteenth century, was a response to the need to adapt to new weaponry, and was also eased by the degree to which the intensity of conflict within the West diminished from 1815 and there was a stronger sense of social stability. Thus, whereas in America during the War of Independence (1775–83), there had been training on campaign, as in the winter quarters at Valley Forge in 1778–9, in 1826 a post for training infantry was established in Jefferson Barracks, Missouri, which was close to the practical frontier with areas under the control of Native Americans. This post, however, was not sustained, and, instead, that barracks became more prominent for cavalry. In 1881, a School of Application for the Infantry and Cavalry was established at Fort Leavenworth, Kansas; a School of Musketry following at Monterey in 1907; and, finally, in 1918, Fort Benning was chosen for an Infantry School of Arms.

There is also the need to consider the use of infantry in combined structures and operations. This was a longstanding practice, seen in both tactical and operational means and doctrine, and reflected accordingly in force structure and in practice across a range of activities. Thus, although foraging by troops could be conducted at a greater distance by cavalry, it was still an important obligation on infantry. Aside from providing the ability to feed the troops, such foraging also enabled them to depart from their lines of support.

Examples of combat cooperation between infantry and cavalry include the skilful use of both in Macedonian armies, tenth century Byzantine opposition to Muslim attacks,[8] and Crusader forces using infantry defence before mounting a cavalry charge when resisting Muslim horse archers.[9] The assessment of such conflict repeatedly proved (and continues to prove) the difficulty of establishing a hierarchy of cavalry versus infantry in relative proficiency, not least due to combined-arms techniques and, separately, to disagreements at the time about what happened in particular battles. In addition, there could be contrasting later verdicts about the results of individual battles as well as differences in success and failure in the case of successive battles.

So also with more recent contexts, circumstances and weaponry. Thus, in the bitter Anglo-Sikh Wars of the 1840s, both sides used combined arms, with British victories owing much to infantry actions with the bayonet, Thomas Pierce recording of the battle of Aliwal in 1846:

> 'We were now within 300 yards of the enemy's batteries which were dealing forth grape and canister without mercy. All of a sudden, they were observed to waver under our severe cannonading and the [British infantry] line giving a wild hurrah, rushed forward, drove them from their guns, which we spiked, pursued them onwards as fast as we were able. They rallied, formed square, the 16th Lancers were ordered to charge.'[10]

They broke the Sikh square, while other Sikh infantry was hit hard by fire from British horse artillery.

In 1909, commenting on the Saxon manoeuvres, part of the German forces, Sir Ian Hamilton, the British Adjutant-General, was most impressed by the co-operation of infantry, cavalry and artillery:

> 'In the earlier stages of a manoeuvre; on the march; during the reconnaissances; at the issue of orders and in the opening phases of an engagement, the co-operation thus secured is the feature which, above all others, renders the German Army so potent an instrument of war.'

However, Hamilton observed that this co-operation (so important to infantry effectiveness) broke down in the final phases of combat.[11]

In February 1945, Field Marshal Bernard Montgomery of the British army argued that close co-operation with infantry was needed for tanks to overcome German anti-tank guns: 'I cannot emphasise too strongly that victory in battle depends not on armoured action alone, but on the intimate co-operation of all arms; the tank by itself can achieve little.'[12] This was scarcely an isolated remark, but rather the doctrinal norm. Thus, in July 1944, Lieutenant General Sir Richard Connor, the commander of British 8th Corps in Normandy and a supporter of motorised infantry,[13] instructed the commander of an armoured division to 'go cautiously with your armour ... Remember what you are doing is not a rush to Paris – it is the capture of a wood by combined armour and infantry.'[14]

Infantry frequently wished not to have armoured support even when available, as it tended to draw enemy fire. Mutual sympathy could be mixed with mutual contempt in this case, not least the differing ability and freedom of both arms to move in order to enhance survivability on or away from the battlefield. Furthermore, attitudes between arms of service, or by senior commanders towards these arms, could influence the course of battle and the learned history of the arms, as in the readiness of cavalry to abandon their own infantry, or of defeated generals to prioritise saving some assets at the expense of others.

Yet the combination can also be seen in broader terms, with infantry not only part of an army structure, but also of a broader set of priorities in the military and, indeed, in civil society. This point has been made with reference to the British army in the Second World War, the topic discussed immediately above in another context. This reminds us how it is possible to address infantry from a number of contexts, a point that automatically contextualises the discussion of all individual episodes. For the Second World War, it has been argued that the limited size of the British army, which bore especially hard on the infantry, to a degree affecting the sustained even remorseless character of its usage,[15] was in part a product of a British focus on support arms that proved beneficial to overall effectiveness.[16] This can be taken further by considering the manpower involved in the British air force and navy, including in the relevant manufacturing of weapons. There was therefore pressure in the British case to use those who did not meet the standard physical criteria for service.[17] The Americans reallocated Army Specialized Training Program trainees to field service before the completion of their training, a standard letter of 19 February 1944 explaining: 'To break the enemies' defences and force their unconditional surrender, it is necessary to hit them with the full weight of America's manpower.'[18]

In contrast, the German focus in the Second World War on combat units was a product not only of poor support arms, but also of the slave labour force used to power the German economy. Moreover, the general and understandable stress on the role of the Soviet army in the defeat of Germany underplays the significance of the Anglo-American war against Germany, which was at sea and in the air as well as on the land, and also of the war on Japan; and in each case deployed far more effort than did the Soviet Union.

Recovering the history of infantry is an important task, both for that of war and for that of the military, the two of which are far from co-terminous. The essential approach here is chronological, and, within that framework, an attempt to offer geographical and functional accounts. This approach, however, can ensure a failure to dissect the very varied cultural significance of infantry, a topic that has attracted far less attention than those of cavalry and artillery. That is unfortunate, for this significance throws light on perceptions and values that were important aspects of the history of infantry and of the total history of the military.

Perceptions are to the fore in the frequently-offered dichotomy, in judging infantry, of an engagement with the future (an approach very much praised now), as opposed to the cultural and practical sway of the past. This sway was particularly pronounced prior to the more explicit and total engagement with modernisation that became pronounced from the mid-nineteenth century and is very much the case now. Thus, in the European Renaissance of the sixteenth century, warfare could be understood in Classical terms and validated accordingly. As the large-scale use of the pike, for example in the victory of Swiss pikemen over French forces at Novara (1513), apparently represented a revival, in weapon, formation and tactics, of the Macedonian *phalanx*, a key development was apparently organisational rather than technological.[19] In his frequently reprinted *Libro dell'Arte della Guerra* [*Art of War*] (1521), the Florentine thinker Niccolò Machiavelli tried to update the Roman writer Flavius Vegetius's fourth- or fifth-century *Epitoma Rei Militaris* [*On Military Matters*] by focusing on the pike and treating the handgun as similar to missile weaponry.

This approach was not surprising as close-proximity action remained the crucial nature of conflict in both battle and small war, because, for long, firearms were not sufficiently effective to clear the battlefield, although they could do considerable damage. Hand-to-hand combat and cold steel were important, but far less scholarly attention has been devoted to them than to firearms, and they are not seen in developmental terms.

In part, indeed, this relative lack of attention was, and remains, a reflection of ideas of military progressivism. These ideas were pushed to the fore, from the 1950s, and, even more, 1980s, with a widespread commitment to the concept of military revolution and the attempt therefore to define particular military revolutions. In turn, these ideas have greatly and repeatedly affected the treatment of infantry, notably influencing assumptions about best practice in combat.

Yet military progressivism does not only play a role in discussions of that topic. Progressivism can also be seen in other respects, for example in organisation and recruitment and indeed the context within which they should be viewed. Thus, military progressivism tends to emphasise state-directed regular forces and skilled service. However, as a form of labour, infantry not so much bestrides the boundary between skilled and unskilled work, as reflects the continuum that encompasses the two. Furthermore, an emphasis on soldiering as labour should ensure that, alongside the discussion of state-directed regular forces, a private role in recruiting and managing soldiers is also fully understandable.[20]

Progressivism was seen again with the emphasis on armour as opposed to infantry in much twentieth-century commentary. Arguably, the same is being repeated now with the drone, which is widely presented as the present and future of warfare, although it is also being superseded in that role with reference to Artificial Intelligence (AI).

The best form of infantry has long been discussed, including being publicly debated, although the impact of that debate can be limited. Views of the best form have been presented either in terms of transformation through the potential gained by change, the tendency from the nineteenth and, still more, twentieth century; or framed in terms of continuity; or discussed in terms of a backward-looking revival. An instance of the last was provided by Sir John Smythe's *Certain Discourses … concerning the Forms and Effects of Divers Sorts of Weapons* (1590), which focused on the retention of the longbow. Smythe's argument, that the longbow was both useful militarily and associated with true manliness, recalled wider currents of uneasiness with firearms, an uneasiness also seen in Japan, China and Mamluk Egypt. At the same time, Smythe failed to take proper account of the social changes that had reduced the willingness to provide the protracted practice essential to the successful employment of the longbow. There is a parallel with some current discussion of the benefits of reviving conscription.

In assessing infantry capability, it is important to give due weight to the difficulties of assessing success and, indeed, what happened. To take an 1813 battle that does not relate to contentious modern identity politics, as do so many, Crysler's Farm was a British victory in the War of 1812 over a larger American invading force on the Canadian frontier. Launched in miserable rain, the American attack was not coordinated, the troops became disordered, and the superior fire discipline of the British regulars powerfully contributed to the failure of the American assault. The close-range rolling volleys from the British infantry were supplemented by cannon firing shrapnel shells. After suffering heavier casualties, the Americans drew back. To the late David Chandler, the doyen of British military historians for the period, the battle established 'the superiority of British linear tactics in the open against less well-trained opponents used to forest warfare' and was 'a superb and salutary action.'[21]

In practice, however, it is dangerous to read general conclusions about military quality from individual engagements, just as it is unhelpful to explain the result of such engagements by virtue of a supposed understanding of aggregate military quality. Instead, it is necessary to give due weight to the circumstances of the day, to individual units, commanders, and terrain, and to their interaction. Crucial to this, in the case of this battle, the defence was well-balanced, with a linear position, that was also a defence in depth, faced by inadequate command, inexperienced troops and poor deployment on the part of the attackers.[22]

The quality of command at every level (including NCOs) was important to infantry capability. It was much more difficult to create or imitate efficient infantry performance than to spread weapons and tactics. Officers and NCOs had to be dedicated to their job and to put an emphasis on recruitment and training. Unit cohesion was greatly enhanced if soldiers understood that officers who might be hard drill-masters gave them the best insurance against defeat and death in combat. Commanders (and rulers) had to be careful in recruiting new officers, and giving them proper training and reproducing the proper attitude, in order to maintain organisational efficiency. These notions, in turn, were culturally conditioned.

An emphasis on shock, variously based on cultural and functional factors, does not necessarily lessen the value of firepower, especially because the latter could be used to prepare for the assault. Moreover, the issues of shock 'versus' firepower – of offensive efficiency or effectiveness in causing casualties – were not as important as a unit remaining able to act, and tractable to its commander, while receiving casualties. The real point of drill and discipline was defensive: to prepare a unit to remain intact in the face of death, regardless of casualties. Some of the standard dichotomies in the discussion of infantry, notably firepower versus shock, drill versus undrilled, and close order versus open order, set up contrasts that are overly stark. In the last, for example, the history of combined arms operations at the tactical level shows how they have worked together.

The evaluation of weapons' effectiveness can also be problematic, as in the comparison of rifles and muskets, for example during the two Anglo-American wars of 1775–1815. Rifles had greater range and accuracy, but, in judging weapons, much depended on the nature of the terrain, cover and weather, the quality of the troops involved, the quality and morale of their opposition, and the proximity of the two sides. Muskets could bear bayonets, which gave infantry an advantage over those with slower-firing rifles, as the latter did not usually have bayonets, although British Baker rifles were equipped with a sword bayonet. The degree of accuracy needed for shooting in wooded terrain depended on length of line-of-sight between trees.

In thickly-wooded terrain, where fighting was conducted at close quarters, a slow-loading rifle with a range of 200–300 yards was outclassed by a quick-loading musket whose bayonet also turned it into a pike. At close quarters, the superior accuracy of rifles could be superfluous, whereas the rate of fire could mean the difference between life and death, giving musketeers an advantage. General Anthony Wayne, who defeated the Ohio Native Americans at Fallen Timbers in 1794, claimed that the rifle and the tomahawk were unavailing when confronted by the musket-bayonet in close quarters,[23] as the bayonet was more rapid and lethal. Wayne's troops had the bayonets.

Alongside similarities, it is also pertinent to consider the very varied contexts within which infantry operated, and that affected attitudes to its use. A key element was the size of population and its nature, an element that became more significant when there was conflict with other societies able to recruit and deploy more troops. Thus, for example, until the nineteenth century in non-Western societies in North America, Amazonia, Patagonia, Australasia, the Pacific and parts of South-West Africa, all areas with limited state development, there was no specialisation of the military, and all fit adult males were expected to act as warriors. This increased the significance of disease. As the economies of these regions were also limited, mostly dependent on pastoral or shifting cultivation, they supported only relatively small populations, primitive governmental systems, and a resource base that could carry neither a large army nor what would later be termed a military-industrial complex. This context was more significant than the weaponry used, and notably so in contrast with the resources deployed by the Europeans.

The situation of contrasting forms of infantry-conflict, and the challenge to outsiders of unusual campaigning environments, encouraged a use of hybrid infantry forces that has comparisons with that of hybrid infantry-cavalry armies. Thus, in seventeenth-century Angola, an area of sustained infantry conflict, the Portuguese were effective against native opponents only in combination with African soldiers. The Portuguese troops were all organised together into a single unit, with its own command structure, while the Africans, either mercenaries, subject forces or allies, were separately organised in their own units with their own command structure. It was only at the level of the army as a whole that Portuguese officers had command, providing control for entire operations.

Alongside the standard emphasis on weaponry, it is important to focus on the means by which infantry was recruited. There were two main forms of military service, that for pay in which there was a degree of volition; and service that was compulsory, although that also could earn pay. The latter might be rewarded with money, but the cash nexus was not the main rationale explaining service. Compulsory military service was generally for the ruler of the state or his representative. Such service was therefore 'national', although that is to employ a terminology that was anachronistic for most of history, as, indeed, for related reasons, was that of mercenary.

Furthermore, service from foreign captives could be significant, and included slaves from abroad, often an important source of manpower, as well as combatants captured in war, as with Portuguese troops captured by the Moroccans in 1578 or Chinese Ming soldiers joining the Manchu victors in the 1640s. For Indians in the British army, capture led to them joining the Indian Volunteer Corps fighting for the Ottomans in the First World War and the Indian National Army fighting for the Japanese in the Second World War. The use of captives, which, historically, was particularly prominent for infantry rather than cavalry, has continued to be important since the Second World War, as with the use of Nationalist Chinese (Kuomintang) captives in the Korean War (1950–3), with such service not necessarily being unwelcome to those captured.

A separate, and more significant, form of compulsory service was that for landlords. The position of leaders within kinship networks added another element. In contrast, voluntary service for pay was of the essence of mercenary payment. However, such service has been redefined across history, and employed in rhetorical and polemical terms, in order to ensure that such service is seen as virtuous if for one's own state/country/people/lord, and very much not so if for someone else's. This construction means much in the modern world, and helps locate private military service in an ambiguous light; but the situation is far less secure in terms of the historical judgment of the past. Thus, a modern distinction of troops serving as mercenaries for pay, as with the Russian Wagner Group, rather than for reasons of patriotism or ideology, does not capture the nature of military service across most of history in large part because it rests on a social politics and ideology that is largely true for the modern world (modern understood as essentially beginning with the French Revolution), but not earlier.

Moreover, the modern stigma of fighting for a foreign ruler meant less when foreignness was not such a clear concept as in the subsequent age of nationalism that was also part of this modernity.[24] The distinction between such units and those raised by members of the social élite for the service of their sovereign was not always as clear as the use of the term mercenary might imply. Although money is generally seen as the prime nexus of mercenary activity, this ignores the extent to which commanders were frequently rewarded with land and the accompanying social status. More specifically, the fact that soldiers (and their commanders) were serving for money was not inherently incompatible with feudalism, a socio-military system that had linked the provision of military service to the receipt from the sovereign of land and other feudal rights.

The very varied cost of military labour at any given moment (as well as across time) is an aspect of modern military capability, which in large part is focused on infantry, the most numerous branch of the military and one generally less expensive than other branches. As part of the equation, there is also the very varied skill set required of infantry (and others) and the resulting costs, not only of employment but also of training.

Whether as feudal levies, militia, mercenaries or permanent armed forces, recruited voluntarily or by conscription, the social dimension of war included an assumption that soldiers and sailors would serve at the behest and under the control of their social superiors. Although there was dissatisfaction and mutinies, the soldiery were not consulted about their conditions or instructions. Morale was generally under pressure, and more so in infantry forces which were generally less glamorous and less well paid than other branches.

Yet infantry forces were still affected by the issues of personal and collective honour, comradeship, and social position within the unit, that were repeatedly significant.[25] Infantry service can therefore be approached in terms of loyalty, but there was also the experience of transferring affiliation. In part this was a matter of being captured and changing imperial master as discussed above, but mercenary units generally changed allegiance without being captured.

The attitudes of soldiers can be difficult to exhume. A collection of Napoleonic-era letters from the *Archives de l'Etat à Liège*, all written by soldiers from the Ourthe department, conquered by France in 1794, the vast majority by conscripts, shows that, alongside comradeship, alcohol and sexual freedom, the conscripts mostly perceived compulsory service as a heavy burden. Soldiers were often poorly dressed, dirty and exhausted, and felt themselves as such. As for other forces, for example the Hessians during the American War of Independence (1775–83), combat was far less common than boring guard duty. Scabies, fever and sexual diseases killed far more soldiers from the Ourthe than the wounds suffered on the battlefield, while there was both draft-dodging and desertion.[26]

The military 'politics' of infantry service was also in part an aspect of an apparently blunt attitude toward casualties, although, in practice, most commanders did not wish to squander their forces. In 1760, Captain William Fawcett of the British army, serving in Germany against the French during the Seven Years' War (1756–63), remarked:

> 'The destruction of two or three hundred poor wretches is looked upon as a mere trifle here, wherever there is any point to be carried which is thought of consequence … 500 or 1000 fine fellows in full bloom and vigour ordered to march up, to possess themselves of an eminence, an old house, or windmill, or other particular piece of ground, with a certainty of one half of them at least being at the same time, exposed to certain death, in the doing of it.'[27]

An infantry officer by background, Fawcett was to be Adjutant-General from 1781 to 1799, introducing the much-reprinted *Regulations for the*

Exercise of Riflemen and Light Infantry, and Instructions for Their Conduct in the Field (1799) and translating their Prussian counterparts.

At the same time, in part due to infantry service being a family matter, soldiers were not reduced to unthinking ciphers, and officers had to take steps to maintain morale, and therefore cohesion. The latter element was particularly important given the significance of experienced troops for ensuring military capability. Thus, despite being slaves, the Ottoman *janissaries* were able to force attention to their wishes by staging mutinies due to the location of many of them in the capital, or the main field army. So, in 1622, Shah Osman was obliged to turn back from a journey the *janissaries* believed was intended to lead to his collecting an army in order to disband them. In 1606, an expedition sent into Anatolia had been abandoned when the unpaid troops mutinied.[28]

Slave soldiers were common in the Islamic world and were also found in large numbers in sub-Saharan Africa.[29] They were far less common in the European colonies in the New World. Convict-soldiers were a form of slave, as in the case of the Russian army today.

In contrast to regulars, militias as well as other forces recruited at the outbreak of hostilities were regarded as less combat-ready, in terms of both experience and training. When tested on campaign, militia repeatedly lacked the skill of professionals. Nevertheless, despite the greater experience of mercenaries, there were important advantages to be found in using alternatives. A reliance on militia ensured larger forces as the soldiers raised from conscription were less expensive than mercenaries, and, linked to this, were less likely to transfer allegiance than mercenaries. For example, the issue of relative cost played a role in the Swedish reliance on militia from the 1540s with the men increasingly given peace-time training by the king's officers. By the 1550s, this militia had become an operational army which could defend any part of the country. Moreover, in the 1560s, it proved possible for Sweden to deploy larger forces than its rival Denmark, which, instead, relied on more expensive professionals.[30]

The political dimension was also seen in America. Thus, in the early American republic, Thomas Jefferson and the Democratic Republicans who gained power in the 1800 election rejected the Federalist idea of a professional army which they saw as authoritarian and expensive. Instead, replacing the Federalists, Jefferson, President from 1801 to 1809, limited the peacetime army establishment to 3,284 men and sought to rely on a citizen soldiery organised in the militia and supposedly committed to a republican view of America. This approach, however, caused problems when needing to turn to offensive conflicts, as against Britain in Canada during the 'War of 1812' (in fact 1812–15) and against Mexico in 1846–8. Indeed, this transition meant a heavy emphasis on the calibre of junior officers and non-commissioned officers in turning recruits and volunteers into effective soldiers, which was better achieved in 1846–8 than in the War of 1812.

Richard Rush, the Comptroller of the Treasury, was told in 1813 that of the 700 troops from which Brigadier General Alexander Smythe of Virginia formed a regiment of riflemen the previous year, 'There was not a man fit to make a Sergeant or Corporal.... And every officer ... was as ignorant, and unable to give any just instruction.'[31] In 1812, President James Madison complained about 'the fluctuating resource in the militia,' while William Henry Harrison found his command 'absolutely ignorant of every military evolution.'[32] On the whole, militia across the world were dominated by infantry (although there were exceptions) while regular forces could have a greater component of artillery and cavalry.

It would be mistaken to adopt too schematic an approach to recruitment, not least because armed forces varied greatly, not only between peace and war, but also within individual years of peace or war. With infantry, a complex interaction of opportunity and motivation, involving factors such as the reliability of pay, the season, the proximity of the harvest, and, at times, the prospect of loot encouraged recruitment or desertion, and the size of units could vary very greatly. If this situation encouraged a reliance on paid professionals, the variation in the size of armed forces could also be accentuated by their use.

There were major cultural, geographical, social and political variations in the willingness to be recruited, whether indeed as volunteers or as conscripts. In 1746, Sir Peter Warren, the Governor of Cape Breton Island, captured the previous year from France with the help of volunteers from Massachusetts, expressed his scepticism about the enthusiasm of British colonists in North America to act as regulars: 'I could not apprehend it was possible to raise two regiments in America at any rate, such is their aversion to enlist as soldiers.'[33] The situation would have been very different for militia service.

There is a strong tendency to treat the history of infantry in terms of factors specific to it, not least weaponry, as is very apparent in accounts of combat. At the same time, infantry operations and capabilities were very much affected by contexts that were not necessarily focused on combat or, indeed, particularly, on infantry. Thus, in his 1927 inaugural lecture as the Professor of Military Studies at King's College London, Sir Frederick Barton Maurice, a former Major-General, declared:

> 'History shows that great changes in the character of war are normally brought about by other forces than the power of weapons (I am here speaking of war as a whole, not of the tactics of the battlefield), for the tendency is that sooner or later an antidote is found for each new form of attack … the deadlock of trench warfare of 1915–1918 was a revolution, which changed the character of war. But the prime cause of that change was only partly weapons, it was still more numbers; and the reason why armies of millions could be maintained in the field was, I think, first the development of railways, roads, and mechanised transport of all kinds, which enabled supplies to be brought to the front in almost unlimited quantities, and secondly the progress of medical science, which has almost eliminated the danger of epidemic disease.'[34]

Separately, the variations in types of infantry ensured that conflict was as much between different forms of infantry as between infantry and other arms. Thus, as an instance of the former, Dean Mahomet, a quartermaster with the Bengal army of the British East India Company, recorded an advance from Bihar to Calcutta in 1772–3, and the response to resistance by the hill people of the passes through which the force passed:

> 'Our men, arranged in military order, fired … the greater part of them, after a feeble resistance with their bows, arrows, and swords, giving way to our superior courage and discipline, fled … prisoners … severely punished for their crimes; some having their ears and noses cut off, and others hung in gibbets.'[35]

However, this was also an external view of the 'hill people.' Furthermore, in this more general pattern, experience could be conveyed by publications, but the latter could also be misleading. They provide historians with commentary from the outside, as with the *Treatise on the Mode and Manner of Indian War* (1812) by Colonel James Smith, a Pennsylvanian frontierman who had been captured by Delaware Native Americans in 1755, and been an officer in the Pennsylvania militia during the American War of Independence. In his treatise, he summarised for the Native Americans: 'Their tactics, discipline and encampments, the various methods they practice, in order to obtain the advantage by ambush, surprising, surrounding etc. Ways and Means to prevent [them] … from obtaining the advantage.' Smith emphasised the value of tree cover when fighting Native Americans.

The role of tasking repeatedly emerged in the use of infantry and therefore in their doctrine, training, weaponry, organisation and, indeed, force structure. For example, the American military was configured, as mass militia armies, for symmetrical conflict during the Civil War (1861–5). However, thereafter, asymmetrical warfare, in the shape of field service against Native Americans, provided education neither in the manner in which firearms became more deadly in the last third of the nineteenth century, nor in the problems of handling large numbers of troops. Instead, there was then, in American military thought, more emphasis on morale and spiritual qualities, than on massive firepower support or the indirect approach, as the means to get across the killing zone provided by opposing firepower. This doctrine and practice helped cause heavy casualties for the American infantry when attacking the Germans on the Western Front in 1918.

This discussion suffers from the failure to emphasise the multiple and often heavy taskings on infantry posed by domestic policy, as in Dublin in 1789:

> 'A very melancholy affair happened last Thursday. The mob were baiting a bull in one of the streets and were ordered by the sheriff to disperse but to no purpose, and he was obliged to send for a party from the Castle Guard which unfortunately were the 64th [Regiment]. They were ill used by the mob, and the sheriff ordered them to fire over their heads, which they did, but, instead of alarming them [the mob], it had a very different effect. They swore they had only powder in their pieces and began pelting them with bricks and

> stones. The sheriff ordered a part of the party to fire which they did and killed four … we are now called the bloody 64th.'[36]

In 1763, an official had reported from Dublin: 'The Lords Justices have at the request of the Earl of Hillsborough [Wills, 1st Earl] ordered a company of foot to Lisburn for the preservation of the public peace … a mob of weavers in that town.'[37]

In many ways, indeed, infantry is the 'default' troop type, both in its use for domestic order and in all the cases where the armed forces operate *in extremis*, as in a very serious defensive situation against external or internal threats. For example, rear-area or support forces can go into combat as infantry but rarely as much else.

The French Revolution brought to the fore in the 1790s both domestic control, as by Revolutionary regulars against Royalist insurgents in the Vendée and Paris, and also the use of infantry in total warfare. Such warfare is generally associated with the French but was also seen with their opponents. In 1796, Major-General David Dundas produced a memorandum outlining the total war envisaged if the French invaded England, as was indeed planned:

> 'When an enemy lands, all the difficulties of civil government and the restraint of forms cease; every thing must give way to the supplying and strengthening the army, repelling…. the strongest and most effectual measures are necessary…. The great object must be constantly to harass, alarm and fire on an enemy, and to impede his progress till a sufficient force assembles to attack him … every inch of ground, every field may to a degree be disputed, even by inferior numbers…. The country must be driven, and every thing useful within his reach destroyed without mercy.'[38]

Like the First World War, the French Revolutionary War is an obvious subject for any book on infantry, but that also begs the broader question of what to include in such a work, and, in particular, the danger of assuming that there are clear paradigm states, situations and periods, whether for geographical areas, chronological periods, or even particular conflicts. Thus, for the late nineteenth century, it is easy to focus on the Franco-Prussian War (1870–1), on wars of European imperial conquest in Africa, and then on the conflicts of 1898–1905 that are readily recognised: the Spanish-American War, the (Second) Boer War, and the Russo-Japanese War. Yet there are also conflicts generally ignored, such as war between Bulgaria and Serbia in 1885 or Greece and Turkey in 1897. Such wars, like those in Latin America after the War of the Pacific (1879–82), are easy to neglect, as is the Third Carlist War in Spain (1873–6). In practice, however, it is not helpful to simplify the period in terms of the legacy of the Franco-Prussian War or of preparing for the First World War.

Whatever the period, in many countries there was a sense, sometimes explicit, that infantry service was less prestigious, pleasant, and well-regarded, the echoes of which continue: 'The top brass prevail over the poor bloody infantry, however,' wrote Charles Moore in 2024, referring to the Church of England mistakenly atoning financially for past involvement in the slave trade, rather than spending the money on ordinary Anglicans, poor parishes and Christian ministry.'[39] It was, and continues to be, generally argued that the 'Poor Bloody Infantry' or the 'Grunts' got worse circumstances. Marching, a core activity for foot soldiers, is hard and demanding. 'Far too good for a bloke from the line,'[40] was the line in one the First World War song, and 'If you want to find the private I know where he is. He's hanging on the old barbed wire' from anothe'. This is their history.

Chapter 2

Antiquity

In conflict on land, infantry, operating and fighting on foot, was the sole game in town for most of human history. This was because the domestication of animals that offered the alternative of cavalry, whether horses, elephants, camels or other animals, only came relatively late. Prior to that, nevertheless, there was still a range in infantry conflict, not least as a result of the continuum from individual to group activity. Both were involved in a decisive form of conflict, that with animals, a competition that arose from the drive for food, water and shelter. Humans were able to operate not only as individuals but also in groups, with the latter eased by the ability to communicate through language. This was important in conflict with other predators, in hunting megafauna, especially mastodons and mammoths, and in helping ensure that plans were formulated and implemented, and innovations spread.

Hunting long remained important in many cultures, for example those of Native Americans, providing a form of training, for hunting developed both individual and collective skills. The image of the hunter, moreover, continued to affect the perception and presentation of the warrior in many cultures and contexts. This could extend to the twentieth century, as with the 1944 report by a British Military Mission on how best to fight the Japanese:

> 'Each individual infantry soldier must be trained to be a self-reliant big game hunter imbued with a deep desire to seek out and kill his quarry.'[1]

Over the long centuries of early conflict, weapons were developed, as the properties offered by stone, wood (itself a very varied category), bone, hide, antler, obsidian, metal, clay and fire were utilised. Flint stones proved especially valuable, particularly for making axe heads; and techniques of working on and with them improved. Composite tools, notably points and blades mounted in wood or bone hafts, were very important. For example, spears and arrows were stone-tipped, providing greater penetrative power for the weight. Furthermore, throwing weapons helped not only in hunting but also for humans to overcome animals with stronger combat characteristics, including innate deadly weapons and protection, such as claws, antlers, tusks, teeth, hides and scales. Weapons served for protection against animals but also other humans, the dagger, with its ease of use as an edged weapon, proving particularly ubiquitous against both, as it has remained to the present. Weapons could also be used for butchering the carcasses of dead animals, thus increasing the value of killing them.

As human populations rose, and as rival carnivorous animals were driven to the margins, so fighting with other humans became absolutely and relatively more significant. The animal dimension, however, is still pertinent, as such behaviour was very much seen in combat. This infantry conflict witnessed weaponry that became more lethal and easier to use, including axes. The replacement, at different times across the world, of the Stone Age by successive ages of metal (Bronze then Iron), saw Stone Age weapons, such as those fashioned from flint and obsidian, gradually superseded. Metal weapons were easier to use and more mobile, notably being less heavy than flint ones. These metal weapons provide stronger penetration and weight, the key requirements for success in hand-to-hand combat. Flint weapons were sharper, but did not hold their edge with use. In 7000–5000 BCE, in both West Asia and South-East Europe, it was discovered that heating could be used to isolate, smelt and work metals found in ore-bearing deposits, a process that occurred at greatly different times across the world. In Sumer in Southern Mesopotamia (modern Iraq), in the fifth to the third millennium BCE, there were armies several thousand strong deployed by city states with the troops equipped with spears, axes and daggers, the spearmen in close-order, and lighter infantry with bows and javelins, the numerous bowmen not wearing bronze and copper helmets and armour to the extent seen with the heavy infantry.[2]

Meanwhile, as a reminder that there was not simply one trajectory of change, the domestication of horses, initially as early as 4000 BCE north of the Black Sea, was to differentiate soldiery fundamentally, by creating the possibility of cavalry and chariots, although the latter obviously only for societies that had the horse in some numbers. Horses were used for riding and also pulling chariots from about 2000 BCE.

The use of the horse also created a new challenge for infantry in the shape of how best to respond to the mobility, shock power, height and firepower that could be deployed as a result of horses and chariots. However, the emphasis should be on could, as there was no single use of cavalry and charioteers. This point remained more generally the case when discussing the relative capability of infantry and other arms. Other animals could also be used to carry soldiers for combat, notably camels and elephants.

The dependence of cavalry and chariots on environmental considerations, such as grassland and the presence of horses or other animals, ensured that relative infantry capabilities also took on a fresh environmental context. One approach to the history of infantry is that of the interaction with physical and human environments, notably the response to other arms, or, at least, the interaction with them. These, indeed, are important and will play a role in what follows.

Nevertheless, it is also necessary to remember that most infantry combat was with other infantry. This was certainly so when cavalry were absent, as in particular environments, for example the Americas until the sixteenth century. A focus on infantry versus infantry conflict is in part a matter of environmental constraints but, separately, related to the decisions, over force-structures and tactics, taken by states and commanders as they responded to circumstances. Thus, it is important to avoid deterministic accounts.

As another trajectory of the development of infantry, the establishment of states or sub-state polities provided the opportunity to group larger numbers of troops; and also, as a different task and challenge, to construct fortifications. This was the case for example with the Assyrians of modern Iraq who rose to being an important imperial power in the Middle East in the period 911–609 BCE.

The general nature of military tasking was significant for infantry, in the responses to environmental considerations and to governmental developments. Thus, throughout history, fortifications took on value when defended by infantry, and were best attacked by it. Artillery, of whatever form, could be damaging in defence and attack, but, to hold or take fortified positions, it was necessary to use infantry, a point later also relevant when assessing the capabilities of armour. In Mesopotamia, early battles were fought in taking fortifications, with exchange of archery a means to gain superiority and thus clear walls and terrain, in order to provide an opportunity to build a siege mound from which to storm the wall. This storming employed spearmen.[3]

Infantry, moreover, had a range of clear functional attractions and values. On the whole, aside from the particular costs of building chariots, it was less expensive to deploy infantry than cavalry, not least due to the costs of horses and forage; while the transition cost of the mobilisation of infantry for conflict was generally less. All of this helped in the assaults on chariot forces in the Near East and Greece in the Late Bronze Age in the twelfth century BCE;[4] although infantry, while manoeuvrable and able to operate over many terrains, moved more slowly.

These, and other, factors, however, varied greatly, notably in terms of environmental and social contexts, and were also affected by norms and ideals of masculinity and by the taskings for the military. As a result, it is necessary to adapt general accounts of change through time, to the multiplicity of contexts and contingencies that reflected and helped cause both the choice for particular infantry forms and the use of them.

This use became more specialised with the development of the sword, which was a weapon for killing men, as opposed to earlier weapons, such as the bow and the spear, which were originally employed against animals. Swords served to kill and also to proclaim status, the latter a key element in claiming and wielding command. The use of swords from the Bronze Age required proximity conflict which encouraged for protection the carrying of shields and the wearing of armour, including helmets and corselets. These were already useful against arrows, but sword conflict provided a greater need for such protection, while also potentially slowing down the pace of the conflict.

In turn, 'swords' entailed a variety of types, in large part due to an emphasis on different purposes notably stabbing or slashing. This was a point also relevant for later weapon types. In Mesopotamia, the Near East and Egypt, an initial emphasis on sickle swords for slashing was replaced by the shorter stabbing swords that were easier to use in close-combat.[5] The growing cheapness of bronze played a role as swords used more of the metal than did bronze-tipped spears. The weapons' cost of components is always a relevant factor.

Swords were valuable because they did not always require two arms, as did bows and arrows, slings, large axes, and pikes. As a result, swords, like spears and javelins, could be combined with shields, so that the infantryman wielded both an attacking and a defending weapon simultaneously. As an instance of the trade-offs involved in weaponry, and the absence of any one obvious development, larger shields offered a greater ability to deflect blows or missiles, and their weight could make them a weapon, but there was also a loss, with large shields, of mobility, manoeuvrability and the capacity to use offensive weapons simultaneously.

The multiplication of the specific advantages of a weapon, and notably so when confronted with numbers of others, meant that, to be best effective, weapons generally had to be wielded by large numbers of trained men, the training providing both individual use according to best practice, and coordination in order to produce unit results. This was especially so as combat styles developed, which was an aspect of the adaptation and application of human skills in warfare. Thus, slings, which were relatively short range, and notably so compared to the bow, were improved by sling staffs. These performed a role akin to spear throwers which, in effect, extended the throwing arm. Nevertheless, bows, which were more readily aimed than throwing spears, and the power of which benefited from the tensile strength of the bow, appear to have become more significant, as in Egypt and Mesopotamia.[6]

Numbers meant requirements to feed, water, house and equip infantry, which entailed significant burdens for states, lords, individual soldiers, and occupied areas. As such, again, it is variety that was to the fore, not least as a result of the implicit or explicit negotiation of both terms of service for the military, and relations with the rest of society. This is a situation that continues to the present. The nature of these relations, and the direction of influence, can both be a matter of considerable debate, as with Classical Greece and the deployment of *hoplites*, infantry with shields and body armour fighting close-packed and with mutual protection in *phalanxes*. This was a process seen in some contexts as an aspect of a shift from warrior groups to soldier societies fighting more organised battles.[7] The *hoplites*, with their rimmed circular shields and bronze helmets, can be found in Greece from about 700 BCE with *phalanx* formations possibly soon after, although probably not until the early fifth century. By then, the Greek emphasis was on *phalanxes*, and not on individual champions.[8] Cavalry was not good against *hoplites* as horses were unwilling to charge them. The discipline of troops in a *phalanx* provided greater value after success as it was easier to turn on opponents elsewhere on a battlefield and thus beat them, turning what might be apparent defeat in an early stage of battle into eventual victory.

The alleged relationship between this development and the political system of city states, notably Sparta, has been much discussed. The particular issue has been that of a relationship between this development and democracy, but the nature of military circumstances changed with time.[9] In addition, such a force structure and tactics appear to have been more widespread. Moreover, alongside *hoplite* close order, which, it has been argued, caused about 5 per cent losses for victors in battle and 15–20 per cent for the defeated, mainly in flight,[10] came such soldiers fighting in a more open order, as well as the use of light infantry, with the latter emphasising javelins.[11] In Sparta, the lower-status *helots* fought as light infantry, notably protecting the flanks of the *hoplites*.

The range of Greek infantry indicates the need to be wary of the idea of prototypes, paradigms, or essential models, as if building blocks for the description and analysis of infantry. Thus, there was not so much a typical engagement as a diverse range of action, with the frictions of battle pushing unpredictability to the fore.[12] So also with the extent to which there were regular forces as opposed to militia levies.

Hoplites were not so good on rough terrain, and tended not to fight there, as the difficulties of forming up and fighting there risking disordering their formations which made them vulnerable. Moreover, *hoplites* were vulnerable to flank attack, which could be limited by providing flank protection through terrain features, or by using cavalry and/or lightly armed troops to that end. Cavalry could cover retreating infantry if pursuing infantry broke ranks, and could also inflict serious damage in pursuit. As a result, there was more vulnerability on open plains, as in much of Asia, and if supporting cavalry and light infantry were defeated.

In Antiquity, the major Eurasian empires had mixed military systems, with cavalry repeatedly important, but not necessarily at the expense of infantry. Similarly, chariots not only carried archers but were also accompanied by light infantry, who, in particular, wielded spears or daggers and served to attack the crew of opposing chariots that had been stopped. These infantry, known now as chariot runners, in turn fought and were challenged by the runners of the opponents.[13] Heavy and light infantry were complementary at the tactical level, for example during a battle, while at the operational level they marched together.

The reliability of the literary and visual sources as a description of the situation can be problematic, not least due to the focus on individual conflict by warriors, so that the visual representation of *phalanxes* on vases, which were prominent in the sixth century but out of fashion from the fifth, is lacking; although, as a reminder of the range of factors that might be involved, that might be an aspect of the problems of depicting them, or even the degree to which they were not used. Related to that depiction came an emphasis on horse-borne fighters, including charioteers, and not, for example, chariot runners. The latter were the peasants of conflict. The heroic account of warriors downplays light infantry as a whole. The most famous literary source, Homer's *Iliad*, made much of individual combat in the midst of conflict involving large numbers of troops, a theme also seen for example in Icelandic and Japanese chronicles, and one that drew in part on the idea of competing gods and, therefore, in parallel, heroes.

In China, there was a stress on chariots, but in the Warring States Period (403–221 BCE), as part of a wider reaction in favour of scale, mass, disciplined infantry formations, largely armed with spears, were important as was the crossbow. So also in the early Iron Age in the Near East and Mediterranean from about 1200 BCE, where infantry in disciplined lines helped provide a stabilisation in the face of attack by cavalry, chariots or infantry. The use of spears, shields and armour were important to providing greater strength. Meanwhile, discipline provided amateurs with professionalism. Discipline also made it easier to plan for formations capable of offensive tactical manoeuvres, as well as using deeper formations better able to resist attack. In a fashion that was long to be important for cavalry, the scale of conflict helped ensure that chariots became relatively less significant than infantry. A key element was the politico-institutional development offered by the extension of state authority over the countryside and the ability, as a result, to conscript large infantry armies, with their scale offsetting the advantages offered by chariots. Moreover, the challenge from nomadic steppe people led to the construction of fortifications, including walls, the defence of which required infantry. In the field, meanwhile, the infantry, especially the light infantry, offered the possibility of swarming tactics. As such, they provided an important offensive capability.

Heavy infantry with armour, helmets and stronger weapons became a significant component on the battlefield. The heavy infantry of the Assyrians had long metal-tipped spears and shields, and wore armour; whereas the conscripts raised for campaigns lacked body armour and tended to provide firepower from archers and slingers.

The Persians lacked such heavy infantry, emphasising instead cavalry, which wreaked havoc on opposing units, and archers who broke the enemy formation as a prelude to the cavalry attack. The archers, who doubled as spearmen, would then wade in to help complete the victory. Although it has been argued that the Persian infantry was not inferior to that of the Greeks, there is no evidence to that end, and the judgment appears more a scholarly reaction to Greek triumphalism than an accurate reading from the battles fought. At Marathon (490 BCE), the Persian cavalry was absent and their archers ineffective against the armour of the advancing Greek *hoplites*. At Plataea (479 BCE), the major land battle during the second Persian invasion, the Greeks chose not to fight on cavalry terrain and, instead, drew the Persians into foothills where their cavalry was ineffective, and then defeated the lightly-armed and armoured Persian infantry.

A key instance of infantry as part of an effective combined-arms system that included a powerful infantry component was provided by the Macedonian army under Alexander the Great (r. 336–323 BCE) which conquered Egypt and South-West Asia from the Persians. This army had cavalry, and Alexander very much presented himself as a cavalry leader, but they operated alongside effective infantry, not least disciplined *phalanx* formations of pikemen with their *sarissas* (long spears). The Macedonian infantry also offered firepower, with javelin throwers, who were useful for example against Persian cavalry at the decisive battle of Gaugamela (331 BCE), and rapid-firing archers, who provided helpful covering fire, as at the successful siege of Tyre in 332 BCE.

Alexander's infantry suffered its greatest number of casualties subsequently in the battle of Hydaspes (326 BCE) when invading India, even though their opponent, Porus, was eventually defeated there. Later, in 305–303 BCE, Chandragupta Maurya's infantry was able to limit the success of the *phalanx* of Seleucus I Nicator, one of Alexander's generals, once it had crossed the River Indus. Indian infantry, deployed in linear formation and equipped with big bamboo bows and heavy swords, were quite effective, and were strengthened with chariots equipped with scythes and elephants along with *sataghnis* (dart throwers). 'Kautilya' in the *Arthashastra*, written at a variety of dates between 150 BCE and 300 CE, speaks of training the infantry.[14]

Alexander's generals set up a number of Hellenistic kingdoms as they competed after his death in 323 BCE, and dominated much of the western portion of his empire until the Roman conquest in the first century BCE. The Hellenistic armies drew on the different resource bases of the particular kingdoms, although their cores, reliant on the *phalanx* of pikemen, fought in a similar style, which was a testimony to the prestige of the legacy, as well as to its continuing value. At the same time, infantry recruitment, formations, weaponry, and tactics also varied in the Hellenistic world, with circumstances helping ensure these changes. Thus, the length of the *sarissa* became greater, which, however, to an extent limited unit, let alone individual, tactical flexibility. Changes in infantry tactics and weaponry in the same period can also be seen in Rome and, although there are issues with the availability and analysis of literary, iconographic and archaeological sources, there was again an emphasis on heavy infantry and heavy javelins.[15]

The employment of auxiliaries from conquered or allied areas was important not only in Hellenistic kingdoms but also more generally in empires and for expansionist states, such as Assyria, and later Rome, which used a range of peoples. These offered particular weapons and tactics, as, for the Assyrians, with Gurrean lightly-armed spearmen and Itu'ean archers.[16] As in part autonomous, auxiliary forces were also easier to hire, maintain and dismiss than the standing units that were the central core.

The conquering Romans had their emphasis clearly on infantry, and it was more relatively and consistently significant (as opposed to cavalry) than had been the case for Alexander. Alongside their short iron swords, which were useful for stabbing, heavy javelins, shields and body armour, it was the well-honed discipline of the Romans that was a key element in their repeated success across a wide range of environments both in frontier warfare and against rebellions.

Fighting together shoulder to shoulder provided battlefield cohesion, but other skills had to be deployed for skirmishing. The Roman infantry required a broad tactical flexibility because of the range of opponents they faced. This situation helped ensure that skirmishing requires more attention in the discussion of Roman warfare than it generally receives.

While evidence is perforce partial, it appears that Roman combat of this type still employed group dynamics through formations, however much in loose order.[17] The ability of the Roman infantry to confront challenges was eased by the diverse range of their infantry which included auxiliaries armed with differing weapons.

Invading England under Julius Caesar in 55 and 54 BCE, the disciplined Roman infantry, with its body armour, javelins, and short swords, fighting in ranks, with veterans often in reserve, was more effective than that of the British, who had little body armour and lacked effective missile power. As fighting then and in the successful invasion from 43 CE was to show, the chariots of the Britons were vulnerable to Roman archers, and their hill forts to the siegecraft made possible by the disciplined Roman infantry. Furthermore, as a demonstration of the problems posed by universal military service when in conflict with regulars, the Britons' farmer-soldiers could not afford to be soldiers all the time, and their farming made them vulnerable to devastation by the Roman regulars.

Like the Han rulers of China, the Romans believed in a mass army based on the adult males of the farming population, a citizenship that offers a 'professionalism' different to that of full-time soldiers.[18] This provided huge reserves of manpower, for example for use against Hannibal of Carthage in the Second Punic War of 218–201 BCE. These reserves made it possible for the Romans to take heavy casualties in defeat, notably when tactically outmanoeuvred and totally defeated at Cannae (216 BCE), but then to sustain the struggle. The Roman army was based on the organisation of the peoples of Italy into various citizen and allied statuses, all of which were required to serve in the Roman army. The Roman Republic proved able to mobilise large numbers of men for less money than their Mediterranean rivals, in part thanks to the use of citizen soldiers, but also due to the exploitation of Italian subjects for military service. Citizenship was the prize on discharge.[19] Maybe up to a quarter of a million Italians were in the Roman army in 31 BCE, nearly a quarter of the men of military age.

The infantry was the leading element, but the Romans won thanks to the range of factors thus summarised. For example, they defeated the Macedonians not because of the superiority of the legion over the *phalanx*, as the historian Polybius (*c.*200-*c.*118 BCE) claimed in his *Histories*, but became of better manpower, resources, willpower, organisation and tactical flexibility. Even so, the three most serious battles, Cynoscephalae (197 BCE), Magnesia (190 BCE) and Pydna (168 BCE), were all close-run. Moreover, at Heraclea (280 BCE) and Asculum (279 BCC), Pyrrhus, king of Epirus, a relative of the Macedonian royal house, had won victories over the Roman legions by utilising the *phalanx*; although at Heraclea his losses were so heavy that it became the source of the term 'Pyrrhic victory,' one that could not be afforded. The Roman infantry was also important in storming positions and in defending fortifications.

This infantry continued as the key element in the early Roman empire, an infantry of legions and auxiliaries, as with the victory at Mons Grapius, Scotland, over the Caledonians in about 83 CE. The historian Tacitus, the son-in-law of the victorious general, Agricola, wrote:

> 'Agricola then encouraged three Batavian [Dutch] and two Tungrian cohorts to fall in and come to close quarters; a method of fighting familiar to these veteran soldiers, but embarrassing to the enemy from the nature of their armour; for the enormous British swords, blunt at the point, are unfit for close grappling, and engaging in a confined space.'

Yet the accuracy of battle accounts is a matter of contention.[20]

Roman weapons and tactics were far from unchanging. Thus, the Romans had originally used swords, thrusting spears, and shields, but, for most units, javelins replaced the thrusting swords during the Republic, the javelins providing firepower. There were also changes in organisation.[21]

The height of unit deployment played a major role in affecting tactical effectiveness. In using missiles, whether stones, javelins, slingshot, arrows or shot, height gave greater range, aided aim, made it easier to fire on the rear ranks of opponents, and reduced air resistance. As far as stabbing or slashing weapons were concerned, height potentially provided much greater downward impact; while dynamism was given by the real and apparent advantages of advancing downhill with a greater speed and force obtainable for the effort expended. Conversely, those firing or advancing uphill, or defending against those attacking with the advantage of slope, were at a disadvantage in each of these respects. Yet, the vulnerability of hilltop positions was shown with their successful blockade, as with the capture of Vercingetorix's stronghold at Alesia in 52 BCE during Julius

Caesar's conquest of Gaul. Defended positions helped to fix opponents, which was a major requirement for the attacking Roman forces.

However, the Romans were far less effective against mounted archers, notably on the plains of Asia. At Carrhae (modern Harran in Turkey) in 53 BCE, the Parthian horse archers operated effectively in concert with Parthian heavy cavalry, with the Roman army crushed.

From the late second century CE, the Romans were increasingly on the defensive, a changing context for the fitness-for-purpose of force structures and tactics. Being on the defensive led to a greater focus on mobility, one in which cavalry played a more important role as it could offer a movable defence-in-depth, rather than the infantry-strong wall- and fortress-based system of linear defence. Nevertheless, infantry remained important, although the extent to which in battle the Romans maintained their traditional formation of one main battle line, with the infantry in the centre flanked by cavalry, and with a reserve in the rear, is unclear. Instead, late Roman infantry was probably deployed as a *phalanx*, which was an aspect of the system's capacity to change. That 'barbarian' armies became a greater problem may have been linked to the Roman choice of different infantry formations and tactics, and the use of a longer sword (the *spatha*).[22]

Yet, as so often with infantry, it is appropriate to employ care in explaining changes when there is scant, if any, evidence for why decisions were taken. At any rate, it is not helpful, when assessing the development or capabilities of infantry, to refer to the Roman way of war, as that changed in tactical, operational and strategic ways. Again, this point is relevant for subsequent periods including the present day.

The Western Roman empire succumbed to 'barbarian invasion' in the fifth century, while in China there was also an instability due to invaders from the steppes. In response, there was a turn to cavalry in both areas, first for defence and then, linked to this but also a development from it, as an aspect of a hybridisation of political systems and military methods. At the same time, this hybridisation did not preclude a continued use of infantry and of infantry-centric war including in particular for sieges.[23]

This was another aspect of the hybridisation so characteristic in military systems. Thus, in the Western Roman Empire, the situation before its 'fall' included a decline in the conventional method of recruitment as local landowners kept potential recruits for their own service. Instead, 'barbarian' units were employed as mercenaries while there was also a reliance on local militia organised in particular around cities. The militia, like the landowners who provided more professional forces, led to a local focus that undercut the imperial nature of regular troops, weakening both the field army and imperial consciousness. This looked toward the situation of the transition over the 'fall' of the Western Roman Empire, however defined and dated. Indeed, this was a long transition that involved the adaptation of earlier techniques by Romans and 'barbarians' alike.

Moreover, in Europe, the 'barbarians,' who were far from homogenous in their methods, relied on infantry as well as cavalry, with the Goths more reliant on infantry than the Huns who drove them westward. The Huns' emphasis on mounted archery, like that earlier of the Parthians, posed a major threat to infantry that could not take shelter in fortifications. That the situation was more cavalry-orientated in the case of China's assailants underlines the need for caution before thinking of only one pattern of development. Cavalry brought a mobility and range that could challenge the friction of distance, but also led to particular environmental and logistical issues. Northern China was closer to the steppes than Western Europe.

Alongside the emphasis on means of fighting comes the concern with organisational practices. Each were in transition in Western Europe, and clearly also more generally, but the evidence for particular elements varied.

Further, emphasising this need for caution comes the extent to which the description of ages of metal has no relevance for much of the world where, because the Iron Age did not come until much later, other substances, notably stone, wood and bone, served instead. So also with the lack of animals to provide cavalry. Both were the case with the New World, Australasia and Oceania. A different material culture meant contrasting weapons for both hand-to-hand combat and as missiles. Thus, in the Americas there could be, as in Central America, an emphasis on throwing stones, some of which were employed with slings.

As with different protective clothing, the consequences of such weaponry for specific tactics may have been less significant than shared tasking. One such was provided by the use of combat to acquire captives, for sacrifices as well as for slaves.[24] The quest for captives, however, did not prevent very violent conflict, as shown by the human remains from the period.[25] This was a violence encouraged by the use of rituals to assert a clear difference in identity, value and purpose between warriors and their opponents, one in which supernatural animal forces were channelled. There were similar elements in Australasia and Oceania, but evidence for them is relatively limited prior to recent centuries. This situation is more generally true for much of the history of infantry, and helps ensure a potentially distorting focus on particular episodes and strands.

Chapter 3

Medieval

The fifth century fall of the Western Roman Empire produced in Western Europe a geopolitical plurality, one of many independent polities, that, with only brief exceptions under Napoleon and Hitler, has lasted to the present. The most dramatic change in the aftermath was presented by the seventh century expansion of Islam. This has permanently altered the cultural space of South-West Asia and North Africa, and was fundamental for centuries to the geopolitics of much of Eurasia.

It is conventional to note the significance of Arab cavalry in Islamic expansion, not least the use of bridle and stirrup, but the role of cavalry in Arab armies in the early seventh century is not at all clear. Infantry was certainly significant in the Arab conquests, although it can be difficult to evaluate the respective importance of individual arms. Thus, the key victories over the Byzantines at Yarmuk and the Sassanian Persians at Al Qadisiya, both probably in 636, may have been in part due to the impact of the Arab archers. However, as so often for even major battles prior to the late nineteenth century, the nature of the surviving sources, including the conventions of narrative accounts,[1] are such that it is difficult to make comments about force structure or size, weapons and tactics. In explaining success and failure, it is important to look at both sides and many factors. Thus, in 750, at Kushaf in Iraq, in a major battle between Arab rivals, the outnumbered Abbasids dismounted, forming a spear wall from behind which archers fired, but, as a reminder of the range of factors involved in battle, disunity ruined the Umayyad response and the Caliph was overthrown. The importance of infantry tactics in the battle was characteristic of much early Islamic warfare which was less dominated by cavalry than generally considered. Thus, the Abbasids, who ruled much of the Middle East, specifically Iraq, from 750 to 1258, had cavalry, but also infantry.

At the same time as an instance of more general hybridisation, the Arab forces of the seventh century were, if largely infantry, mostly mounted infantry, using horses and camels to provide a mobility that their opponents perhaps generally lacked, notably the Byzantine (Eastern Roman) forces of this period. In turn, both sides increasingly turned to mounted archers, in large part in response to each other. Indeed, capabilities generally produce a response.

Yet this emphasis was far from fixed, which was not surprising as warfare is never static; and this was certainly so of the often unreasonably disparaged early-medieval period. Indeed, in the tenth century the Byzantine army saw not only the development of heavy cavalry but also of heavy infantry able to act in battle in providing and resisting shock.[2]

The following century, the expansionist Almoravids of Morocco (r. 1050s-1147) focused on infantry using curved swords and spears, both javelins and pikes. They apparently fought with a *phalanx*, flanked by cavalry. Their cavalry was both camel and horsed. The Almoravids benefited greatly from tactical flexibility. Their major defeat of Alfonso VI of Castile at Zalaca/Sagrajas in Spain in 1086 involved the Almoravid infantry using javelins and curved swords, but victory may have owed more to the envelopment possible thanks to far larger numbers.[3]

The image of medieval warfare is dominated by cavalry: the light cavalry of Inner Asia, notably the Mongols who came to prominence under Chinggis (c.1162–1227), and the feudal cavalry of Western Europe. Feudalism, a system of vassals (sworn followers) holding land in return for military service, was associated with heavy cavalry, and this remains the case in the public attitude in the West where the period is generally seen as an age of knights.

Yet now it is better appreciated among scholars that a combination, indeed hybridisation, of infantry and cavalry forces and techniques was important to force structure, capability and success, not least in addressing different physical, social and political environments and contexts.[4] In particular, infantry played a major role in European operations, and notably in amphibious operations and in sieges. A focus on the significance of these two, especially sieges which were more common than amphibious operations, increases the prominence of infantry. While cavalry might be crucial in sweeping territory, and could help blockade positions, infantry was important to the advance of siege equipment and to mounting a siege, including sustaining any blockade, not least manning lines as well as siegeworks, for which digging was intrinsic. This required significant numbers of infantry of modest social origins.[5] The need for forage in supporting a cavalry force was a factor limiting its appeal, but cavalry could seek supplies over a far wider area than infantry.

Moreover, emphasising the difficulties of classification, knights frequently dismounted to fight in battle, as did their Japanese counterparts. Thus, English victories in the Hundred Years War with France (1337–1453) involved dismounted men-at-arms as well as longbowmen.[6] This underlines the need to abandon any simple definition of infantry or cavalry, and any clear-cut distinction between the two. Moreover, at Hastings (1066), the English *thegns* (landowners) wore much the same kind of mail armour as William the Conqueror's knights, and also used spears and swords, while the *thegns* travelled on horseback. However, their tradition of fighting on foot in a densely packed 'shield-wall' was reinforced in this instance by King Harold of England's defensive position on a ridge. The 'shieldwall' held its own until it fell victim to the Norman tactics of feigned retreats and the use of archers. Ironically, given the emphasis on William's cavalry, it was possibly his more numerous archers who proved decisive by the chance event of Harold being fatally struck by an arrow, although the depiction of his being killed this way is contentious.

As another instance of the lack of a clear distinction between infantry and cavalry, mounted archers could, if necessary fight dismounted. Although far less commonly, archers who usually fought on foot could be mounted.

A standard narrative is that of cavalry dominance in Europe in the early Middle Ages followed by the rise of infantry in the later Middle Ages, notably with Scottish and Swiss pikemen, English longbowmen, Italian crossbowmen, Hussite wagon forts, and other infantry forces. There is much of value in this account, and we will return to it. However, the key point at this juncture is that infantry usage was already strong and was not only some marginal survival in environments, such as much of Scandinavia, that were largely unsuited to cavalry and where there were few horses. The Vikings were infantry who reached their targets via their longboats, although frequently stealing horses once landed. Battles between Viking rivals were often fought at sea. They were still essentially infantry battles, but fought on the decks of ships, such as the battle of

Skiklestad (1030) where King Olaf II Haraldson of Norway was killed, although others, were fought on land.

The Scandinavian military world, that of the Vikings, one that spanned from Muscovy to Greenland, was not only important but also interacted with others that had similar features, such as Anglo-Saxon England and Gaelic Ireland and Scotland. These had considerable resilience as shown in 1066, prior to Hastings, by Harold of England's defeat of an invading Norwegian army at Stamford Bridge in which, apparently, the Norwegian shieldwall was overcome by the more numerous attacking English shieldwall, with both armies armed with the same weapons: two-handed, long-shafted axes, spears, swords and shields.

In East Asia, in contrast, there was a clearer emphasis on cavalry, although that did not mean that infantry was of minor significance. Thus, in China under the Tang dynasty (618–907), alongside the reliance on cavalry, there was an important infantry most of whom used spears, with crossbows also common. Crossbows were very widely used from Han times (202 BE-220 CE) and very fine bronze locks can be found in Chinese museums. The crossbow could be an effective response against steppe cavalry. Chinese troops were increasingly equipped with armour under the Tang. Under the Northern Song (960–1127), the emphasis was more clearly on defence than had been the case with the Tang, who had expanded westwards into the steppe, and this encouraged the stress on infantry, which focused on crossbowmen as the main defence against nomadic cavalry: the Song themselves had relatively few cavalry.

Infantry were important to Song fortifications, and vice versa, not least with the latter providing killing zones for fire from archers. More generally, this was true for fortifications across the world. They were a means of providing infantry with enhanced defensive capabilities against both infantry and cavalry. This role has continued to the present, albeit with cavalry now seen in terms of vehicles.

Song China was to be overcome by the Mongol cavalry in the thirteenth century, which reflected the potential strength of steppe forces and their ability to adapt to different environments, not least by developing siege weapons and recruiting Chinese engineers and infantry. The Mongols were also successful across much of Eurasia. Furthermore, this success was repeated by other Inner Asian cavalry forces, notably the Seljuk Turks in the Near East, and those that conquered much of northern India, such as the Ghaznavids in the early eleventh century, the Ghurids in the late twelfth, and Timur in 1398. Unlike the earlier Huns and Sakas, the Ghurids were able to conquer northern India because they integrated elephants and crossbow-equipped infantry with mobile mounted archers. Timur went on to defeat decisively the Ottoman (Turkish) army at Ankara in 1402, the Ottoman infantry being finally broken after their cavalry had been beaten.

However, infantry remained part of the situation, not least in conflict over fortifications. Thus, the Mongols had to acquire an ability to take fortified cities in order to conquer southern China in the thirteenth century. Furthermore, the Inner Asian cavalry forces were not successful everywhere, the Mongols failing in India and Syria, and they did not lead necessarily to other militaries following their example. In Japan, where Mongol invasion attempts in 1274 and 1281 failed, largely due to storms at sea, these attacks appear to have triggered changes in styles of armour better suited to fighting on foot; in weapons, with swords now having a shorter, heavier blade; and in tactics, such as the use of more coordinated infantry movements. The terrain and vegetation of Southeast Asia, which was not suited to invading Mongol forces, as was shown in 1285 and 1288 by Dai Viêt victories, gave rise to light skirmishing infantry supported by elephants. Timur's army contained significant numbers of infantry and in battle these could contain the opposing centre while the cavalry enveloped the opposing army as a whole.[7] This was a classic infantry-cavalry co-operation.

There were infantry-cavalry clashes during the Crusades of the 1090s-1290s. Western forces were stronger in infantry and heavy cavalry, their opponents having both, but focusing on mounted archers who were light cavalry. The tightly-packed Western infantry provided mutual protection, but also had to be able to manoeuvre, marching in this protective fashion. The crossbow was introduced into Western armies during the second half of the eleventh century, and used in conjunction with pavises, large shields which provided protection for the crossbow men when loading. Crossbows were highly effective against the light horse archers of the Middle East during the Crusades, and in the defence of cities, especially Italian ones.[8]

The infantry developments of the later Middle Ages, both in Europe and in Japan, increasingly emphasised infantry means and solutions. In

Japan, and notably in the age of *Sengoku* (Warring States) from 1467 to 1615, a period of internal conflict, there were a series of major changes including larger armies, a greater preponderance of infantry, and alterations in weaponry, especially the spear and armour. The combination of larger armies and an emphasis on infantry was linked to a move away from the largely individualistic style of fighting hitherto followed, and, instead, toward a focus on massed formations. Spears were the key infantry weapon in Japan, paralleling the role of the pike in Western Europe. This underlines the extent to which mass formations, unit fighting and discipline were not necessarily linked to firepower, whether archery or handguns. Meanwhile, in response to spears, as earlier to arrows, body armour sought to combine flexibility with protection.

In Western Europe, infantry was reliant, as before, on both edged weapons and firearms, with each showing developments in some spheres. That does not mean that the introduction of new weapons was perforce required for success. Instead, as is normally the case, commentators, both then and later, were most interested in novelty, and inclined to focus on assessment accordingly, a process that was to be particularly prominent with the diffusion of gunpowder weaponry.

Such an approach, however, could, and can, lead to a downplaying of the continued use, indeed successful employment, of pre-existing weaponry, a pattern separately seen with fortifications and, indeed, siegecraft. 'Traditional' weapons played a role in many infantry victories, for example at Legnano in 1176 by the Italian Lombard League, its infantry benefiting from fighting from a fortified camp, against the Emperor Barbarossa (Frederick I) whose army was more cavalry-strong,[9] although that result was no indication of what would have happened in the absence of such a camp. So also with Swiss halberds and spears proving very effective against Habsburg (Austrian) knights at Morgarten in 1315 and Sempach in 1386; and with the gallowglass heavy (armoured) infantry from west Scotland wielding swords and two-handled axes in Ireland in the thirteenth century that prevailed against Norman heavy cavalry and light infantry. The wagon-camps of Eastern Europe, as used, for example, by the Hussites of Bohemia in the early fifteenth century, were also a successful defensive deployment that remained significant until the early eighteenth century when infantry firepower increased.[10] Thus, it was not necessary to adopt longbows, crossbows or pikes in order for infantry to be effective. Moreover, the greater effectiveness in Western Europe of staff weapons, notably spears, halberds and pikes, offered a wall of points providing a defence that did not depend on shields and was therefore less encumbered. Tactical and organisational changes were significant as well as technological ones.[11]

These weapons, not themselves new, did offer significant advantages. The employment of pikes had a lengthy genesis, with continuities with spears and halberds (a combined spear and battleaxe), which were employed successfully by the Swiss in the fourteenth century, by the Flemings, as at Courtrai (1302), and by the Scots, as in major triumphs over the English at Stirling (1296) and Bannockburn (1314). The halberd was shorter than the pike, but the tactics developed were initially similar, both being used as defensive weapons.

The particular value of pikemen, however, related not only to their ability to sustain a defence, but also to their potential for effective attack. Useless as an individual weapon, because it was heavy and inflexible, and could not provide all-round protection, the pike was devastating *en masse* in disciplined formations, its mass providing momentum in attack, while pike squares, whether in attack or defence, were, if prepared, not vulnerable to flank attacks; although they benefited, in avoiding envelopment, from cavalry on their flanks.

In defence, pikemen could give protection against cavalry, as the pike outreached the lance. Furthermore, while benefiting from their protective firepower, pikemen provided archers, musketeers and halberdiers with the defensive strength otherwise offered by walls or field entrenchments. Other infantry weapons were less able to do so. However, pikemen did not emerge in China, India or Persia due to the presence of large numbers of fast-moving, swarming mounted archers which were absent in Western Europe.[12] Such archers had proved destructive to the Romans at Parthian hands at Carrhae in 53 BCE, and were later a challenge to the Crusaders.

The operation of units focused on pikemen required concerted actions that rested on drill and, as with musketry, methodical training, which led to a need for trained, professional infantry that were far superior to most medieval levies. This requirement rewarded unit cohesion, and thus the professionalism linked to continuity. The major role of advancing Swiss pikemen in victories over Charles the Bold of Burgundy, a formidable opponent, at Grandson (1476) and Murten (1476), led other powers to hire (France) or emulate (several German rulers) the Swiss in establishing mobile infantry forces largely composed of pikemen. At Guinegate (1479), Maximilian, Archduke of Austria, later Emperor Maximilian I, used Flemish pikemen, their pikes copying those of the Swiss, to defeat the French. The German *landsknechte* units, strong in pikemen, defeated far larger Frisian forces in 1496 and 1498.

Meanwhile, combining infantry with firepower, on a long-established pattern, the English developed archery. Their longbowmen being infantry, however, lacked the tactical and operational flexibility of Central Asian archers who were cavalry. The longbowmen were sometimes mounted for movement on campaign, but could not fire from the saddle and, even if they rode to the battle, tended to fight on the defensive, which meant that the men-at-arms required to help protect them also fought on foot. This ensured that armies with longbowmen as their core component benefited from being attacked, a general issue with infantry forces in the period. They could not so readily force battle on their opponents unless besieging fortifications, which fixed the defenders.

Longbowmen were the key element at the expense of the Scots at Falkirk (1298) and Halidon Hill (1333), and at that of the French at Crécy (1346), Poitiers (1356), and Agincourt (1415);[13] whereas the English handled their archers very badly at Bannockburn (1314), a crucial Scottish victory. Battle accounts are frequently contradictory, but the propensity of the French to launch ill-considered and poorly-executed attacks were important to English victories. In short, poor leadership was to blame for failure, notably the French failure to cope with English tactics of fighting from strong defensive positions. Once Bertrand du Guesclin, as Constable of France in 1370–80, stopped the attacking practice, the English lost a significant advantage and were defeated at Pontvallain (1370) and Chizé (1373). However, at Nicopolis (1396), French commanders repeated the same error, rushing headlong into the attack, only to be soundly beaten by the Ottoman infantry who were in a fortified position. Hubris was/is a major feature in failure, and therefore success.

Longbowmen could keep up a continuous fire for about two minutes, according to modern re-enactors, emptying their quivers of their 25 arrows. At Crécy and, to a lesser extent, Poitiers, the arrows could penetrate most armour, especially mail armour. However, as armour improved, as it certainly had by the time of Agincourt (1415), the penetrative power was less effective. Nonetheless, a storm of arrows forced attacking men at arms to keep their visors down, and made them bunch up. This appears to have happened at Agincourt, where the main attack was launched by the French on foot. Also, as the French, fighting on foot, through heavy mud, got closer, the penetrative powers of the arrows became greater. The ability of the lightly-clad and -equipped archers to join the melee that was unfolding in front of them, may have been one of the deciding factors in that battle.

At Verneuil (1424), the well-armoured Milanese in French service, with their fully armoured horses, rode through the English but then attacked their baggage train looking for loot. The English, showing remarkable discipline, then reformed their ranks and attacked the largely Scottish force that opposed them. The archers joined in this bitter hand-to-hand fight, which eventually turned into a major victory, arrows having proved less important to victory than archers operating as light infantry. Despite the apparent inability of the longbow to penetrate plate armour, archers continued to prove a vital part of English armies, and played a critical role in the Wars of the Roses, notably in the victory of Edward IV at Towton in 1461.

The longbow had a major disadvantage in that, with a draw weight of between 81 and 185 pounds (37 and 84 kg) force, it required considerable effort to use, and thus much strength and practice; which, in effect, increased the problems and cost of that option, although much of the cost was born by the male public through making practice compulsory. This is a reminder of the need to contextualise infantry firepower rather than treating it as a magic bullet to military proficiency.

Longbowmen, like crossbowmen, had considerable accuracy and a high fire-rate. Traditionally made out of a single piece of yew wood, although there was no uniformity in wood type or arrowhead,[14] longbows were easier and cheaper to make than crossbows, and an experienced archer could fire an arrow every five seconds. At Crécy, the Genoese crossbowmen in French service were, as a result, seriously outfired while vulnerable because they were separated from their pavises (protected shields), and were shot down by the English before being scattered by ill-disciplined French cavalry.[15] But, aside from the strength and expertise required, the specifications of longbows never improved, unlike those of crossbows. The use of steel in the construction of the crossbow frame, which improved the range and velocity of crossbows, and the variety of spanning methods for loading the weapon are examples of such development and help to explain the continued popularity of crossbows.

At the same time, infantry forces could be defeated by well-led combined arms armies, as with the Flemings at Mons-en-Pevele (1304), the Scots at Dupplin Moor (1332) and Neville's Cross (1346), the English at Otterburn (1388), and the City Militia of Verona at Castagnaro (1387).

A trajectory of European/Western infantry development focused on Western Europe looks different if a broader definition of Europe is adopted, and that whether the context or content is in terms of weaponry, organisation, society or politics. Thus, in the case of Hungary, until the early fifteenth century, some of the retainers of the nobility and clergy fought on foot, as did those of petty nobles who lacked the means to buy a warhorse and proper weapons. In turn, most of the Hungarian infantry from the mid-fifteenth to early sixteenth were Bohemian mercenaries, such as Hussite refugees, many of whom had firearms.

Matthias Corvinus, king of Hungary from 1458 until 1490, and of Bohemia from 1469 to 1490, showed great interest in his infantry. According to the chronicler Antonio Bonfini in 1487, Matthias had an army of 20,000 cavalry and 8,000 infantry, the latter divided between *armati*, armed with pikes or other types of hafted weapons, *clipeati* (shield bearers), and handgunners. The percentage was increased because Matthias was fighting against the Habsburgs (against whom the Bohemians had experience), and needed to adapt to the requirements of siege warfare. The shield bearers used their pavises to cover both crossbowmen and handgunners. Considerable success was achieved against the Ottomans, but the cost of maintaining paid forces proved prohibitive, and the army broke up after the sudden death of Corvinus in 1490, aged 47, when their pay stopped.[16]

Under Louis II of Hungary (r. 1516–26), German *landsknechte* (pikemen) were also hired. While foreign mercenaries were often employed, Hungarian kings had the means to raise local infantry by a system introduced in 1397 involving one soldier for every twenty peasant tenants, although the recruitment ratio and type of soldier varied over time. Mounted soldiers alternated with infantry depending on the particular context, a decree of 1454 mentioning infantry armed with bows, shields and spears, and one of 1518 referring to infantry with handguns.[17]

In Moldovia, the cavalry could also dismount and fight on foot when needed. In Wallachia, there was a use of peasant infantry, and in 1479, in the battle of the Breadfield, as part of an Ottoman raiding force, this infantry fought, in a variation of later 'pike and shot,' with spearmen in front and archers in the rear, being defeated only with difficulty by Hungarian and Transylvanian heavy cavalry.[18]

Alongside any emphasis on infantry limitations, it is worth noting that successive polities, even empires, in the New World showed what could be achieved by infantry-based armies. The Inca of Peru, who created a far-flung empire along the Andes in the fifteenth century, used spears, bows, clubs, slings, swords and battle axes, the forces raised by conscription; with most of the troops from subject peoples, which, as with the Romans, led to much variety in fighting technique and weaponry. So also elsewhere. The New Orleans Museum holds a Central American terracotta warrior depicted wearing armour and a removable mask bearing an image to create terror, and holding an axe and a circular shield. In 1517, a Maya force beat Spaniards who landed on the Yucatán, the Maya equipped with quilted cotton armour and carrying bows, slings, stone-tipped spears, and flint or obsidian-edged swords: there was no worked iron in the Americas. In Florida, Spanish expeditions were repelled by archers in 1513 and 1528. More generally, the strong and sometimes successful resistance faced by the Spaniards in the Americas was a testimony to the vigour of native fighting techniques, and, in the absence of native horses, the strength of particular infantry traditions. So also in sub-Saharan Africa with frequently-successful opposition to the Portuguese.

The range of infantry weaponry was also to be shown in Australasia and Oceania, and unsurprisingly so as this was a very large area indeed. It was also one with a range of natural materials that could be worked. This range was linked to usage, but, in turn, the latter helped influence the weapons produced: as usual, there was a permissive relationship rather than a deterministic one. In particular, again on a normal pattern seen across contrasting environments, but presenting in different ways, there was an important distinction between the use of projectiles, such as slings and stones, and that of contact weaponry. The Hawaiians tended to use the former (although they also had spears, clubs and daggers), while the Tongans and the Māori of New Zealand made use of contact weapons, including clubs, from whalebone and jade, and adzes made from jade.

Shark teeth were also used to edge swords, spears and daggers. The Australian Aborigines used spears. Coconut fibre could be employed for armour, as on Kiribati, where it was worn by the key warriors, and thus became a way to differentiate among the troops.

These variations can be taken further to emphasise those of natural and human environments, each of which could be classified in greater detail. As a result, it is unsurprising that it is unhelpful to distinguish gunpowder from pre-gunpowder weaponry, tactics, doctrine and much else, as if there was a clear developmental process with obvious situational units and stages, and clearcut relative capabilities.

So also in the case of gunpowder weaponry, as that had a variety of characteristics, contexts and consequences, and took a while to stabilise even in part. This was true of weapons and of their usage. Handguns, developed in China, where they were differentiated from cannon by the fourteenth century, and had greater penetrative power than either longbows or crossbows. Gunpowder-driven projectiles have markedly higher velocity. Indeed, arrows are much closer to hand-thrown spears in terms of velocity than projectiles fired from handguns which were far deadlier. The Ming put a major emphasis on firearms. In Europe, handguns were definitely used from the 1370s, but were not in general use until the second half of the fifteenth century. Artillery weapons were employed in battle and siege from the fourteenth century, but, as metallurgy and black powder improved, so also did handguns. The Hussites used them, along with crossbows, halberds and flails, while, in the siege of Constantinople in 1453, they were used by both sides, notably the defending Genoese mercenaries of Giovanni Giustiniani Longo. Charles the Bold of Burgundy attempted to introduce handgunners into his all-arms forces, and the Swiss also had handgunners attached to their pike columns, although only a small percentage, as clearly seen in the illustrations of Diebold Schilling in his *Amtliche Berner Chronik* of 1483.

Handguns had deficiencies. They had a limited range and a low rate of fire, being less accurate, shorter-range and slower than bows, and were affected by bad weather as rain doused burning matches, affecting ignition, and also damped powder. Handguns were also harder to make than bows, more dangerous to use, and, as a widespread and persistent problem, required a supply of powder and shot, with both needing to be in adequate condition. There were also characteristics of firearms that interacted with a poor use that was understandable under the strain of combat. Individual soldiers might be poor shots, or unsteady in igniting the fuse, or otherwise in the firing process.

The use of the arquebus, the first effective hand-held firearm in Europe, spread from the early fifteenth century. This spread appears to have been due not to an instant acceptance of the overwhelming capability of firearms, but to the use of the arquebus in a particular niche and by a specific group: militia who guarded city walls. As in earlier periods, fortifications provided a key need for infantry. From this, the use of the arquebus spread. Rather than assuming that a shift from bows to arquebuses took place because they were more deadly weapons, cost may also have been significant. In general, the desirable specifications of weaponry rarely aligned. Thus, crossbows, which required far less training and physical strength than longbows, gained more penetrative power in the fifteenth century as a result of the development of steel bows, but these were expensive as tempered spring steel was a costly material to make and one that required much skill and needed elaborate pulleys to cock them.[19]

The arquebus was a significant technical improvement on what had gone before, as it used the matchlock firing mechanism, as opposed to the primitive methods of firing employed in early handguns. It could be effectively fired by one man, rather than two, and was more manageable and more lethal. The arquebus was also relatively easy and safe to fire, but cost more to produce in terms of money and skill, had a slow rate of fire of one round per 40 seconds, and was only really effective when used in large numbers. The arquebus only really proved its worth on the battlefield in the early sixteenth century.

We will follow that spread in the next chapter. This might appear a misleading break, and, in truth, 1500 did not mark any fundamental change in infantry development or conflict, although Spanish victories in Italy from 1503 over French heavy cavalry were significant. More generally for infantry warfare, the centuries on either side of 1500 were ones of combined-armed forces. This situation had existed ever since the distinction between firepower and contact weaponry developed, and is one that continued to be strongly the case in Europe until the start of the eighteenth century with hand-to-hand combat and cold steel both still important alongside firepower. In that context, and definitely prior to the spread of the bayonet in the late seventeenth century, it was not necessarily the novelty of individual weapons that is of note. Instead, and this was also to be true for the bayonet, new infantry weaponry, techniques and tactics worked best when they could be fitted into existing military practices and structures, and certainly so without transforming the socio-political structures.

In assessing infantry, it is important, as for the previous chapter, to note that, across much of the world, there was a low density of population. This ensured the tendency for all fit adult males to be warriors, and for conflict to be local in extent; but also favoured élites with the time to train and develop athletic strength and the wealth to acquire the best weapons. There was no static situation, but a fundamental continuity in the social context of warfare in these areas, many of which were stateless. Personal ownership of weaponry was a feature of these societies and crucial to their military character. This ownership, and the limited control wielded by tribal authorities, made the borrowing of outside techniques by such societies highly unlikely. Partly as a consequence, the West defined 'barbarians' as militarised, but individualistic; while the civilised, in contrast, were members of states created by war and in which battlefield combat and arms were centrally organised. In practice, conditions in both types of society varied greatly and also overlapped in part.

Despite the value of firm governmental control, seen notably with both Ottoman forces and the Chinese, there was no clear developmental pattern in military organisation. The tendency in Western literature is to place a progressive interpretation on the rise of the state and on what is discerned as its attempt to monopolise force and to develop a professionalised state-run military. This approach, however, fails to give sufficient weight to the vitality of other military systems and developments. In particular, there was the professionalism and adaptability of mercenaries. This was a form of military service noted for the West.[20] So also, however, for other areas, particularly with well-developed labour markets, such as north and south India, but not only there. In the expeditions against Suwār of Dhu'l-Kadr in the late 1460s and early 1470s, the Mamluk sultan Qaytbay found it difficult to get his Egyptian cavalry fief-holders to serve and, instead, hired infantry, including archers, in Syria, closer to the sphere of hostilities.[21] Mercenary service spanned, and could bring together, both infantry and cavalry, including in the same units. This is a reminder of the problems involved in treating them separately, instead of the value of complementary attention.

Although voluntary paid soldiers were the key element in Western Europe, obligatory levies played a major role in many parts of the world, including in Europe, where in Saxony in the fifteenth century every houseowner had to keep their arms in good order. As a reminder of the multiple purposes of infantry, an element that continues to the present, such levies did not necessarily provide effective forces for field armies. Instead, these levies were more important in local defence than in expeditionary warfare, and obligation could be as much owed to the local community as to the distant ruler. As today, the military activity of local forces overlapped with the maintenance of law and order. Thus, in the Ottoman empire, peasant village militias were significant in providing defence against robbers and brigands.[22]

A variant, again focused on infantry, was that of soldier colonies. In particular, much of the Chinese army was based in such positions, mostly near the frontiers. Soldier-farmers, provided by the government with seeds, animals and tools, produced food while also manning the fortified strongholds that the colonies contained, strongholds that, in turn, protected the storehouses and granaries.

However, as an aspect of the coercive control of infantry, seen most clearly with slave soldiers, this system deteriorated, in China from the fifteenth century, largely because the officers tended to take over the colonies, using the soldiers as a labour force. Thus, the military came to approximate to the landed system found more generally. This economic convergence remains an aspect of infantry service. It is a branch of the military that particularly replicates social patterns, and notably so when officers were essentially hereditary. So also in China, where much of the army was raised in the fifteenth century from a hereditary soldiery, although mercenaries became more important in China during the sixteenth, in part in response to the deterioration of the hereditary element, including large-scale desertion.

Across the world, alongside the stress on group combat and the realities of the shared experiences and interests of military professionals,[23] came the cult of the individual warrior, and the related emphasis on hand-to-hand fighting. Whether for cavalry or infantry, any focus on the individual warrior risked undermining the often complex pattern of order in military systems. For concepts of subordination meant relatively little when the focus was on individual prowess, a focus that was not necessarily compatible with organised systems of warfare. However, forms of warfare, whether old or new, served to display valour, and to provide leadership, moral and otherwise.

The evaluation of infantry in what subsequently have been termed the Middle Ages is one that has been far from fixed, which, indeed, is also the situation for the so-called Dark Ages. That is certainly the case for Europe, which raises further the question of how best to fit in the remainder of the world to any analysis of Europe, and vice versa. There is also the question of what the broader, and more varied, area of Eurasia means in this context, and also how best to assess environmental issues and their impact on the choice for infantry or cavalry.

The latter question can be applied to cavalry, with the implication, explicit or implicit, that infantry somehow was a form of rump, prominent only in areas where cavalry could not then operate. In geographical terms, this was most of the world, although the situation was different once space is remapped in terms of demographic distribution, an approach that puts an emphasis on Asia. However, it is far from clear that this is a helpful way to look at the situation, as a focus on geography alone leaves out other elements of tasking and capability; while the perceptions of appropriate force structure and context were far from set then, or in other periods, in an apparent mechanistic fashion of obvious optimalisation and clearcut best practice. These factors suggest that more attention should be devoted to reasons for infantry and for particular types and tactics, but do not make clear what the nature of this attention should be, nor how an account of change in and through infantry could be constructed and an analysis established.

There is also the longer-term problem of the relationship across time not only within the lengthy Middle Ages, but also between them, however defined, and other periods. This relationship had 'real', functional and perceptual elements. In particular, there is the degree to which medieval infantry is presented, or 'constructed,' as a primitive prelude to the musketeers of the sixteenth century or, indeed, as an interlude between the Roman age and that of 'modernity,' the latter defined at first in terms of sixteenth-century warfare. This approach apparently becomes a way to view not only the medieval centuries but also what came later.

Moreover, late medieval warfare and weaponry can be seen as a prelude to the 'modern,' with longbows, crossbows and pikes in particular presented accordingly. That may in part be the case, but is not an approach that is sufficient as an analysis of late medieval warfare. Furthermore, the late medieval warfare of Western Europe is not a guide to Eastern Europe, let alone further afield.

These are by no means the sole conceptual, methodological, historiographical and empirical questions that should be to the fore, but they capture the degree to which time and space offer an uncertain matrix within which to plot infantry. Instead, each of these axes is up for debate in this case. A similar point can be made for other periods. The more specific one for this period is that infantry was not simply a weak rump or geographical safety-feature in a pre-musketeer age dominated, where it could operate, by cavalry. Instead, the situation was more complex. That looks toward the present age and the impact of armour and air power, however much the latter is now being redefined by drones, some classes of which can be operated by infantry as light mortars and machine guns were hitherto. Throughout this book, there will be an emphasis on complexity, which, in turn, should make the discussion of causes for change more tentative.

Chapter 4

Sixteenth Century

Firearms dominate our attention from here on, but they were only one of the classes of infantry weapons in use, and, far from being survivors, the others were significant in tactics and doctrine, as was cavalry. Furthermore, this was not solely a matter of remaining significant but could also involve an increase in relevance. Thus, for example, the pike became more important from the fifteenth century, continuing to play a major role on the European battlefield until the close of the seventeenth. This was a marked response to need, notably for a shock infantry able to prevail in combat against other shock infantry. In other areas, spearmen provided this capability, or swordsmen, or those wielding other stabbing, slashing, or hitting weapons. Moreover, pikemen provided protection from attack for musketeers, especially while they reloaded. Organising infantry deployments to provide protecting pikemen was significant, as were field fortifications which also helped musketeers, and were best defended by them and by pikemen. No other type of infantry offered this level of protection for musketeers.

There are significant problems in assessing the relationships between technological change and infantry weaponry. Then, and in other periods, weapons should be understood as parts of a tactical system that helped incorporate new developments into existing patterns of use. It is also always difficult to assess how much weight to put on the potential for change represented by the specifications of a given weapon and how much to focus on the constraints of the situation. These elements help explain why gunpowder weaponry did not significantly replace edged weapons in Western armies until the sixteenth century. Rate of fire, logistics and cost were all crucial issues, as were versatility of use and tactical awareness, and the lack of any influential social group or military interest committed to firearms. A considerable body of experience and knowledge existed for the exploitation of all manner of edged weapons, but a similar knowledge and skill base had to be built up for firearms.

Meanwhile, the use of handguns was guided not only by the need to secure and maintain protection but also by interlinked issues over range, accuracy and killing power. Muskets had both a short range and a low rate of fire. They had to be resighted for each individual shot, a process involving effort and running the risk of error. These problems were exacerbated by the serious and persistent difficulties associated with poor sights, eccentric bullets, heavy musket droops (which led to firing short), recoil, overheating, and misfiring in wet weather when damp powder could be a problem.

Effectiveness was seen to depend on volume of fire, not individual accuracy and lethality; and the absence of individual accuracy lessened the need for lengthy training, thus encouraging ease of usage. This absence accorded with the poor specifications of firearms for accuracy. Spherical bullets were less aerodynamically effective than their nineteenth-century replacements. The ball could roll out if the barrel was pointed towards the ground. Recharging and reloading from the muzzle (rather than, as later, the breech) increased the time taken to fire, and the reloading cycle led to acute vulnerability for the musketeers. Accuracy would have been increased by rifling the barrel, which helps give a controlled spin to the projectile fire, but this was not practical because of the difficulty of muzzle loading if the shot had to be pushed down rifled grooves.

The ability of spherical shot to inflict lethal wounds at other than short range was limited, and was further decreased by the impact on muzzle velocity of the large windage (gap between projectile and inside the barrel) made necessary by the difficulty of casting accurate shot. The windage meant that part of the explosive force of the gunpowder charge was dissipated, so that the speed of the shot was not high, while its direction was uncertain. This was a particular problem at longer range as velocity fell while the musket balls spread out more. Non-standardised manufacture, a result of the necessary craft-production techniques, was a problem. As a result, a tight windage caused a risk of muzzle explosions.

This limited ability to inflict lethal wounds helped account for the continued popularity of armour, as it could provide protection against most gunshot wounds, as well as against swords and pikes. Thanks to quenching rather than air cooling, improved armour was produced in sixteenth-century Europe. The popularity of armour helped ensure a very different look among the troops to those on the twentieth-century battlefield. Conversely, body armour increased for some forces in the twenty-first. Modern body armour is designed to dissipate the energy of bullets and, to that end, is composed of a number of materials.

Sixteenth-century developments in the West made gunpowder weaponry normative there, alongside pikes or stabbing or other slashing weapons, notably for regular forces, those of states. That is to say that aspects of drill, tactics and assumptions concerning infantry conflict were all increasingly focused on a particular way of firing, while remaining far from identical. Yet, the cost of the new weaponry, which in part reflected the absence of the later economies of scale offered by mass production, acted as a constraint, indeed drag, and notably so given the lack of liquidity and credit enjoyed by most states. It is possible that there would have been far less investment in new weaponry but for the consequences of obtaining bullion from the Americas and thereby expanding the European money supply. For example, Tudor muster rolls reveal that archers were still the mainstay of the late Elizabethan militia because the government was reluctant to face up to the cost implications of training and equipping musketeers,[1] while James I's emphasis on archery in the *Book of Sports* (1618) was in part to ensure that archers were trained for warfare. There are numerous modern equivalents of finance acting as a drag, although it can also be regarded as an aspect of debating and defining fitness for purpose.

Outside Europe, alongside the diffusion of firearms, as in North America and West Africa, the focus on firepower could be different and the standardisation less pronounced. In both, volley fire (never easy to arrange) from densely-packed formations was less appropriate, and fighting and firing were in more open order. This was the case for example in the conflict between Portugal and African forces in Angola. Musketeers were but part of a wider range of weapons. Thus, Idris Aloma, *Mai* (ruler) of Bornu (r. 1569-*c.*1600), a Muslim state based in the region of Lake Chad, who obtained muskets from North Africa, also had archers and shield bearers, as well as cavalry and camel-borne troops. Although musketeers helped give the Moroccans victory over the larger Songhai army at Tondibi on the River Niger in 1591, Songhai archers and spearmen proved effective subsequently, not least because the swampy terrain of the Niger valley did not favour the Moroccan musketeers.[2]

In the more coastal parts of West Africa, armies fought in close order, with javelin-men in the front line and with archers behind providing overhead fire. The javelins could be thrown or used as pikes, and the javelin-men were also equipped with swords, so that they were able to fight as individuals in 'open' order. Shock warfare prevailed: lacking shields, and therefore vulnerable, the archers were essentially support troops, as was so often the case with infantry bowmen; and the bow lacked the prestige of the javelin and sword, which conveyed greater warrior status. Indeed, the Portuguese conflict with the kingdom of Ndongo in modern Angola in the late sixteenth century, while it saw the Portuguese role resting in part on firearms, probably focused more on their skill as swordsmen, which was also important in the Spanish operations against the Aztecs and the Incas, and in battle the Portuguese formed a heavy infantry core with local archers deployed on the flanks. Combined arms infantry was more generally important in Africa, as with the archers and shield-bearers of Jolof formations in West Africa.

Issues such as finance and the availability of gunpowder, shot, and muskets were significant across the world, in Europe as well as beyond. There was also the nature of particular military environments. Moreover, cultural factors appear to have played a role in the adoption or otherwise of firearms, not least the emphasis in some societies on riding as an élite activity where horses were available, with the infantry reserved for other, lower, strata in society. This was apparently true of Mamluk Egypt in the early sixteenth century, while in Japan there came to be an aversion to firearms as socially and culturally disruptive. The extent to which cultural preferences guided the response to pragmatic issues, or vice versa, or with little essential relationship between the two, can be very difficult to evaluate; and is certainly not answered by a simple process of assertion which has been the case in some of the literature. Furthermore, cultural preferences are not incompatible with change and adaptation.

A very different infantry to that which commonly gains attention, was that of the Oromo warriors of East Africa. This might seem primitive to outsiders, but, far from being static, their fighting techniques developed, as in the 1580s when they adopted the use of body-length shields made of stiff-ox-hide, which protected them from archers. The practice of Oromo warriors shaving most of their head to show that they had killed someone was different in form to that seen elsewhere, but matched a widespread pattern of displaying prowess at the individual and collective levels.[3] More generally, it is not only for the Oromo that the standard emphasis on the proficiency of gunpowder infantry deployed by developed, bureaucratic states fails to give sufficient weight to the strength and vitality of other militaries, including infantries.

Close-proximity remained the crucial nature of conflict in both battle and 'small war.' Firearms did not greatly lessen that as they were not sufficiently effective to clear the battlefield. While firearms could do considerable damage, hand-to-hand combat and cold steel remained important. As a result, firearms fitted into established patterns of warmaking, infantry and cavalry, rather than transforming them, again in large part because they represented new iterations of the firepower already offered by archery.

A considerable body of experience and knowledge existed for the exploitation of all manner of edged weapons, but a similar knowledge and skill base had to be built for firearms, both infantry and cavalry. Tactics countered the limitations of handguns, and this was easier for infantry than cavalry: the use of densely packed soldiers fighting at close range, so as to build up the volume of shot likely to hit a target, thus offsetting the effects of low individual accuracy. Moreover, the use of firearms became more important as they were integrated into combined arms tactics, with training accordingly. As a result, firepower came to have greater significance than the manpower offered by other infantry, although this was far from invariable.

Much said about infantry was perforce also the case for cavalry and artillery, but that does not make it any less pertinent in a study on infantry. Battle, like smaller-scale clashes, but often more so for infantry, due to its closeness to the ground, revealed the difficulties of controlling engagements, both from a distance and on the ground, as well as the role of risk. Commanders took the chance of battle or were forced into it, but found it difficult to control the flow and tempo, let alone to get inside the decision loop of opponents, notably because of the problems of battlefield communications, in both speed and reliability.

The absence of smokeless powder meant that all firearms were badly affected by smoke. After the first shots, battlefield visibility was limited, contributing to a confusion commanders sought to counter with tight formations. The problem of battlefield visibility put a premium on the fire discipline required to delay shooting until a short range had been reached.

The noise and smell experienced by infantry are less easy to recreate than the sights, for illustrations and, later, photography and film provide insights into the latter. Comparisons, however, might be forced and therefore potentially misleading. Thus, describing the battle of Waterloo in 1815, Edward Neville Macready of the 13th Foot found that the roaring of the cannon and the shouting together produced the impression 'of a labouring volcano.'[4] The disorientating contrast between the sight and sound of battle was given by the novelist Stendhal [Henri Beyle, who served in the French army in 1800–14] in his account of Waterloo (where in fact he did not fight), in his novel *La Chartreuse de Parme* (1839):

> 'Our hero realised that it was shot from the guns that was making the earth fly up all around him. He looked in vain in the direction from which the shots were coming. He saw the white smoke of the battery an enormous distance away, and, in the midst of the steady and continuous rumble produced by the firing of the guns, he seemed to hear volleys of shot much closer at hand. He could not make head or tail of what was happening.'[5]

As the same time as elements of continuity, there were consequences from the use of firearms in terms of recruitment and payment, and both were related to issues of governmental development and related effort. The case of the Ottomans was instructive, for their background was similar to that of many Inner Asian peoples, but the outcome was different. At the same time, the reasons for this contrast can be debated, including as they do sociological changes, political choices, and military needs in the context of the particular opponents faced. Initially, the Ottomans relied on mounted archers, *akincis* (raiders), who were essentially freelance. In turn, they established an infantry that had become a centrally-paid standing army eventually armed with field cannon and handguns. Yet, it is difficult to establish how far this should be seen as a linked process because the army was created before the use of handguns. The governmental control over resources made possible a standing army, but the growing emphasis on handguns appears to have developed when the Ottomans encountered Christian European forces using guns in battle. Nevertheless, when the

Ottomans later fought the Aqquyunlu of Iraq in 1473, much of their infantry was not yet armed with handguns (the same was true of the Aqquyunlu), and, when Sultan Mehmed II had earlier crossed the Taurus mountains in the face of Aqquyunlu opposition, he did so with archers and spearmen in his vanguard. In the 1510s, when the Ottomans fought the Safavids of Persia and the Mamluks of Egypt and Syria, most of the *janissaries* still carried bows, and many of those who successfully invaded Egypt in 1517 were armed with spears.[6]

Yet, Ottoman infantry firepower played a role in victories over largely cavalry armies in the 1510s: over the Safavids at Chaldiran in 1514, and the Mamluks at Marj Dabiq in 1516 and Raydaniyya in 1517. At the same time, other factors were significant, not least Mamluk divisions in 1516. As far as firepower was concerned, infantry firepower can be difficult to separate from the impact of the impressive Ottoman cannon, as in their victories at Chaldiran and over the Hungarians at Mohács in 1526. In the latter, the Ottoman *janissaries* included kneeling musketeers.[7]

The Ottoman infantry centred on an élite corps, the *janissaries*, who demonstrated the value of professionalism. There was some *janissary* cavalry but most was infantry. The availability of the *janissaries* lessened the potential independence of the Türkmen cavalry. Indeed, as so often, it is the political element that should play a major role in the history of infantry. Thus, the true value of the *janissaries* lay in the fact that they were a full-time, regular, professional force, who owed their allegiance solely to the Sultan; as opposed to the traditional feudal and regional troops which made up the bulk of the Ottoman armies.

The discipline of the *janissaries*, especially when on the march and when in camp, was commented on by numerous Christian observers who witnessed their operations. The perseverance and loyalty of the common soldiers (as of their opponents) owed much to incentives, bonuses, booty and ceremonial. The Ottomans were also quick to adopt firearms, and, during the siege of Malta (1565), their accuracy with them was considered by the defending Knights of St John to be superior to those of the Christian troops. Although it was not until the mid-sixteenth century that the majority of the *janissaries* carried firearms, the Ottomans made stronger and more reliable musket barrels than their Western counterparts, which were constructed with longitudinal seams, whereas the Ottomans used flat sheets of steel coiled into a spiral which produced great strength in the barrel. In Christian Europe, in comparison, the cost of maintaining a full-time body of soldiers proved onerous, other than for small guard units.

The *janissaries* never wore armour, and therefore suffered heavy casualties, including during major siege operations, as at Malta where the Ottomans were defeated. However, the organisation of the *devshirme* (levy on Christian households) and its administration was such that a steady stream of new recruits was always available in the cadet schools to replenish the combat units, and this ensured that they remained at the core of all Ottoman armies: however significant, any infantry type of unit requires fresh recruitment. With time, the emphasis for the Ottoman infantry on firepower increased, in part in response to a comparable development for the Austrian rival. The Ottomans had both an increase in the relevant infantry and, by 1605, an ability to deliver volley fire, possibly as a result of the diffusion of Western techniques but possibly as a consequence of developing the new technique themselves.[8]

East Asia was also an area where there was an emphasis on infantry, notably in China, but even more in Japan where there was not access to steppe cavalry, a situation shared by South-East Asia. In 1555–8, China deployed large numbers of troops armed with traditional weapons – bows, lances and swords, to capture the coastal bases of the *wako* pirates. Infantry was also crucial for the fortifications used by the Chinese to provide defences against the Mongols, and, later, the Manchus, both fortresses and walls.

In South-East Asia and the East Indies, there was a reliance on infantry alongside the warrior élites, some of whom duelled on war elephants. Effectiveness in the use of handguns, which were low-precision weapons, required their employment in a regular manner in order to provide concentrated fire, but heavy thunderstorms and dense jungle affected the value of matchlock guns. Furthermore, the necessary discipline and drill did not match social assumptions about warfare in the region, because they subordinated individual skill and social rank to the collective, the disciplined unit. Firearms there were expected to fit into existing tactics, which was a response not only to cultural conservatism but also to the social norms influencing military service and warfare, as well as to the difficulty of training troops for new tactics.

This was also the case with Japan, where effective guns were introduced in the sixteenth century as a result of trade with Europeans and the Chinese. In many respects, however, firearms mostly just replaced bows one-for-one, thus maintaining the size of other arms. This tactical shift also included the need for protection when reloading, which took longer for musketeers. In Japan, spearmen provided handgunners with protection while archers maintained firepower. The importance of guns was shown operationally, as well as tactically, as Oda Nobunaga, a leading *daimyo* who rose to power in the 1560s, seized control of major gun foundries at Sakai and Kunitomo. So also in Europe with arms-producing sites such as the metallurgical centre of Liège.

In India, cavalry was far more significant than in China, not least because of the importance of mounted archers. However, by the reign of Akbar (1556–1605), the Mughals also had a infantry much of which was armed with handguns. They had already used matchlockmen with great success in conclusively defeating the Lodi at Panipat in 1526, although their cannon had also been important there.

Yet, any capability gap disappeared. The widespread distribution of firearms among the Indian states ensured that the key to success, for both Mughals and others, was not the possession of such weapons, which indeed became widespread, but, rather, organisation: among those who fought, as well as in terms of exploiting agricultural resources and sustaining effective alliances.

In Europe, infantry played a major role in the Italian Wars (1494–1559), with differing combinations of weaponry offering contrasting effectiveness in specific contexts and being encoded in particular units and armies.[9] Thus, at the battle of Cerignola (1503), the greatly-outnumbered Spaniards were held in defence behind a trench and earth parapet, which stopped three attacks by the French cavalry, exposing them, and the Swiss pikemen in support, to heavy Spanish fire from arquebuses: handguns in which the powder was ignited by a length of slow-burning match, the matchlock. The revival of the art of field fortification transformed the possibilities for infantry, although, as was often the case, it was necessary to have the attack mounted to suit the defending infantry in order to enable the latter to realise their potential. This was to be seen with machine guns in the First World War and anti-tank guns in the Second World War

The effectiveness of pikes depended on the existence of disciplined units that were able to use them, such as those of the Swiss. The particular value of pikemen related to their value in attack and defence. Pikes were far more impressive, effective and intimidating than earlier infantry edged weaponry, such as swords and halberds, whereas gunpowder firearms were not a comparable advance on longbows and crossbows. Yet, the battles of Cerignola (1503), Marignano (1515) and Bicocca (1522), the dense blocs of Swiss pikemen were shown as vulnerable, not least because they offered a concentrated target. Combined armed formations and tactics were far more effective at Cerignola, musketeers and swordsmen beating cavalry and pikemen, while at Pavia (1525) the Spanish infantry was in the ratio of 2:2:1 for pikemen, musketeers and swordsmen, whereas the French force was cavalry-strong and only ten per cent of their infantry were musketeers. The French were heavily defeated in what was a long battle, where, aside from the force structure and weapons used, the Spanish proficiency in small-unit engagements emerged anew, the battle in part being an amalgamation of such engagements. The Spanish forces were reorganised into *tercios* in 1534, a combination of companies of pikemen and musketeers that brought tactical flexibility. The initial ratio was towards pikemen, which indicated the ancillary role of firepower at this point.

So also elsewhere. Thus, as Flodden (1513), the attacking Scottish pikemen were unable to develop momentum, and the more mobile English billmen defeated them. The Scottish centre was further pressed as other English troops, victorious over the Scottish right, attacked it in the rear. James IV, much of the nobility and at least 5,000 Scots were defeated.[10] Followed by another major defeat at Pinkie (1547), this suggested that the Scots were not in a position to defeat the English field army. Yet Flodden was more than simply a pike failure. The Scots also had less firepower than the English: in addition to their longstanding inability to match English archery, the Scots lacked the resources, expertise and experience to match them in gunpowder weaponry, although the English army in each battle was dominated by archers, not handgunners. Moreover, as was the case in other battles, there were important factors in this infantry warfare that were not linked to weaponry: the Scots' diverse forces lacked the ability to act as a coherent unit, and some individual sections, especially the Highlanders, were disinclined to accept the discipline of remaining on the defensive under fire, advancing, instead, into a vulnerable position. Henry VIII (r. 1509–47) had a predominantly archer-based army when he invaded France in 1513 and later at the siege of Boulogne in 1544. English archers and billmen were also very effective as part of a Spanish army against the outnumbered French at St Quentin in 1557.[11]

While underlining the value of archery practice in 1511, Henry wanted troops trained in the use of firearms, addressing this by hiring Continental mercenaries, a costly policy continued into the 1550s, that did not, however, always produce reliable units.[12] At the same time, these mercenaries helped bring victories over peasant armies in 1549 in Norfolk and South-West England: at Dussindale near Norwich, *landsknechte* (German pikemen) and German handgunners were crucial. The English government from the 1560s sought to rearm garrisons and key militia units with handguns, although the militia system limited government control over weaponry and force structure.[13]

In Eastern Europe, native infantry never adopted the pike, instead usually being lightly-equipped musketeers or using shorter hafted weapons such as spears or poleaxes. In Transylvania, native infantry were mostly lightly armed musketeers with additional weapons for close combat, deployed in battle on the flanks because the emphasis was on cavalry.[14] Politics played a role in the development of infantry warfare in Eastern Europe in that it gained more importance as the nature of political boundaries changed. As the loose and generally vague medieval frontiers became firmer there was a shift from cavalry defence to border fortifications defended by infantry garrisons well-supported with gunpowder weaponry. This change was associated in Transylvania and nearby with a new type of infantry, the guardsman.[15]

For battle and other needs, it was possible at the time to suggest that various conclusions could be drawn from the combination of arms and tactical formations, not least when assessing firepower, pikemen, cavalry, artillery, the offensive and the defensive. Whichever arms and formations were used, discipline, cohesion, resilience and command skills were all significant and presented as such. Thus, Paolo Giovio, in his book on the Schmalkaldic War (1546–7), emphasised the importance of drill and praised the *landsknechte* for their discipline. So with the Spanish Army of Flanders, the impressive force that fought the French and Dutch rebels with repeated success in the second half of the century. In 1587, François de la Noue (1531–91), a major Huguenot commander in the French Wars of Religion, published his *Discours politiques et militaires*, a work, also appearing in English and German, that argued the possibility for pike and musket squares to beat off mounted archers.

The shift to musketeers and pikemen could be inappropriate if supplies of gunpowder were lacking, as for the Irish rebels in 1593–1603. In addition, there was the limited value of pikes to the rebels in mêlée combat. Indeed, this provided an instance of the danger of transforming infantry: the rebels were overcome in 1601 at the battle of Kinsale in which deployment in a *tercio* proved mistaken while cavalry was crucial to the English victory over them.[16]

Improvements in handguns reflected an important flexibility with firearms. Thus, the musket, a heavier version of the arquebus, capable of firing a heavier shot farther, and therefore penetrating armour, was used in Europe from the 1520s, and its use became widespread by mid-century. Heavier shot is less affected by deviations than lighter shot, and this made it more accurate, although, at long range, accuracy was still poor. The lead ball of about 15 grams (half an ounce) that was fired could kill at 180 metres (200 yards), but it was very difficult to hit a target at more than 55 metres (60 yards).

At the same time, the tactical advantage of particular infantry formations and weaponry was challenged by the degree to which large infantry forces posed serious operational problems due to the support they required.[17] Nevertheless, the ability to provide this support helped to make both the major Ottoman field army and the Spanish Army of Flanders impressive, as each had an effective organisational structure and good logistical support system. Each were professional forces, well-disciplined on the battlefield, and characterised by a meritocratic ethos in which, for officers, aristocratic background was no substitute for expertise.[18] In each case, infantry was at a premium due to the significance of sieges: in the Danube Valley and the Low Countries respectively.

The leading opponent of the Army of Flanders were Dutch forces that put an emphasis on infantry, as opposed to the cavalry-strong French who were the other opponent. These Dutch forces were to be associated with a particular improvement in the tactical use of infantry firepower, one that raised its volume and consistency by using particular deployments and routines, contributing to the idea of an 'Early Modern Military

Revolution'. The Dutch were heavily defeated in their initial battles with the Spaniards, which led to a dependence on their part on fortifications, but subsequently improved their battlefield reliability. They introduced broader and shallower troops formations which permitted more soldiers to fire at once, and, in the 1590s, they developed continuous fire by using a volley technique, so that one rank of soldiers fired simultaneously and then reloaded, while other ranks fired in turn, providing protection by means of continuous fire. The Japanese also developed the same method.

William of Nassau, a scholar of Classical literature, drew on the *Tactica* of the Roman writer Aelian written in about 100 CE, which provided an account of the drill of pikemen and slingers, and this model influenced Count Maurice of Nassau, the Dutch commanding general. He was encouraged to improve firepower and standards of both weapons and drill. The military reformers linked to the House of Nassau in the Dutch Republic, as well as to certain German Protestant territories, including Hesse-Cassel and Nassau, consciously used ancient Greek and Roman models for their efforts to improve military organisations. Their limited sense of changing conditions was matched by the contemporary writings of Justus Lipsius and others on the ancient Roman military.

The Dutch introduction of volley fire potentially had a major impact.[19] Prior to the Nassau reforms, firearms could be important, but played only a supporting role in many battles, while pikemen, swordsmen and cavalry frequently decided the outcome of the battle. In contrast, it has been argued, the drill and tactics developed by the Nassau reformers helped the musketeers to operate successfully in close formations in the open field.

At the same time, the significance of these changes is a matter of debate. To end with the account of Dutch improvements might lead to a marked failure to consider not only their atypicality, but also the extent to which they did not amount to a clear stage in an obvious progressive narrative. This point will be probed in the next chapter. It serves as a reminder that significance is a movable feast, not least looking different in prospect and in retrospect, as well as being inherently contentious.

The Dutch Revolt itself moved from being an instance of rebellion to that of conflict between states. The former was often the responsibility of infantry. The use of troops in policing was seen across the world, and reflected the lack of alternative police forces able to maintain order. Thus, large-scale operations against bandits south of Beijing from 1509 were only successful in 1512, while banditry was a common feature in many European rural regions, as in Albania, Apulia, Calabria, Jülich and Sicily. Frontier zones, including inner frontiers, as in India, provided particular cover for often large-scale brigandage. The means of coercion and defence were crucial for government, and the use of troops, infantry and cavalry, in these contexts scarcely approximated to battlefield maxims.

Chapter 5

Seventeenth Century

The most significant campaigns in the century were those in which the Manchus conquered Ming China in the 1640s and 1650s, resisted an attempt to reverse their success in the late 1670s, and defeated the Dzungars, their principal steppe rival, in the 1690s. In all of these, cavalry, in which the Manchus were strong, was to the fore, underlining the extent to which it would be foolish to see the century as one of the steadily or inevitably greater success of infantry.

So also with the effectiveness of Maratha light cavalry in seventeenth-century India, where it was estimated that a mounted archer could fire six arrows in the time it took a musketeer, armed with a matchlock musket, to fire one shot.[1] However, all such estimates should be tentative, not least as they are evaluating two separate criteria. The Marathas proved particularly effective against Mughal forces, not because the latter focused on infantry but rather on heavy cavalry. Indeed, there can be a tendency to see matters as infantry rather than cavalry, when it should rather be heavy or light cavalry.

In a very different context, the spread of the horse in the Americas was another key indication of a continued role for cavalry. Cavalry also dominated warfare in much of Central and South-West Asia, the savannah belt of Africa, and Eastern Europe.

At the same time, infantry became proportionately more significant in Europe in the late seventeenth century, in part due to the increase in the size of armies; and this set a pattern that was to be important to the Western system. Yet, aside from the inherent flexibility of deployments affected by topography and opponents,[2] it is also necessary to note differences of emphasis such that it is not necessarily always helpful to refer to a Western system. In particular, cavalry was far more significant for some states than others, for France for example rather than the Dutch Republic, while the role of musketeers as opposed to pikemen also varied. The idea of a basic paradigm or model requires qualification.

Alongside important geographical variations, there were also significant chronological ones.

And so also in the world scale, where infantry conflict in coastal West Africa, Amazonia, Sri Lanka, the Himalayas, and South-East Asia, in each of which it was the dominant type, was different to the most common Western European pattern. Differences in the use of firearms were not the sole point. For example, whereas pikes were used in Europe, the more flexible spear was still employed extensively in Africa, indeed into the nineteenth century; while, in Bengal, *paiks*, light infantry armed with spears, proved effective in the often waterlogged terrain. So also with the adaptation to the terrain seen in the forested valley of the Brahmaputra in which the outnumbered Ahom resisted the Mughals. The Ahom relied on infantry armed with muskets or bows and arrows, used flexible tactics, including surprise night attacks, and rapidly created fortified positions based on bamboo stockades which made attacking them a costly and difficult task. The riverine and jungle terrains were very different to the cavalry-helpful plains and low hills of Rajasthan where the Mughals had campaigned extensively in the sixteenth century, as well as the plains of Gujarat. There is a parallel with the major problems that faced the British Indian Army, a force used largely for conflict on the dry upland terrain of India's North-West Frontier, when it was sent in 1941–2 to resist Japanese advances in the jungles of Malaya and Burma, only to be seriously outfought.[3]

Weaponry was only one of the variables in the employment and significance of infantry. Environmental factors were important to differences in tactical, operational, and strategic goals and possibilities. Thus, at the tactical level, the skilful use of stockades in Arakan, Burma, Kerala and Nepal to magnify defensive advantages reflected the plentiful availability of timber. Organisational differences were also significant, with a contrast between the use of conscript troops, as in Arakan, Burma and Nepal, and of mercenaries, as in northern India.

Whatever the region, the course of conflict unsurprisingly revealed that, while weaponry and tactics were important to infantry effectiveness, experienced troops were more useful. This was not least if they were employed by commanders able to direct the flow of the battle by seizing and using the initiative. This also involved responding to the moves of opponents in a fashion that denied them control of the tempo.

Furthermore, it is appropriate to be sceptical about the supposed, almost automatic, superiority of novel formations assumed by protagonists of the Military Revolution thesis. Instead, in the Thirty Years' War in Europe (1618–48), the more innovative linear formations, only five or six ranks deep, those of the Dutch, were in practice far more vulnerable to flank and rear attack than the long-established blocs of troops, for example those formed by the Spanish *tercios* and others based on that model. Rather than rewarding new tactics and formations, victory in that conflict tended to go to larger and more experienced armies, size providing mass in attack and defence, as well as the ability to extend the front. In addition, Duke Bernard of Saxe-Weimar, won a number of battles, such as Rheinfelden (1638), essentially by successful manoeuvre and, significantly, did not adopt Dutch-style tactics or formations. The weakness of Dutch tactics was also seen in Brazil in the 1630s, as the Neapolitan troops in Spanish/Portuguese service proved better able than their invading Dutch opponents to adapt to the possibilities of the terrain, adopting far more open formations as well as mounting frequent ambushes.[4]

More generally, far from being redundant or novel, the range of tactics employed left room for both musketeers and pikemen to show their skill. For example, pike formations were more open than normally assumed, suggesting that the effectiveness of pikemen depended on individual skills in hand-to-hand combat as well as the sheer weight of mass.

Whatever the formations employed – and the square was not much used in Russia – the general deployment on the European battlefield was linear, with infantry in the centre and cavalry on the flanks. Cavalry victory there helped support the (slower) infantry assault (and defence) in the centre, and to that end, seizing and using the initiative, and the local advantages of height, slope and surface drainage were all significant. Yet there was not an equivalent to the greater significance of cavalry in conflict in India.

Numbers of infantry were an important factor, but also posed serious longstanding issues of use. They could be unwieldy on the battlefield, there were problems in ensuring sufficient numbers of infantry, let alone experienced infantry, and logistical difficulties gravely affected their operational capability by encouraging campaigning focused on a search for supplies. In the seventeenth century, in contrast to the norm in the twentieth and twenty-first, this search pressed on a situation of demographic and economic stagnation, which was worldwide and could not be readily addressed by recruiting soldiers elsewhere; although, as today, cultural norms and preferences played a role. In the seventeenth century, there is an instructive contrast between the willingness of Islamic societies to raise slave forces, principally infantry, and that of (Christian) Europeans to do so for manual work in the Americas, but not for military work for soldiers. Galley slaves were used in the Mediterranean and there were dockyard slaves in the Caribbean, but a major effort was made to keep from using slaves as troops unless in exceptional circumstances.

In a more detailed viewpoint, demographic variations ensured that the ability of individual powers to raise large numbers of infantry was far from identical. There was also the impact of epidemics, or disease more generally, on recruitment and on existing forces. These epidemics hit armies hard and could greatly affect numbers and fighting quality, as with the War of the Mantuan Succession in Italy in 1628–31. Disease helped bring that conflict involving Austrian, French and Spanish forces to a close.

That was not the sole constraint on infantry conflict. There were also issues with tactical and operational indecisiveness. Thus, the extent to which, in the Thirty Years' War, experienced and well-deployed infantry were usually safe against frontal attack threatened a tactical impasse in infantry conflict, one that prefigured, on a very different scale, the trench warfare of the First World War. In the former case (as in the latter), this impasse led to a particular need for skills in generalship and also directed attention to differences in infantry and cavalry capabilities in particular circumstances. In the First World War, however, unlike in this earlier period, there was a testing of new weapons systems including aircraft and tanks.

In the mid-century British civil wars, it is appropriate to note the importance of success in the cavalry conflict on the wings, as with the Parliamentary victories at Marston Moor in 1644 and Naseby in 1645; but this success was significant only because the infantry had held off their Royalist counterparts in the centre. At Marston Moor, the 'Parliamentary' force was in fact the Allied Army of Both Kingdoms, and many of the Scots were veterans, not least of conflict in the Thirty Years' War on the Continent.[5] Like the Swiss, infantry formations had been a staple of Scots warfare for centuries.

At Naseby, the Royalist infantry, although heavily outnumbered, had advanced and driven back the front line of their Parliamentary opponents, but the most experienced troops were deployed in the second line, and they held fast, stopping the Royalist infantry. It was this struggle that the cavalry under Oliver Cromwell swayed by attacking the flank and rear of the Royalist infantry, which succumbed with about 5,000 men taken prisoner.

As a reminder that the subject of infantry combat is far from static, suggestions that pike combat was anachronistic in the face of rising firepower have been challenged in recent work arguing that pikemen retained an offensive capacity, rather than being essentially defensive, to protect musketeers from cavalry.[6]

Despite battles such as Naseby, the bulk of the fighting was small-scale, which required formations, tactics, and combat and command skills that were more ad hoc than those of major battles. About 47 per cent of the soldiers who died in conflict in England in 1642–6 died in skirmishes in which fewer than 250 died, while only 15 per cent died in major battles.

In Europe, infantry played a significant role in the 'small war' of raids and skirmishes that helped establish or challenge control. This warfare saw many contact engagements, with most infantry actions decided within minutes of the first volley. In much, but far from all, 'small war', regular formations fought using the same volley fire tactics employed by troops in large battles. Indeed, in a situation that looks to the present, notably with urban conflict, large battles can be thought of as a series of small engagements in which, despite their proximity, units, even individual men, fought in relative isolation from one another.[7]

At the same time, individual troops and small units are affected by what happens round them, notably on their flanks and, even more, in their rear, and by the extent of supporting fire and action. The grouping of men and units into larger formations was important to their success in these circumstances, as was discipline and, even more, training. All contributed to resilience.

Resilience was made more important by the difficulties of reinforcement which included limited communications on the battlefield. Bugle calls had only a few uses, in the smoke of the battlefield it was difficult to signal by flags, and commanders were usually reliant on mounted aides-de-camp who were vulnerable to fire and attack. There was a general absence of subordinate tactical units such as divisions or brigades, and scant experience of manoeuvring in ad hoc subordinate units.

Once engaged, it was difficult to retain central directions of the units, and to control their manoeuvres, especially if it was hoped to disengage and adopt a new position. There was a great danger that any changes in formation would interrupt fire, threaten morale, and create gaps in the line that could be exploited by opponents, as with the total Moroccan victory over the Portuguese at Alcácer Quibir (1578), or the Scottish Highlander victories at Kilsyth (1645) and Prestonpans (1745). As earlier with the *phalanx*, cohesion and tactical continuity in the use of linear formations were not therefore necessarily a sign of rigidity, but in part a wish to avoid gaps and the resulting multiplication of flanks to attack.

'Small war' was more characteristic of contexts in which there were relatively few soldiers, although, in those, the threshold to 'battle' was also lower. As with most aspects of infantry, it remains the case that there was no fixed definition of battle. 'Small war' was also characteristic of European colonial conflict with non-Europeans, in part, as in North America, due to the numbers involved, and in part as a result of the physical and military environments, as for Europeans fighting Natives and escaped slaves in the Caribbean.

On the global scale, the ability to acquire the relevant equipment was important to the diffusion of infantry techniques. Thus, Native Americans learned to repair muskets, cast bullets and make gunflints. North America was a key area as there was a range of types of conflict greater than in Europe: that of conflict between Native Americans, between them and Europeans (whether regulars or settlers), and between the Europeans, notably the English and the French. The Natives' general lack of fixed battle positions made it difficult for the Europeans to devise clear military goals, and ensured there was only a limited role for volley fire. As experts with bows and arrows, the Native Americans were adept at missile warfare, and thus more readily able to make the transition to muskets, which were easier to aim, and the bullets of which, unlike arrows, were less likely to be deflected by brush, and also could not be dodged.

Native use of weapons and tactics allowed for considerable autonomy on the part of individual warriors.[8] Yet, in the context of a cultural approach to Native warfare as individual, in contrast to a machine-like European system, it is important not to underrate the role of organised tactics and discipline among Native Americans, nor of leadership by officers. This is a counterpart to the need to be very cautious in assuming that Asian forces were in some way 'hordes', an approach that can be treated as 'Orientalism in warfare.' Native American military potential was considerable, given their hunter-warrior training. Their battlefield manoeuvring made expert use of flanking movements proceeding from the half-moon formation into which they flowed from files upon contact. These movements could be used for advance or retreat. Natives were adept at ambushes, feints and ruses. The half-moon formation was not dissimilar to the impressive Zulu 'Horns of the Buffalo' formation in the nineteenth century.

Conflict in the seventeenth century in North America was essentially on foot, and, far from readily implementing European methods, European success in frontier warfare there greatly depended on Native assistance or on adaptation to the Native way of war. Thus, in King Philip's War in New England in 1675–6, the English colonists moved in loose order, adapted to the available cover, fired at specific targets, and benefited from Native support against rival Natives. The latter were crushed with considerable savagery, which in part reflected fear of their opposition.

The situation for Europeans versus non-Europeans was different in sub-Saharan Africa, another infantry zone in part due to the tsetse fly limiting the possibility of using horses. This difference was not least due to a population gradient that was very unfavourable to the Europeans, especially when their greater propensity to disease is taken into account. The Portuguese found the Africans well-armed with well-worked iron weapons, as good in some ways as Portuguese steel weaponry, and certainly better than the Native wood and obsidian weapons of the New World. Both the slow rate of fire of Portuguese muskets, and the openness of African fighting formations, reduced the effectiveness of the Portuguese firearms; their inability to deploy anything larger than a small force of cavalry ensured that they could not counter this open order. As in North America, where the process was greatly helped by rivalry between the European powers, firearms were diffused rapidly, and Africans in Angola possibly even had them in equal numbers to the Portuguese as early as the 1620s. Certainly quantities of them were reported in 1626–8 in the first war against the formidable Queen Njinga of Ndongo who challenged the Portuguese position in Angola.

As a result, for the Portuguese, the value of firearms in creating a capability gap was limited, especially in the absence of combined forces. The Portuguese victory over the shield-bearing heavy infantry of the kingdom of Kongo at the battle of Mbumbi (1622) was the result of overwhelming numerical superiority, notably due to alliance with the Imbangala, cannibal mercenaries; and not of weapons superiority. When, however, they were left without African light infantry, Portuguese forces could well be destroyed, as by the forces of Queen Njinga at the battle of Ngolomene (1644). In contrast, the combination of Africans and European infantry, with its body armour and swordsmanship, as well as firepower, was effective, as in the Portuguese victories over Njinga at Cavanga (1646) and over Antonio I of Kongo at Ambuila (1665); in the latter, the Portuguese deployed 400 Europeans and 4,000 African slave soldiers. There was a parallel with the earlier warfighting of many powers, for example Sparta.

Firearms also played an important role in infantry conflict between African states, notably with an increasing preponderance of firepower over hand-to-hand combat. At the same time, this could mean a reliance on archers rather than musketeers. Thus, from the mid-seventeenth century, their role increased in Akwamu and Denkyira, inland states of West Africa, and, as firepower became more significant, this led to a more open formation and a wider battle frontage, with archers in the front line flanking the javelin-men. As a result, missile tactics came to prevail in West Africa, even before the widespread use of firearms, the former, as in North America, helping ease the eventual path of the latter. The new emphasis on archers spread in West Africa, for example to the kingdom of Asante (in the interior of modern Ghana) in the 1670s. Javelin-men came to play a tactical role subordinate to that of the bowmen, and, between the 1660s and the 1690s, the javelin was discarded as a weapon, becoming (like the halberd in Europe) essentially ceremonial. The emphasis was different in Europe as the musket was challenged there not by archers or javelins, but by pikemen and cavalry.

In turn, in Africa, the bow came to be supplanted by the musket, although usage was long restricted by the limited availability of shot and power. The use of firearms in West Africa was first reported in the fifteenth century, in Kano, a city that traded across the Sahara, but a regular force of musketeers was not organised there until the 1770s. In contrast, on the West African coast, the Asebu army of the 1620s was the first to include a corps of musketeers, their guns being supplied by the Dutch. Muskets replaced bows on the coast in the 1650s to 1670s, but the tactical shift there towards open-order fighting did not come until later: initially, musketeers were used as a shield for the javelin-men, and tactics centred on gunfire were slow to develop in the coastal armies. Firepower, though, did increase in the 1680s and 1690s, as flintlock muskets replaced matchlocks, but bayonets were not used. In the forest interior of West Africa, muskets replaced bows in the 1690s and 1700.[9]

The discussion of infantry capability suffers to a degree from the extent to which outside observers were able to appreciate the reasons for particular courses. This ensures a slant in the reporting of many regions, although, at the same time, the criteria cited are instructive for the light they throw on what was expected. Thus, in 1685–6, James, 8th Lord Chandos, the English envoy in Constantinople (Istanbul), explained Ottoman failure at the hands of the Austrians in terms of an absence of 'military discipline' and a lack of numbers, whereas, he claimed, in the past, 'their prodigious vast multitudes of men that by the weight of flesh bore down all their enemies before them showed greater spirit in battle.'[10] In practice, the major Ottoman defeat in that war with Austria, Zenta in 1697, reflected a lack of unpreparedness and a very poor defensive position, with the Ottoman infantry exposed by their backs being to the river and the cavalry on the other bank.

The warfare between the Christians and the Ottomans indicated in particular the strength of Christian infantry firepower and the value of its ability to operate in a disciplined fashion on the battlefield, such that Ottoman warmaking no longer had an edge in battle. However, divisions between the Ottoman commanders, as at Vienna in 1683, were also important. It is important to focus on such specific factors, rather than adopt a generic cultural approach. Indeed, in the two Austro-Ottoman wars of the early eighteenth century, those of 1716–18 and 1737–9, the Ottomans were heavily defeated in the first but successful in the second, losing Belgrade in the first and regaining it in the second.

As in the sixteenth century, firepower provided a significant advantage for regular forces. Thus, in 1685, at Sedgemoor in England, a poorly-organised rebel army, commanded by James, Duke of Monmouth, was heavily defeated by its experienced opponents' superior firepower, whereas previously in that campaign the militia, which had lower morale and less commitment as well as training, had failed to do so. More generally, where regular forces were relatively small, this helped with equipment and training, and thus made it easier to respond to changes in the methods of fighting, although at Killiecrankie in 1689 the government troops, some of whom were inexperienced, were defeated by an attacking Jacobite force. About a third of the government troops there had pikes.

In Christian Europe, there was a major change in infantry weaponry in this period, with the divided system of pikemen and musketeers replaced in the 1690s in part thanks to the development of an effective bayonet, one of the most important and underrated innovations in military technology. To a degree, the bayonet was a response to problems: the combination of pikemen and musketeers was complex and led to a degree of tactical inflexibility as well as a density of formation that limited the possibilities of linear deployment over an extensive front. Such a front was appropriate in order to maximise firepower. The role of responses to problems was to be shown in a very different context with the turn to trench warfare in the First World War.

Whereas with the plug bayonets devised earlier in the seventeenth century that were inserted in the barrel of the musket, it had been necessary to remove the bayonet before firing the musket, the ring-and-socket bayonet, developed in the 1680s, enabled firing with the bayonet blade in place, as the bayonet was attached to a ring fitted round the musket barrel. Furthermore, the bayonet was turned and locked in place, providing firmness in combat. Shooting with the bayonet fixed, however, posed the problem of extra weight, which not only increased the physical burden but decreased accuracy (such as it was) partly because tiredness made the musketeer drop the muzzle even lower. The transition to the bayonet in Western Europe was very rapid, with Russia following in the 1700s. There were elements of responding to the decisions made by others, but also to the particular circumstances of specific military environments. Thus, the Austrians abandoned the pike in Italy and the Balkans in about 1691, when Field Marshal Aeneas Caprara, the Austrian Commander-in-Chief in northern Italy, changed pikemen companies into musketeer ones. In the West, pikes remained in the Austrian ordinances until 1703, but were not used against the French from about 1690.[11]

All infantry were thus armed with a weapon that combined firepower and steel. However, this did not greatly encourage attacks, because bayonet drills were, for a long time, based on pike drills, with the weapon held high and an emphasis on receiving advances, although they were used offensively on occasion.[12] It was not until the 1750s that a new bayonet drill, with the weapon held waist-high, made it easier for the English infantry to mount attacks. In turn, in France, the drills and formations of the age of musket and pike continued into the eighteenth century and tactical changes were slow.[13]

Indeed, in practice the move from the use of the pike had been gradual, with the proportion of pikemen decreasing during the seventeenth century as that of musketeers increased. Already, in 1642, on the basis of his experience on the Continent where he had been a military chaplain, Donald Lupton had suggested moving from the pike to muskets.[14] The number of pikemen, which, at the start of the century formed most of the Austrian infantry, fell during the Thirty Years' War (1618–48) and, by 1670, their percentage was down to a third. Yet Count Raimondo Montecuccoli, the leading mid-seventeenth century Austrian general, retained his belief that pikes were important as he did not think that musketeers alone could repel cavalry attack, and he accordingly deployed his pikemen in six ranks. At the same time, the challenge posed by the Ottoman cavalry to infantry was diminished both by the pikemen and by the enhanced Austrian firepower. Montecuccoli observed that, when fighting the Ottomans, it was necessary to use cavalry against their infantry and infantry against their cavalry. Organisational factors were also significant. Austrian units benefited from the extent to which the ratio of officers to rank-and-file was much greater than in the Ottoman army, thus ensuring that the Austrian army was better controlled and more agile.[15]

The percentage of pikemen in French infantry units fell from 50 at the start of the century to a third by 1650, a quarter by 1680, and a fifth by 1690, and formations accordingly became longer and thinner.[16] At the battle of Neerwinden in 1693, a long and difficult struggle in which infantry, cavalry and artillery were all heavily involved, the French successfully used their bayonets in attack, Brigadier-General James Douglass arguing that the British and Dutch suffered from a lack of socket bayonets whereas the French were able to be 'both pushed and fired at once and of a much better defence than our pikes were.' After the battle, in which William III was defeated, Douglass pressed for permission to arm his troops with socket bayonets.[17] Yet many pikes have been discovered in the silt on the battlefield of Blenheim which was fought in 1704 between a French-Bavarian army and an Anglo-Austrian one.

As pikes were replaced by muskets equipped with socket bayonets, so matchlock muskets were replaced by flintlocks which were more reliable and fired faster. The process of loading was complex but less vulnerable to wind, rain and general humidity than with matchlocks. In a normal flintlock loading, the regular procedure was to tear off the end of the greased paper cartridge, prime and shut the frizzen, thus covering the primed pan, and pull the hammer to half cock (a safety position to prevent premature sparking), cast about to bring the muzzle to chest level, pour the remaining powder from the cartridge down the barrel, stuff the opened end of the cartridge into the muzzle (the ball would be encased in the opposite end of the cartridge and, depending on the manufacturing method, crimped in place by twists to the cartridge above and below the ball or by a thread), draw the rammer, and ram down the charge so as to seat the ball and cartridge firmly, usually by means of two or three solid tamps to ensure it was all the way down and properly seated. The greased paper cartridge provided the wadding that both ensured increased compression and held the ball in place until the main charge exploded.

Then to fire, the soldier would pull the hammer to full cock, present the muzzle down range on command, and, on the command 'Give fire!', pull the trigger. The soldier would return back down to the prime and load position with the flintlock at the waist ready to load and fire it all over again. When weapons were loaded and to prevent the powder from getting wet, a wooden plug called the tampion (the origins of the word tampon) was inserted to plug the muzzle, while the closed frizzen cover held the powder in the pan and hopefully kept the priming powder dry.

Flintlocks, developed in the early seventeenth century, were used for hunting and for pistols, which further underlined their characterisation as a luxury weapon. This issue of cost was magnified by the marked increase in the size of most Western armies from the 1660s which meant that it took longer to introduce the flintlock as a major military weapon, and that moreover in a period of widespread economic stagnation. The cost of a flintlock musket was equal to the annual wages of an agricultural labourer.

Instead, the less expensive bayonet, which was also a clearer force-multiplier, was pushed first. Nevertheless, as an indication of competitive pressure in the West, of the clear advantage of the flintlock, and of the existing firearms' tactics, units, and doctrine that could guide its use, the adoption of flintlocks was quicker than that of the arquebus.

All the new English regiments raised from 1689 were equipped with flintlocks and in 1699 a French ordinance ordered that the flintlocks be adopted by all, the pike being abandoned in 1703. The new English Land Pattern Musket could be fired at least twice a minute and weighed one pound less than the matchlock previously used. The speed of fire, which could lead to inflicting higher casualties, resulted in new tactical formations, with the infantry generally deployed first in four ranks, and then in three. However, in practice, there were many variations due to the specific needs of an individual engagement and the troops available. European armies were not to experience a comparable change in weaponry until the introduction of rifled guns in the nineteenth century.

As all the Western European armies followed a similar pattern of re-equipment, however, capability gaps between them did not emerge, a situation that has been more generally true of infantry in recent centuries. In contrast, the enhanced weaponry was potentially useful, indeed very useful, for conflict overseas against non-Westerners who lacked such weapons, for example in North America. Furthermore, the tactical mobility and flexibility of European troops were increased by the fusion of musketeer and pikemen into a soldier wielding a flintlock carrying a bayonet.

Much of the rest of the world did not follow the European pattern of development, with neither China nor South-East Asia (unlike India) moving from matchlocks to flintlocks. Indeed, hand-to-hand weapons remained more important, there and elsewhere, than is frequently appreciated. These weapons were employed not simply by weak or apparently unchanging powers, but also by dynamic powers and people, such as the Nepalese Gurkhas who used swords (*kukris*). In South-East Asia, pikes, swords, spears and daggers, such as the Malay *kris*, were still important, and firearms made scant impact on tactics.

Yet, firepower West versus shock non-West is not only an aspect of a misleading Western designation of non-Western forces as hordes, but also a product of a tendency to underplay the continuing role of shock in

European conflict. Thus, in 1689 a Jacobite force of Scottish Highlanders defeated at Killiecrankie a far larger Williamite force by charging with their broadswords against static musketeers. This was a tactical success, but the death of the Jacobite commander contributed to a strategic failure. Such tactics were not only seen with such marginal forces. Attacking infantry armed with muskets was also important, as with the British success over the French at Blenheim in 1704.

Defensive positions provided the opportunity for firepower, but, however much the logic of musketry might lead in that direction, the balance was not yet necessarily in favour of such an infantry doctrine. Thus, the major battles in William III's conquest of Ireland in 1690–1, the Boyne (1690) and Aughrim (1691), were won by the attacking forces. In both cases, tactical considerations relating to the terrain, and to the ability to take advantage of developments, had been crucial, and the vulnerability of defending armies to flanking attacks by opponents that retained the initiative was clearly demonstrated. William's forces were well armed with flintlock muskets, and many had bayonets as well.

The significance of the latter was also seen at Narva (1700), with the attacking Swedes rapidly coming to hand-to-hand combat with the Russians and proving adept with their bayonets. The Russians were heavily defeated. As with the total Ottoman defeat at Vienna in 1683, the battle demonstrated the continued vulnerability of the defence, in the case of Vienna, however, to cavalry attack.

The attack brought the potential euphoria of the advance, but there were other factors significant to success, and for infantry as well as cavalry, including maintaining control of the flow of a battle, as well as the extent to which many battles lasted for a while. This duration placed a premium on the experience and determination of the troops and, more specifically, on their ability to take casualties and go on fighting, and to a tactical purpose, including altering formation and even position, rather than simply for survival. Although uniformity might have been the objective of drill that focused on repetitive movements and formulaic tactics, patterned training and battlefield dispositions did not define what, in practice, was a far more varied military experience, both in battle and elsewhere.[18]

A different version of uniformity was seen with uniforms. The West's adoption of military uniform began as badges and later livery for particular groups, commonly the retainers of specific warlords. There was a borrowing of this from the East during the Crusades, but the practice did not increase greatly until the mid-seventeenth century when military uniform became a particular dress-genre. In the later seventeenth century, proto-national uniforms were adopted in a number of countries. Uniforms were of value in the confusion of smoke-shrouded battlefields, and in making desertion more difficult, while also presenting military service as more attractive to recruits.

The seventeenth century saw widespread and destructive civil war in what has been termed a mid-century crisis. Thereafter, there was a period of recovery and consolidation, notably in China, Europe, the Ottoman Empire and India. This period witnessed a marked increase in the size of armies, which, in effect, principally meant infantry at least in so far as numbers were concerned. Thus, in the early 1660s, Duke Charles Emmanuel III of Savoy-Piedmont declared six infantry regiments a standing, or permanent, force. Such developments ensured that the military establishment created for the wars earlier in the century was sustained. They were seen more generally, for example in England and, on a far greater scale, France.

Indeed, France was the dominant power in Western Europe in the late seventeenth century, in part because it was able to fight on several fronts simultaneously. Despite the fame of its cavalry, the scale of the French army was very much that of its infantry. This reflected the size of its population, the greatest in Western Europe, but also the ability of the governmental system to raise such a number. Politics was the great enabler. At the same time, as in Eastern Europe, India and China, cavalry was far more prestigious. There were a few prestigious old regiments of infantry in the French army, such as the *Regiment du Roi*, but infantry was regarded as necessary and worthy, rather than inherently prestigious. This was to remain the case throughout the European *ancien régime*, but was not an accurate guide to relative importance.

Chapter 6

Eighteenth Century

'As the superiority of English sepoys over their enemies, as likewise their own safety, consist entirely in their steadiness and attentiveness to the commands of their officers, it is ordered that no black officer or sepoy pretend to act or quit his post without positive orders to that purpose from an European officer … should any man fire without orders, he is to be put to death upon the spot … regularity and obedience to orders are our grand and only superiority.'

Captain Robert Stuart, commander of a *sepoy* battalion in the army of the East India Company, 1773.[1] Serving in India from 1764, Stuart became a general and gained great wealth.

The image of eighteenth-century warfare in Western Europe, that of a move from lines of infantry to one with columns as well, scarcely matches the situation for India. The latter deserves attention for the century there saw much conflict and it was of great consequence for significant political developments in India. There was plentiful infantry in India, including in battle, but the role of cavalry was more pronounced, and in relative terms far more than in Europe. It might appear that the redundancy of the Indian force structure is readily apparent, with British infantry victorious across India by 1820. Yet that view, of victory and redundancy, can mean reading from later consequences, for, across most of the eighteenth century, the principal challenge to Indian states was not that of Britain, which only became militarily significant from the 1750s, but rather cavalry-strong forces successfully invading from across the Indus. These were, first, in 1739–40, under Nader Shah of Persia, and then, from the 1750s, armies led by the Durrani ruling dynasty of Afghanistan. Nader Shah (r. 1736–47) also had an infantry, but their firearms lacked bayonets, which made them vulnerable to cavalry; whereas his mounted musketeers had mobility.[2] Within India, the Marathas emphasised cavalry, but their infantry was also valuable, and notably in sieges, as in those of Portuguese bases in 1737–40. Disciplined and drilled infantry could be found in the Indian tradition. Moreover, masses of matchlock-armed infantry allowed the local and regional power-brokers to persist such as the various *zamindars* who acted as de facto warlords.

As elsewhere, attack by cavalry in India did not necessarily force a cavalry response, as, instead, the emphasis could be on infantry configured to oppose cavalry attacks. However, even if the response was infantry, the organising context in India was that of the reply to a cavalry threat, while cavalry was indeed the key response in India for much of the century. Nevertheless, in the closing decades of the eighteenth century, that context became less pertinent, and there was a growing emphasis on field artillery and infantry, although it is necessary to note the continued significance of cavalry. Thus, in 1781, John Bristow, the British Resident in Lucknow, estimated that the forces of Alam II, the Mughal Emperor, included thirty battalions of *sepoys*, while there was also both infantry and cavalry among the troops supplied by dependant lords. In 1795 at Kharda, Asif Jah II, the Nizam of Hyderabad, the leading ruler in south-central India, was defeated by the Marathas, retreating after his infantry and artillery were unable to prevail against those of his opponents in terrain that was not conducive to the use of cavalry,[3] terrain being a highly-important determinant of battle choices.

From mid-century, the Marathas had felt it increasingly necessary to supplement their cavalry with infantry and artillery, particularly in order to be more effective against fortresses and to counter the advantages of British-trained infantry and artillery. This was an instance of infantry as symmetry, but it greatly increased the cost of their more numerous armed forces and thus disrupted the political economy of Maratha states, as well as slowing down their armies.[4] In conflicts between Maratha rulers, infantry became more significant.

There have been claims that these forces were foredoomed to failure, not least due to a lack of unit cohesion among the infantry and inadequate weaponry,[5] but it was far from inevitable that such infantry-strong forces would be defeated by the British and there was considerable proficiency not least in the army of Mahadji Shinde which was successful in campaigning in Rajputana in the 1780s and early 1790s. He hired in 1784 Benoit de Boigne, a Frenchman and, under a new contract in 1790, gave him a large land grant thanks to which by 1793 he had trained 27,000 troops in Western methods. At Laslot in 1787, de Boigne's infantry and cavalry routed a far larger body of Rajput cavalry which attacked the defensive square without preparatory fire. The following year, outside Agra, the cavalry charges of Ismail Baig, a Mughal noble opposed to Mahadji, were similarly defeated, at Patun in 1790 de Boigne's infantry, advancing firing by platoons, defeated Rajput cavalry, and at Merta in 1790, Rajput cavalry attacks on de Boigne's square were beaten off.[6] In response, Tukoji Holkar, another Maratha leader, raised a *sepoy* force under a French mercenary. Mahadji Shinde's victory over Holkar at the battle of Lakheri in 1793 was largely settled by the superior quality of the former's infantry under de Boigne.

Local circumstances were crucial to the broader question of the relationships between infantry weapon capabilities and success. Thus, in central Amazonia in the 1760s and 1770s, the Portuguese were unable to defeat the guerrilla attacks of the mobile Muras with their ambushes of Portuguese canoes and attacks on isolated settlements. The Muras did not learn the use of firearms, but were very effective with their bows and arrows, although they could not defeat the Portuguese.[7] In contrast, at Arequipa in Peru in 1780, superior firepower led to the defeat of local rebels armed with lances, sticks, and the traditional Andean weapon, the sling. Earlier in the century, in south-west Brazil, the Paiaguá used their bows more effectively than the Portuguese did their muskets in conflict in the late 1720s and 1730s. The eventual failure of the Paiaguá was due not so much to military advantages for the Portuguese, as to disease and Native foes. However, evaluating such a range of factors is far from easy. This range, nevertheless, helps frame the significance of infantry as well as a hierarchy of infantry, indeed military, proficiency. So also, for example, with conflict between the Spaniards and the Maya in the Yucatán.[8]

At a very different scale, in South-East Asia as a whole in the eighteenth century, the use of firearms by non-Europeans was very extensive, but the volley technique was not adopted. The war elephant, pikes, swords and spears were still the dominant weaponry, and firearms made little impact on tactics, while flintlock mechanisms were not reproduced in local foundries.[9] In Myanmar (Burma), a permanent force, hereditary in membership and leadership, was supplemented during a war by conscript levies. The permanent troops, provided with state land, were obliged to grow their own food, a crucial operational restraint as it took much time. Pitched battles were generally avoided, and most fighting was with bludgeon, spears, sword and bow, although firearms also played an important role from the 1750s, first for the permanent force and then for some of the levies.

The necessary flexibility of infantry was shown by the Dutch in Sri Lanka. After an expedition against inland Kandy failed in 1764, the Dutch attacked anew in 1765, replacing swords and bayonets with less cumbersome machetes, providing troops with a more practical uniform, and moving more rapidly. Speed helped in gaining the initiative and also lessened the impact of disease. The deserted capital of Kandy was captured rather as Napoleon was to occupy Moscow in 1812 and the British Washington in 1814; but, differently to the other two cases, the Kandyan refusal to engage in battle led to a dissipation of Dutch strength, the basis for a peace in 1766. Kandy did not fall finally until 1815, and then to the British. Similarly, Chinese invasions of Myanmar in 1766–7 failed to win success, and were wrecked by disease. The Chinese did not operate there again until the Second World War, and then, against the Japanese, in very different circumstances.

In West Africa in the eighteenth century, muskets, powder and shot were important import goods, although there is little evidence that Europeans provided real training in the use of firearms. Rulers felt a keen interest in seeing European troops and their local auxiliaries exercise in formation, while Latsukabe, the founder of the Geej dynasty in Senegambia in the 1690s, sought to borrow advisers to train soldiers in the use of firearms. Local auxiliaries who worked seasonably for Europeans, for example on riverboat convoys, were probably the key figures in the transfer. For the kingdom of Kajoor in the Senegal Valley and some other West African states, including those on the Gold Coast, there is good evidence that troops armed with muskets 'exercised' and trained in formation.[10]

Further away from the Atlantic coast and its European influences, there was greater reliance on the traditional military system of forest Africa: shield-carrying, heavily-armed, infantry operating in densely-packed formations and fighting hand-to-hand, especially with swords. In so far as there were missile weapons in support, they were generally bows and javelins. This was true of such armies as those of Matamba, Kasanje, Muzumbo a Kalunga, and Lunda (in modern eastern Angola). Lunda expansionism is a reminder of the folly of assuming that Western-style infantry was necessary to success.[11]

In Madagascar, firearms played a major role in the powerful kingdoms of Menabe and Boina. Plentiful firearms were obtained from Western traders in return for slaves. Major John Corneille noted of the Madagascans in 1754, 'most of them have a gun, powder horn and shot bag, and the rest have spears.' He observed that the religious figures claimed they could provide invulnerability to shot and arrows,[12] an argument also found elsewhere.

In Ethiopia, firearms were important, as at the battles of Azezo and Fagitta in 1769, but could not alone determine battles. Thus, at Sabarkusa in 1771, shock tactics prevailed and in 1787 at Amed Ber, in an Ethiopian civil war, an army strong in firearms was defeated by the cavalry of the Yejju, a branch of the Oromo. It is necessary to consider battles as a whole and not only one in isolation, whether or not it was supposedly decisive.[13]

Meanwhile, across parts of the world, and notably in Europe, the introduction, in the late seventeenth century and early eighteenth, of the flintlock musket made a significant difference to combat. In this musket, powder was ignited by a spark produced through the action of flint on steel. The flintlock was more expensive but lighter, not requiring a stand, more reliable, easier to fire and more rapid-firing, than the earlier matchlock. Helped by the spread of pre-packaged paper cartridges, which provided the correct amount of powder, the rate of fire almost doubled. Without the hazard of the burning matches previously used to ignite powder, musketeers were able to stand closer together; and those matches were readily extinguished by rain.

Accuracy, however, was a major problem for infantry, and the switch to the flintlock did not make much difference. The accuracy of flintlocks, as earlier of matchlocks, was compromised by the nature of the barrel (unrifled and, in order to avoid fouling by powder and recoil, generally a loose fit for the shot); the shot, often elliptical rather than, as it should be, spherical, and thus unlikely to travel as designed; the slow lock time; the need for rapid firing; and the absence of accurate sights. The calibre of individual Prussian muskets ranged between 18 and 20.4 millimetres, while their length varied by up to 8 centimetres. The development of iron, instead of wooden, ramrods was believed to increase the rate of musket fire, but they often bent and jammed in the musket, broke or went rusty;

and frequent use of the ramrod distorted the barrel into an oval shape.[14] Soldiers fired by volley at close range, rather than employing individually aimed shot. Fire rates improved, notably with the adoption of platoon firing,[15] but faced problems. John Hill, who was commissioned into the 23rd Foot (Royal Welsh Fusiliers) in 1796, recorded 'we had the regiment fire ball some time ago, about 4 in an hundred hit the target … some of them do not know how to load their piece. The badness of the musket, the ball not firing.'[16]

Despite the bayonets, hand-to-hand fighting on the battlefield was relatively uncommon, and most casualties were caused by shot, as with the French troops wounded at the battle of Oudenaarde in 1708, and admitted into the Hôtel des Invalides in Paris, with many of the others wounded due to cavalry sabres.[17] Bayonets rather served as a deterrent to such hand-to-hand fighting, which tended to occur when regular formations had broken down, and also in storming attempts during sieges and in skirmishes. At the same time, infantry could advance to attack with cold steel in the face of musket fire, as with the Swedish victory at Klisów (1702) over a larger Saxon army. The Saxons retreated, as defending forces tended to do if they could not keep their attackers at a distance, although they did not break as they were to do when beaten by the Swedes at Fraustadt in 1706. As the Jacobites were also to show in their victories over regular British forces, for example Prestonpans in 1745, linear formations relying on firepower were not designed for close-quarter fighting.

Yet it was necessary to consider how best to use this potential for shock, given the casualties that would be taken in any advance against defensive firepower. There was also the danger that shock action would be absorbed and/or countered by defence in depth, notably the availability of reserves, as with the Russian victory over the Swedes at Poltava in 1709,[18] and that of British regulars over the Jacobites at Culloden in 1746.

The firing drill took time and required training and discipline, especially as it was to be carried out under fire from clearly hostile forces and was expected to be coordinated with other members of the same unit in order to produce volley fire. A close-knit network of tactical rules and customs, and mechanistic creeds, informed the ideas behind linear tactics. The regulations for the First Battalion of the Norfolk Regiment in 1780 stated:

> 'In firing great care to be taken that the battalion is in close order, that the men level well and ram down their cartridges, as a slow well-directed fire is far preferable to an hasty irregular straggling one.'[19]

There was a degree of rationalisation of infantry units, such that they were to have uniform size, armaments, clothing, command strategies, and other features. Such developments made it easier to maintain control not least in order to implement drill techniques that maximised firepower.[20] They were not dependent on a particular political mechanism, for allied and subsidised units could be expected to fight in an identical fashion with 'national units.' This was a marked contrast to the situation in the Asiatic empires where there was a major difference between core and ancillary troops. Thus, there was an obvious contrast between the Allied forces in battles in the War of the Spanish Succession (1701–14), such as Blenheim (1704), and the situation in major engagements in Asia. In the former case, Austrian, British and Dutch forces fought in a similar fashion and combined with little difficulty.

The Europeans extended this model to India, training local units to fight as they did, and thus linking the well-developed Indian military labour market to Western patterns of infantry behaviour. In 1787, Brigadier-General Charles, 2nd Earl Cornwallis, the Governor General of Bengal and Commander-in-Chief of British India, felt less concerned about the threat posed by Tipu Sultan of Mysore, 'since I have seen this brigade of *sepoys*. Major Hay's regiment is one of the finest in every respect that I ever saw in any country ... the facility of obtaining good recruits is so great in this country [India], that we may share almost any numbers of native infantry.'[21] A common element in both Europe and India was the continuous expenditure on permanent forces, expenditure that could not be provided by the fruits of offensive warfare – land and plunder – because such forces were not always engaged in war. This expenditure necessitated particular financial and governmental techniques.

In effect, there was a military labour market in all countries, as well as a transnational one. Nevertheless, these markets, notably the domestic ones, varied greatly in their character, the extent to which they were explicit, and the degree to which they overlapped with issues of discipline and morale. There could be serious breakdowns, some of which reflected systemic problems. Thus, in the Ottoman empire, the infantry, which lacked the financial benefits of cavalry landownership, suffered particularly hard when the Sultan was unable to pay the army. Alongside political tensions, this led to rebellions, notably in 1717–19 and, more seriously, 1730. This problem in part reflected the lack of pillage and fresh land to distribute, as well as a loss of prestige stemming from the absence of new conquests. In turn, desertion affected the number of Ottoman troops and there was an increased need to turn to normal militias as well as to forces raised by local strongmen. This tendency was linked to a lack of discipline and an absence of consistent quality, which is an obvious consequence of using a number of means to raise troops.

The early decades of the century saw a working through of recent tactical developments, not only in terms of evaluating best practice and combined arms possibilities, but also assessing the likely nature of battle fatigue and shock as a result of their use. In the War of the Spanish Succession, in which Britain was engaged in 1702–13, the combat effectiveness of the infantry, both the fire discipline and bayonet skill, owed much to their extensive experience of battle in the 1690s and 1700s, which familiarised the troops to immediate manoeuvre and execution. Drawn up in three ranks, the infantry was organised into three firings, ensuring that continuous fire was maintained which was an important goal.

More consistently, British infantry fire was more effective than that of the French, so that the pressure of battlefield conflict with the British was high, for example in the British victory at Dettingen in 1743. Moreover, at Culloden in 1746, the discipline of the British infantry blunted what might otherwise have been sensible preliminary Jacobite lunges. This was very much a victory won by infantry. Outside Quebec in 1759, the battle was an infantry one. The French advanced in columns, but were hit by British volley fire, and then attacked with a bayonet charge, a participant recording:

> 'About 9 o'clock the French army had drawn up under the walls of the town, and advanced towards us briskly and in good order. We stood to receive them; they began their fire at a distance, we reserved ours, and as they came nearer fired on them by divisions, this did execution and seemed to check them a little, however, they

> still advanced pretty quick, we increased our fire without altering our position, and when they were within less than an hundred yards, gave them a full fire, fixed our bayonets, and under cover of the smoke the whole line charged.'[22]

Earlier that year, at Minden, the French were defeated thanks to the courage and fire discipline of the British infantry, which defeated cavalry and infantry attacks while, despite being ordered to do so, the British cavalry failed to act. Lord George Sackville, the cavalry commander, reported:

> 'The ardour of the English battalions and Hanoverian Guards carried them into the midst of the enemy, and though they found themselves raked by the cannon, and attacked on their flanks and rear by cavalry, they made so brave, and so glorious a resistance, and so often renewed their attacks, that the enemy soon began to give way, and the whole affair was over in two hours.'[23]

Generals in mid-century proved able in Western and Central Europe to deliver victories that had not proved possible in the 1690s in part due to the flexibility brought by flintlock-bayonet soldiers.

Linear tactics were much affected by the details of topography, drainage and vegetation, for uniformity was rare. Thus, the formation of advancing units could be disrupted, broken up, or funnelled, providing opportunities for the defenders, and notably so if the attackers were disrupted, for their fighting effectiveness required cohesion, as was the case for close-packed formations, such as advancing lines of infantry, stopping and firing volleys. There was a psychological significance of advancing in unbroken order under fire and closing on an enemy who would thereby be mastered.[24] This practice, however, did not invariably work as the British showed in their failures at Fontenoy in 1745 and Bunker Hill in 1775, at the hands of the French and the Americans respectively. The very different contexts of these two battles indicates the need for caution in drawing conclusions from individual battles. Bunker Hill indicated how drill did not matter too much for troops behind field fortifications and on the defensive.

Major engagements were less common than smaller-scale clashes. Lieutenant-General Henry Conway described the *petite guerre* against the French in Westphalia in 1761, the frequent clashes around outposts that are too often overlooked: 'small skirmishes, and almost daily marches and counter-marches.' The following year, he described such fighting as heavy: 'the French fought quite close to the point of bayonet.' In such clashes, light troops, such as the British units that drove the French back over the River Lahn in 1762, were at a premium.[25] The Catalan Miquelet militia, irregulars who played a role in successive conflicts from the 1640s, were also instances of the role of light troops.

As with matchlocks, although to a lesser extent, fire from flintlocks, could readily be disrupted by poor weather, especially by rain and, to a lesser extent, wind. Damp powder caused misfires. In 1738, the Austrian 'infantry's arms were rendered almost useless by reason of the rain'[26] when fighting the Ottomans at Cornea. The speed of fire was enhanced by the use of paper cartridges, with the ball, powder and wadding in a single package. This packaging made reloading easier and allowed each soldier to carry more ammunition.

The Brown Bess, the British flintlock musket, had many deficiencies. These included its stiff trigger, powerful recoil, poor performance if the powder became damp, and the large bore that ensured a loose fit for the musket ball and thus decreased its accuracy. Yet they were more effective at a greater distance than French and Prussian flintlocks. Furthermore, the large bore meant that the Brown Bess could take all calibres of musket ammunition, while the loose fit of the ball helped make ramming it down the barrel easy and thus contributed to the rate of fire. Yet despite some (improbable) suggestions of a rate of fire of up to five times a minute in the hands of a trained soldier, the real rate may have been closer to twice a minute.

The use of the bayonet became normal for Western European armies in the early eighteenth century, but that did not settle the tactical deployment of infantry nor indeed what was held to be the optimum weaponry. That uncertainty occurred within the context of a belief in military change, indeed one that, for some commentators, might lead to a return to the arms in use before gunpowder. The last was argued in 1761 by Lieutenant-Colonel Campbell Dalrymple, Governor of conquered Guadeloupe, in his *Military Essay*, which grounded its discussion of the present in Antiquity, as well as showing an awareness of French tactical debates:

> 'The effect of fire begins now to be disputed, at least, it is not believed so formidable, as it was; which in time may produce another military revolution, and send us back to the arms in use before the invention of gunpowder.'[27]

There remained a consistent tension between firepower and shock tactics. The different choices made reflected circumstances, experience, the views of particular generals, and wider assumptions in military society, and were not dictated by technology. The prestige of the attack remained culturally significant but also a product of the need for speed. The tactical offensive in Western Europe was not banished by the enhancement of firepower from the 1690s. Lieutenant-General John Burgoyne, the British commander at Saratoga in 1777, referring to the difficulties he faced, noted: 'The British bayonet was repeatedly tried ineffectually.'[28] In contrast, the same year, British bayonet charges were decisive in the victory at Brandywine, but that reflected both a more open terrain and the British ability there, unlike at Saratoga, to outflank the defenders.

Moreover, there was the use of infantry in the assault in storming positions, and frequently in costly fashion, as in the French storming of Dutch-held Bergen-op-Zoom in 1747. John Deane of the British Foot Guards recorded of the successful but lengthy siege of French-held Lille in 1708, which cost the besiegers 14,000 casualties:

> 'this murdering siege, it is thought, has destroyed more than [the siege of] Namur [1695] did last war, and those that were the flower of the army; for what was not killed or drowned were spoiled by their hellish inventions of throwing of bombs, boiling pitch, tar, oil and brimstone with scalding water and such like combustibles, upon our men, from the outworks, and when our men made any attack. Especially the English Grenadiers have scarce 6 sound men in a company; likewise many other inventions enough to puzzle the Devil to contrive.'[29]

The combination of earlier methods with the weaponry of the gunpowder age thus made the experience of war very unpleasant. In the American War of Independence, Nathanael Greene, the American commander in the South from December 1780, wrote of the difficulties of attacking positions when without heavy artillery and unable to mount a siege:

> 'the idea of storming works which many speak of with as much familiarity and confidence as they would talk of gathering a basket of fruit, unless it can be effected by surprise, affords but a poor prospect of success.'[30]

Key to military history, the relationship between continuity and change varied in form and content, this variation providing much of the guidance to differences in performance. Thus, in Russia, Peter the Great reorganised the army in 1699–1700, creating new-style infantry regiments, and followed up by adopting an effective flintlock musket. This represented a continuance of the rejection of dependence on the cavalry of the feudal host, and, linked to that, another iteration of the Russian establishment of new-model infantry units, as particularly seen in 1550 and 1630. The very need to repeat the exercise casts instructive light on specific steps, but also underlined the continued nature of military revival that is an aspect of maintaining effectiveness.

At the same time, the rapid account of Russia in terms of infantry modernisation, and, indeed, a focus on the infantry, requires a granulation in terms of specifics that emphasise circumstances and difficulties, and are of more general application. Many of the Russian troops, especially in the battles of 1701–4 with the Swedes, were not new-style regiments. Furthermore, although impressive, the developing Russian metallurgical industry could not meet the army's need for muskets until 1712, so that, in 1707, the proportion of pikemen to musketeers was actually increased, while infantry firearms were not standardised in Russia until 1715.[31]

Looking forward with a different aspect of significance, there was a protracted debate over weaponry and tactics from the 1720s in France. This debate was of greater importance as France was the leading and most influential European power on land, although the discussion, which drew heavily on an understanding on past infantry practice, was not limited to France. Indeed, in 1736, the British envoy in Berlin reported: 'They make frequent parallels here between the Macedonian troops and theirs,'[32] which was a way to validate Prussia in opposition to Austria. There was a concern among commentators that a firepower emphasis led to a loss of battlefield mobility and offensive force and, therefore, a wish to restore a role for shock tactics, a wish that could extend to an interest in reintroducing the pike.

Maurice, Comte de Saxe (1696–1750), the leading French general of the 1740s, who had a strong reputation across Europe, was interested in innovation, some of it looking back for its point of references. Thus, he called his ideal formation a legion and was interested in the re-introduction of armour. More significantly, Saxe was committed to the attack. At Rocoux in 1746, Saxe attacked in columns, employing successfully his superiority of numbers at the expense of an Anglo-Dutch-Austrian army.[33]

Jean-Charles Chevalier de Folard (1669–1752) saw his advocacy of shock tactics in part as a commentary on Polybius, specifically on the latter's account of the clash between Macedonian *phalanx* and Roman legion. Folard wanted to bring back the wedge (*cuneus*), while the column he advocated was a form of the *phalanx*. Folard and Saxe were also interested in reviving the pike, as was the *Encyclopédie* (1751–65), the repository of fashionable French opinion; while there was also support for the idea at the time of the French Revolution.

That was not to be the course followed, but interest in column as opposed to line, led, in the manoeuvres of 1778, to the testing of the rival systems. They failed to settle the controversy, and the new French tactical manual issued in 1791 incorporated both. War broke out in 1792 and there was a focus for France in the 1790s on attacking column formations, and, in particular, a relative reduction of the emphasis on firepower. That is a debate that can be followed with relative ease, which raises the question of the extent and nature of the many debates that are more obscure. Separately, the reliance into the nineteenth century, as at Waterloo (1815), on infantry squares to see off attacks, notably by cavalry, was a testimony not only to firepower but also to the tactical value, in the defence, of cold steel, although now that was a case of bayonets, not pikes.

At a broader social level, the prestige of swords and their ease of use, the latter even more true of daggers, ensured that, if the ability to employ violence was a de facto definition of violence (although clearly not a definition restricted to regular soldiers), then the continuity of cutting and thrusting weapons was very apparent. This, however, did not necessarily mean that irregulars had military clout. Thus, in 1715, Daniel Dering observed 'For my part I have no notion that a crowd of peasants got together can make any resistance against standing regular forces,'[34] a reflection made more pertinent by Jacobite opposition to George I. If infantry only means regular forces, then this issue might seem of marginal consequence; but that was not the case for infantry were not thus limited.

Returning to regular forces, tactical discussion was not restricted to lines or columns. A rival of Saxe for attention in the 1740s, Frederick II, Frederick the Great, of Prussia (r. 1740–86) in 1745 developed the attack in oblique order, so as to be able to concentrate overwhelming strength against a portion of the linear formation of the opposing army. Focusing on his infantry, Frederick devised a series of methods for strengthening one end of his line and attacking with it, while minimising the exposure of the weaker end. This method depended on the speedy execution of complex manoeuvres, for which well-drilled and well-disciplined troops were essential. It was essential to move more rapidly than the opposing side in order to maintain the advantage of deployment. Although its impact has been exaggerated, the oblique attack was used to great effect, most notably in defeating the Austrians at Leuthen in 1757 during the Seven Years' War. This was a system or 'school' borrowed by other commanders such as Duke Ferdinand of Brunswick,[35] and this led to the dissemination of Prussian influence, as with the Russian infantry code of 1755 and regulations in 1763–4 which stipulated Prussian-style tactics.

The oblique order was not without precedents, indicating the continuities notable in combat, infantry as well as cavalry. Elements of the Highland charge, especially the 'cluster' or 'wedge' designed to hit at a particular point in the enemy's line were relevant, as also the use in the War of the Spanish Succession of strengthening a wing of an army, and there were relevant suggestions in the writings of some military commentators.

Yet, as so often with infantry, there was the need to retain the capability gap. Colonel Horace St Paul, a perceptive English aide-de-camp to the Austrian Field Marshal Leopold Daun, noted:

> 'at first he [Frederick] only attacks the leading troops of the wing he is assaulting, and because he attacks them in such force he is certain of driving them back, irrespective of their bravery ... he thus tries to take them in detail.'

St Paul also observed that because Frederick 'always launches his attack against one of the two wings of the army he attacks, it is necessary simply to plan a suitable response.'[36] Austrian and Russian defensive positions, as for the Russians at Kunersdorf in 1759, did not necessarily collapse. Furthermore, heavy Prussian casualties in the gruelling campaign of 1757, as with the costly defeat of the Austrians at Prague which entailed a repulsed infantry attack, ensured that many Prussian troops were only hastily trained and therefore little-suited to execute complicated tactical methods. The battle of Zorndorf (1758) showed the difficulty of controlling troops once combat had begun, while once an oblique order attack had failed, it was difficult for the Prussians to regain the initiative. In turn, the Austrian use of dispersed columns helped to bring successes against Prussia in 1758–9, as at Hochkirch in 1758.[37] Yet, as an instance of the response mechanism, or copying or countering, that helped close-capability gaps, at Burkersdorf and Freiberg in 1762, the Prussians used dispersed columns successfully in attack.

That Frederick frequently lost more men than his enemies, compounded organisational issues, namely a shortage of recruits and the degree to which tightly disciplined troops could not be unleashed in a headlong pursuit without the danger of the units becoming less coherent, or even disintegrating because of desertion as soon as they were out of sight of their officers. This was a particular problem because of the Prussian practice of pressganging soldiers from neighbouring principalities, although most of the troops were native.

Infantry tactics were closely linked to formations, with the latter not only a matter of mounting offensive strength but also of providing defensive capability, including in the face of counter-attacks and in the mêlée clashes that could arise. In practice, linear tactics were a general concept, including a substantial variety of precepts among which line formations were only one and their application did not depend on orders from commanding officers, but rather on a nuanced mix of orders, their perception, the decisions of subordinate officers, and, to a great extent, the perceptions, emotions and actions of ordinary troops.[38] In particular, war against the Turks and overseas warfare allowed and even required more frequent deviations from the conventions of linear tactics than warfare in Western and Central Europe. Thus, in their wars with the Turks, especially the successful conflicts in 1768–74 and 1787–92, the Russians used a chequerboard of mutually supporting advancing oblongs in order to counter Turkish counter-attacks.

There was more innovation on these Balkan battlefields than in those in North America during the War of American Independence (1775–83), although the latter tend to receive more attention. The battles of the American War of Independence were similar to those in Western Europe, with lines of infantry, as at Long Island (1776), exchanging volley fire, and the major difference arose from the infrequency of cavalry action on the battlefield. As a result, infantry fought in more open order. The American militia often rode to the Southern battlefields, but then dismounted to fight, as in their success at the battle of King's Mountain in 1780.

The extent to which battle was dependent on deployment was captured at Guilford Court House in 1781, when the American lines were placed too far apart to enable the defence in depth to permit falling back in an orderly fashion thanks to mutual support. The American force was about twice as large as their British assailants. The North Carolina militia in the front line brought down many of the attackers with two volleys, but most fled the British bayonet charge, as expected. The engagement with the stronger American second line was more confused, but it was slowly pushed back, before the third line, which had more experienced troops, repelled the advancing British. To block their attack, the British commander, Charles, Earl Cornwallis, ordered two cannon to fire grapeshot into the mêlée, which led both sides to disengage with casualties. As the British reformed and resumed the attack, the Americans retreated, but the British were too exhausted to mount a pursuit and could not afford their losses.

The confusion of battles was captured later that year at Eutaw Springs when the two forces were about the same strength. The Americans were again drawn-up in three lines and, although the militia in the first gave way before a British bayonet charge, they fought better than their counterparts at Guilford Court House. The North Carolina counterparts sent forward from the second line to fill the gap were similarly broken, but the British were beaten back by their Maryland and Virginia counterparts using the bayonet. However, the American pursuit collapsed in disorder as the hungry Americans looted the British camp, especially for food, enabling the British to rally and drive the Americans back.

Although the American use of a defence-in-depth, as at Guilford Court House, was impressive, it had been prefigured, for example by the Ottomans. The battles of the American War of Independence did not see major tactical innovations. There was no equivalent to the French

Revolutionary use of columns or, earlier, Frederick the Great's employment of the oblique order. Instead, it is the conservatism of the war on the battlefield that is most significant. That, however, does not mean that infantry usage itself was static. Instead, there was a marked employment of harrying techniques by Patriot forces when circumstances permitted, as near Concord in 1775, in the Hudson valley in 1777, and, on a greater scale, in the South in 1781, the last after the regional battle-force of the Revolutionaries had been repeatedly defeated. To a degree, the operations of these forces represented the successful application of 'small war' techniques. The equivalent for the French Revolutionary and Napoleonic forces was the extensive use of skirmishers, but this was usually as part of a battlefield system, notably a harrying prelude to column attacks, rather than as an alternative.

The role of the local environment and of the challenge faced was seen in the War of Independence. The enclosed nature of much of the New England terrain encouraged deployments that reflected the topography. Thus, heavily-encumbered regular units manoeuvring and fighting in their accustomed formations were vulnerable in the face of entrenched positions and were also unsuited to the heavily wooded and hilly terrain of the Canadian frontier. Near Hubbardton in 1777, the Americans 'soon betook themselves to their breastworks, which is a mode of their defence they have adopted ... almost every shot took effect.'[39] The breastworks, field fortifications constructed of logs, were ideal cover.

Captain William Evelyn of the 4th Foot was part of the relief force sent to help the British retreat on Boston from Concord and Lexington in 1775:

> 'they were attacked from the woods and houses on each side of the road and an incessant fire kept up on both sides for several hours, they [Americans] still retiring through the wood whenever our men advanced upon them ... we were attacked on all sides from woods, orchards, stone walls, and from every house on the road side.'[40]

He died in November 1776 as a result of wounds received near White Plains.

At the battle of Long Island earlier in 1776, Captain William Congreve of the British artillery found his cannon vulnerable:

> 'the riflemen being covered by trees and large stones had very much the advantage of us, who were upon the open ground … [had] not the light infantry of the Guards … come up in time I believe we should all have been cut off.'[41]

Indeed, picking up themes of the initially unsuccessful conflict with France in North America in the 1750s,[42] General Thomas Gage, the British Commander-in-Chief in North America, had recommended in October 1774 that the British needed 'a large body of good irregulars such as German huntsmen, picked Canadians etc.'[43] In the event, the British adapted well to the challenge of the war usually firing a single volley before closing quickly, and showing considerable flexibility in formations and tactics.[44]

The engagements in the war showed the usual issues of infantry combat including responses to the detailed topography, morale, resilience, and the interaction of the moves of both sides. Thus, a British army surgeon reported of the battle of Princeton in 1777, in which an outnumbered British force under Lieutenant Colonel Charles Mawhood was handled roughly:

> 'the 17th and 55th [regiments] were on their march from Princeton…. There was a rising ground which commanded the country…. The Americans endeavoured also to gain the rising ground and their first column reached the one side of it rather before the two regiments got to the other, so that just when the 17th reached the top they received the fire of this column. The 55th (who would not advance in line with the 17th in spite of Colonel Mawhood frequently calling out to Capt [ ] who commanded them to mind his orders and come up) as soon as they saw such a slaughter among the first rank of the 17th, immediately ran off on their commanding officer saying it was all over with the others. The 17th returned a very well-levelled fire against the provincial column and instantly leaped over some rails .. and charged them with their bayonets … they ran off…. Upon the whole rebel army, advancing … retreated.'[45]

The experience of conflict in North America for the British in 1775–83 was different to that earlier during the Seven Years' War, where there had been fighting there from 1754, but both ensured the development of light infantry that also drew on wider currents of interest seen in particular in France and Austria.[46]

Separately, and more generally, the greater cost of cavalry (and its need for forage) and the effectiveness of infantry encouraged a shift toward the latter, and notably so in Europe. Shock cavalry could not hold its ground unless supported, which further underlined the need for infantry. Thus, the percentage of infantry in the Spanish and Ottoman forces rose.[47] Such an emphasis was also particularly appropriate for expeditionary warfare involving transport by sea (which was neither easy nor inexpensive for cavalry), and, separately, for militia systems and their use to provide a wartime reserve.

As always with colonial wars, regular infantry could find combat more difficult when facing hostile forces more attuned to the local environment, as for the British in North America, South America, Jamaica and St Vincent. Reflecting on the failure of the 1741 expedition against Spanish-ruled Cartagena de las Indias in modern Colombia, Colonel John Stewart observed:

> 'if ever Britain strikes any considerable stroke in this part of the world the blow must come from the North American colonies not by bringing raw men from thence like those we have had, but by sending officers of experience and good corps to incorporate with and discipline the men to be raised there. These troops as the passage from thence is much shorter might be transported directly to any part of the Spanish West Indies and arrive there with the health and vigour necessary for action, whereas troops sent from home as our own experience has taught us, are by the length of the passage one half disabled with the scurvy and the other laid up with diseases contracted by confinement and the feeding on salt provisions.'[48]

In St Vincent in 1772–3, the British, with good, new flintlocks, advanced against native Caribs, confronting ambushes and disease, and obtaining a satisfactory treaty.[49] However, Governor William Bull of South Carolina reported in 1761 that Anglo-American prisoners released by the Cherokees claimed that:

> 'their young men from their past observations express no very respectable opinion of our manner of fighting them, as by our close order, we present a large object to their fire, and our platoons do little execution as the Indians are thinly scattered, and concealed behind bushes or trees; though they acknowledged our troops thereby show they are not afraid, and that our numbers would be formidable in open ground, where they will never give us an opportunity of engaging them.'[50]

Conflict with Native Americans tested both regulars and colonials, and encouraged the development of experience with small war.[51] In 1790, in the Ohio country, Miami successfully ambushed advancing American forces who suffered from not being prepared for frontier warfare. Their preference for muskets which could bear bayonets, over the slower-firing rifles which could not, was inappropriate, as, in wooded terrain, it was accuracy, not rate of fire, that was important. Seeking to maximise their opportunity to deliver aimed fire and to minimise the target they offered, the Natives fought in open, not close, order; but the Americans lacked the confidence and training to do so. The militia also tended to lack relevant experience, and this was difficult to counter with training as their discipline was weak. In 1791, at the side of the Wabash River, the Natives surprised the poorly-prepared American camp. Unable to offer an effective response with musketry, cannon or bayonet charges, and with the outnumbered but elusive Natives firing from cover and using time to their advantage, the Americans were badly shot up, before abandoning their position, breaking out, and fleeing in disorder with over 600 dead to the Native 21. As in 1790, Native tactical superiority was well-demonstrated at the infantry level.[52]

The key element of training was demonstrated by the response, with a new commander from 1792, Anthony Wayne, focusing on combat-preparation not the parade ground, and the combination of firepower and mobility. This helped lead to a major victory at Fallen Timbers in 1794, with an American bayonet charge crucial. Moreover, a clearer understanding of Native techniques and their limitations helped to deliver further American victories, such as the battle of the Thames in 1813.[53] There was to be a similar trajectory in other conflicts with Native Americans, such as the eventually-successful Seminole Wars in Florida (1817–18, 1835–42,

1855–8), and, indeed, other conflicts between Western and non-Western forces, such as the Java War of 1825–30 for the Dutch.

Native Americans were better at ambushes than at attacking fortified posts, and were vulnerable to attacks on their settlements, which presented targets for their opponents and could be battered by cannon, a key prelude to Western infantry attack and a cover for the infantry. The Natives had very few cannon to use either for siegecraft or for counter-battery fire in defence. As so often with the possibilities for infantry, numbers were a crucial element. The Natives lacked the numbers to man most fortification systems, and individual positions could be seen as traps in which battle could be forced on infantry. As a result, when their positions were approached, the Natives generally tried to attack, rather than simply waiting on the defensive. As so often with war, this in part was a matter of cultural norms about conflicts as well as a response to the balance of military capabilities: the established enhancement of infantry by means of fortification had been lost in the face of European siegecraft capabilities.

The French were successful when they invaded Egypt in 1798, as their Mamluk opponents fought them in battle. This enabled the French to use their firepower with success, their muskets appearing to an opponent 'like a boiling pot on a fierce fire.'[54] Instead of using the linear formations common to European battlefields, Napoleon deployed his infantry in squares (often in practice oblongs), rather as Rumyantsev had successfully done against the Ottomans in 1770, and as the Russians did anew in war with the Turks in 1787–92, for example in victories at Fokshany (1789), Martinishtje (1789) and Machin (1791). The Austrians had limited success against the Ottomans using linear tactics in 1737–9 and 1788, but in 1789 successfully employed square/oblongs, notably at Mehadia.[55] This formation permitted Napoleon and others to combine the firepower of densely packed infantry with a tactical flexibility of formations that could not be put at a disadvantage by being attacked in flank or rear by more mobile cavalry which would have been a problem for columns. The battles of 1798 in Egypt were significant triumphs of infantry over cavalry. Napoleon then advanced into modern Israel. At Mount Tabor in 1799, deployment in squares was again decisive against a far larger Ottoman army.

Very differently toward the close of the century, firearms were introduced to the north-west coast of North America by European and

American traders in the 1780s and the willingness to trade them led the Native Americans to replace bows and arrows. The use of firearms was then spread by intertribal trade, and the Natives, who rapidly became expert in their use, employed them for warfare among themselves and against whites as well.[56]

The column tactics that became important for European forces from the 1790s were not simply a matter of an undisciplined assault, but rather a response to the continued role of shock tactics. The column can be presented as the organised consequence of the *levée en masse*: the addition, by the French Revolutionaries, of large numbers of poorly-trained conscripts to the army.[57] It was easier to train hastily-raised troops to fight in columns. Little time was available or required, and the formation offered a psychological benefit of packing the recruit in with others, which established a sense of security in the midst of battle. Aside from solidarity, columns provided mobility. The deployment of troops in a column allowed for more men to be concentrated in a smaller area than before, which increased the chance of a breakthrough. A number of columns meant the greater disposal of units, ensuring that command and co-ordination skills became more important. The French benefited from young and determined commanders, the war serving as a forcing house for talent.

Yet, although on the defensive the French relied on the line, columns could also be employed on the defensive, and, indeed, were an obvious formation for troops stationed in reserve. Thus, infantry brigades and divisions stationed in the second line would almost always have been in column, this being the best formation for rapid movements, whether plugging a gap, launching a counter-attack, or reinforcing an offensive. But columns were also of use in the front line; while, more generally and for many purposes, it was possible to intermix lines and columns.

These points underline the problems involved in the assessment of infantry 'progress.' Far from presenting columns as a product of a relatively simplistic, indeed barbaric, military organisation, as they were to some critics, a regression from the professionalism, training and sophisticated battlefield manoeuvres of the Frederican army (the military system modelled on the army of Frederick II), it is possible to argue that they were not only effective but a development on what had come before.

A sudden onslaught by a line of columns on an attacking force, and particularly on an attacking force that had been shot up and become somewhat 'blown' and disorganised, was likely to have been pretty devastating. It was possible to change deployment if advancing in column more easily than if attacking in line. Furthermore, columns could still fire, while they could also be placed side by side to present a continuous front.

It is possible to distinguish between shallow columns and deep columns, and between columns of manoeuvre and columns of attack, but these principles were not applied in practice zealously and, anyway, as more generally with infantry combat, everything tended to break down when combat began and Saxe had pointed out that columns could readily become disordered. Yet, there was a contrast between battalion columns and larger units, the former a single block of men while the latter could be made up in many differing ways, not least by varying the spacing of the individual battalions. Some columns had men packed tightly together, while others had less coherent and dense formations.

Columns gave a defender weight, the capacity for local offensive action, and solidity; while troops deployed in line came under enormous psychological strain when under attack by columns.[58] This issue underlines the danger of presenting one form of tactical deployment as necessarily weaker than another, and so also with related organisational matters. There is also a parallel with the British use of attacking line-ahead tactics at sea, notably at Trafalgar in 1805, thus breaching their opponent's line of battle.

The extent to which infantry tactics were contested invites discussion of the nature of debate when we lack relevant evidence. There appears scant reason to believe that debate would have been absent, yet also no reason to anticipate similar levels of debate. Nevertheless, as another instance of doctrine linked to debate, the tactical system adopted by the British in 1792 drew on that of Prussia, and was based on Colonel David Dundas' *Principles of Military Movements, chiefly applied to infantry. Illustrated by manoeuvres of the Prussian troops, and by an outline of the British campaigns in Germany* (1788), in short on the experience of Continental warfare, more particularly the Prussian manoeuvres that focused the attention of many military visitors and commentators.[59] Dundas issued a call for order:

> 'In order to facilitate the movements of great armies, and to enforce their discipline, it is necessary to organise, divide, subdivide them; to establish such general regulations as may prevent the repetition of a tedious but essential detail at times when action and exertion are

> required … to ascertain the duties and attentions of individuals in every situation of march; so that the most concise orders may suffice to put the army in motion; and to place it at all times ready to execute with exactness and alacrity such intentions of its commander as may arise from the circumstances of the moment.'

Dundas praised the instructions of 1760, both of Marshal Broglie and his opponent, Ferdinand of Brunswick, under whom he claimed, troops had moved 'as parts of one and the same great machine,' and criticised any stress on the adoption of a looser, more open tactical system for light infantry.[60]

Dundas's tactical system represented a deliberate rejection of the more flexible tactics of the American War of Independence. Indeed, belonging to what was termed the 'German' rather than the 'American' school of officership, Dundas placed the organised firepower of the close-order line, the epitome of heavy infantry at this point, at the centre of military practice, claiming that such a line could resist cavalry in open country. He was much less concerned with light infantry. Yet, as Richard Brinsley Sheridan declared in Parliament in April 1797, mocking government assurances about the ease with which the French would be defeated:

> 'I will not remind those gentlemen of their declaration so often made, that the French must fly before troops well disciplined and regularly paid. We have fatal experience of the folly of those declarations; we have seen soldiers frequently without pay, and without sufficient provisions, put to rout the best-paid armies in Europe.'[61]

The Russian forces deployed against the French during the French Revolutionary and Napoleonic Wars used methods that were similar to those of the French army, notably a focus on inflicting casualties and destroying opposing formations: the Russian army under Suvorov that advanced into northern Italy in 1799 used repeated attacks in battles, notably Cassano d'Adda, Trebbia and Novi, to find weaknesses in the French position. Employing methods developed successfully against the Ottomans, Suvorov was willing to accept a high rate of casualties and to mount costly frontal attacks with a reliance on bayonet attacks rather than defensive firepower, which contrasted with the tactics against both Turks and French of his more cautious Austrian allies. Like Napoleon, Suvorov was a believer in the tactics of attack, and employed against the French techniques developed earlier in conflict with the Turks. Rather than the wastage of ammunition seen with unaimed volley fire, Suvorov preferred aimed firepower. Russian troops were trained to fight in columns as well as extended order formations, although in practice they did not do the latter that much.[62]

Separately, the French both employed light infantry in a largely separate category on the battlefield and, employing *l'ordre mixte*, integrated close-order and open-order infantry so that every infantry battalion had the capacity to deploy its own skirmishers.[63] Though vulnerable to cavalry, although far less so in broken terrain, skirmishers were not vulnerable to volley fire or artillery. The French chose their best infantry to skirmish as skirmishing was a job for those who knew what they were doing. The key to French infantry tactics was not the column or skirmishers *per se*, but the ability to suit tactics to terrain and situation. They could stand in line, albeit a bit more ragged than the Prussians; or French troops could be arranged in the *l'ordre mixte* combination of line and column for stability or for mobility, depending on circumstances. Additionally, they could deploy as skirmishers. Effective light infantry were not limited to special regiments or particular companies. And most importantly, the French could use line, column and skirmishers in combinations that fitted the situation. Combination in flexibility and flexibility in combination were significant, and important victories were delivered from 1792.

In contrast to the French, Charles Jenkinson, watching a Prussian infantry review in 1792, observed: 'the celerity and precision with which all their movements are performed are inconceivable to those who have not seen them. Every operation they go through is mechanical.' The more caustic French envoy in London referred to new hordes of disciplined slaves, although that stereotype for the Prussians is inaccurate.[64]

Western commentators, nevertheless, presented their militaries as more disciplined and organised than non-Western forces. George Thomas, an Irish adventurer, who in 1797–1802 gained, by conquest, an independent principality north-west of Delhi, wrote of

> 'European troops, or Indian troops disciplined and conducted by European officers ... as a machine actuated and animated by the

> voice of the commander; but in an irregular army, where discipline never obtained [existed], little can be expected...'[65]

The experience of the Anglo-Maratha conflicts of the 1800s and 1810s suggested that Indian forces were far more effective than Thomas claimed, not least with good small arms and artillery.[66]

The infantry of the late eighteenth century can be regarded as an aspect of modernity, but that is less the case for the ways in which they fought. Thus, the American snipers were an extended development of the skirmishers and sharpshooters sent out in front of the line on the battlefield in most later eighteenth-century armies in Europe, a key element in the development of light infantry. The French Revolutionary attack harked back to the Swiss pike square, although now combining firepower with the shock weapon, which was now the bayonet.

Meanwhile, in terms of conditions, infantry remained worse off than cavalry. Thus, the real wages of Western infantrymen were low in the eighteenth century but they received uniforms and accommodation provided in barracks. The military were a section of the community which governments needed and cared for, albeit at a basic level, and troops were the largest group paid by governments. The rations that were specified could be generous: in the 1720s, every French soldier in Roussillon received daily one litre of wine or beer, 500 grams each of meat and vegetables, 25 of fat, and about one kilogram of bread, the basic minimum that virtually all governments seem to have provided. On campaign they were often more limited. At Valley Forge in 1778–9, the American soldiers dined on 'fire cakes,' a baked flour-and-water paste, while in the South in 1779–83 rations were often rice or 'johnny-cake,' or hoe cake, mixed quickly from flour and water and baked over a fire on a hoe.

Troops on campaign generally had worse supplies and circumstances than those on base. In August 1748, Edmund Martin reported from near Eindhoven in the United Provinces about fevers and deaths in the British forces: 'the wetness of this country, the bad food ... we lie in barns and open cowhouses with little or no straw... The Hollanders ... are the same; I hear the French are too.'[67] And this was one of the most favourable areas for campaigning. British troops marching south from Emden in 1758 found East Friesland bare of supplies, the Commissary, Michael Hatton, complaining:

> 'No contractors, no regular magazines ... a continual rain ... the bread for want of covered waggons is dissolved ... as is the two days bread the men had in the knapsacks.... There has not been a pot boiled these two days, the rain put out all the fires ... there are potatoes ... which the men will get if the waters fall a little.'[68]

Following heavy rain in northern Germany in August 1758, Charles, 3rd Duke of Marlborough observed 'the foot have marched the last day almost up to their middle in water the whole way.' In 1762, the British infantry found supplies lacking in allied Portugal and the men 'were fainting with the heat and want of food.'[69] In 1777, Burgoyne's advance south from Canada to the Hudson Valley was threatened by a failure in supplies. As he subsequently told the House of Commons: 'It was soon found that in the situation of the transport system at that time, the army could barely be victualled from day to day, and that there was no prospect of establishing a magazine in due time.' However, so also for his opponents in this campaign, Major General Philip Schuyler noting at one stage 'we have no cartridge paper.'[70] And so also when not on campaign. John, 4th Earl of Loudoun's 1,450 strong regiment garrisoning Fort Augustus in the Scottish Highlands was short 1,057 pairs of shoes. It was not until the mid-nineteenth century that the invention of canned meat, dried milk powder, evaporated milk and margarine changed the perishability and bulk of provisions.

The very slow spread of barracks, an expensive device, ensured that troops were frequently quartered among the civilian population, which made it easier for troops to pursue civilian trades. In Russia, it was not decided to house all Moscow's soldiers in barracks until 1765, while, although there were many barracks in Ireland by the later 1720s, there were very few in Britain prior to 1793. This made it harder to maintain discipline and train troops, and even to develop a distinctive military attitude, while making relations with civilians more contentious. The use of barracks became more important in Austria, France and Prussia in the second half of the century, but barracks were often unpleasant for the soldiers, frequently being gloomy, damp and insanitary.

There was interest in better treatment, in part to improve morale. Russian regulations for officers issued in the 1760s emphasised the need for positive motivation in the process of transforming peasants into soldiers. In 1764, France created invalidity pensions, in 1767 Austria introduced utilitarian uniforms that were easier to maintain, and in the 1780s the pay and conditions of Bavarian soldiers improved.

Discipline could be harsh, although less so than was reported. This was a common feature of law enforcement, which was often tempered and episodic – however savage and arbitrary it might seem. Thus, under Frederick the Great (r. 1740–86), who used the death penalty very sparingly, a small number of hard cases received a disproportionate number of the most severe punishments. The most vivid accounts of the Prussian system's horrors were selective treatments composed by critics. Russian discipline appears to have been more savage, possibly due to service divorcing soldiers from their native communities and treating them as the possessions of their officers. At the battle of Kesseldorf in 1745, Saxon regiment commanders made inspiring speeches and rewarded those who captured flags and cannon, but also ordered the troops acting as file-closers to kill everybody who sought to leave the fight.

Brigadier Cholmondeley recorded of the battle of Falkirk in 1746, in which some of the British troops showed a lack of the expected fighting spirit, that to move some forward 'I was forced to fire a pistol amongst them, before I could get them to do this.'[71] In part, such responses reflected a sense of discipline as precarious. Colonel John Moore noted of his troops in the West Indies in 1796: 'great want of discipline and confidence in their officers.... The men of our regiments are mere recruits – the officers young and without either zeal or experience.'[72]

Youth was certainly a factor. On the eve of the Revolution, half of the French infantry of the line were aged 18 to 25. Yet that left many in their thirties. The army recruited first among the unmarried.[73]

Military disaffection, as seen particularly with the French Revolution, might appear to have a modern tone when, in practice, it was scarcely new. So also with the problems of fighting irregulars and in urban settings. In December 1789, Robert Arbuthnot commented: 'I think that Sovereigns had better all disband their regular troops, as we now find they are no match for a mob.'[74] This was a response not only to developments in France but also in the Austrian Netherlands (Belgium) where, at Turnhout, Austrian troops were defeated by a 'Patriot' force in which snipers and women throwing stones from the rooftops increased the pressure on Austrians unprepared for town fighting.[75]

In practice, such conflict was not new, while 'Patriot' movements were defeated on other occasions, for example the Dutch by the Prussians in

1787, the Poles by the Russians in 1794 and the Irish by the British in 1798. Moreover, there was much continuity in the fighting of the period. The American and French Revolutionary wars were less revolutionary than they might appear.

It is worth altering the perspective at the close from the standard Western narrative, and not only by querying that analysis and narrative. It is appropriate to consider China, because that was far from a marginal power in this period, nor one best regarded as in some regard anachronistic and, because the route to failure in the late nineteenth century overshadows the earlier situation. Aside from this as a problematic account of China as a whole, this approach has limited value from the military perspective. China was one of the most significant military powers of the eighteenth century on land, one that made important territorial gains. Although cavalry was prominent, the bulk of the Chinese army was infantry, but its trajectory was different to that of the West. However, a crucial factor for China as for Britain (but not Austria nor Prussia) was the ability to deliver power at a great distance. Western weaponry was better, although as China was not confronted by stronger-armed infantry, the significance of this is unclear. Chinese soldiers were frequently armed with muskets, but these were poor matchlocks as the Chinese had not made the transition to flintlocks, while their gunpowder was low-grade. Partly as a result, the Chinese continued to use bows, swords, spears, pikes, halberds and spears.

The tendency to end an account of warfare in this century with the French Revolutionary Wars is well-established. And yet, they were of scant significance for the practice of war across much of the world. Thus China, which in the last fifteen years of the century fought in Nepal and Vietnam and faced the large-scale White Lotus rebellion, was on a different page in infantry conflict.

There is therefore no one model of war for this period, a point that could be further expanded were we to consider sub-Saharan Africa and India, in each of which there were high rates of conflict. The overall conclusion is that infantry was the prime arm and, in particular, of greater importance than hitherto in India. This was the case even before the major changes in firearms during the nineteenth century.

Chapter 7

Nineteenth Century

Colonel James Stanhope of the First Foot Guards reported the day after the British victory at Waterloo in 1815:

> 'When the French cavalry attacked us in our squares … our men behaved as if they were at a field day, firing by ranks and with the best possible aim. Under a most destructive cannonade and having several shells burst in the middle of us, not a man moved from his place.… At the last we became exposed to the united efforts of all their arms and changed from line to squares and from squares to lines, as the circumstances of the case required.… There was a moment peculiarly critical and where nothing but the extraordinary steadiness of the troops saved the day.'[1]

The nineteenth century appears as the great century of infantry, in part due to the relative, indeed absolute, decline of cavalry, and to the extent to which mechanisation and air power are not yet to the fore, although a different form of mechanisation to that of petrol engines could be seen with infantry firepower. Rail as an instance of mechanisation was important precisely because it played a major role in the movement of infantry and in logistical support, as was very apparent for example in the American Civil War (1861–5). Yet, rail offered movement toward the battle zone, rather than on the battlefield.

Infantry was also affected by the spread of Western models, both with Western imperialism and with emulation by other powers seeking to keep up and respond, for example Egypt and China. As a result, military modernisation for infantry was understood in terms of firepower, a process furthered by the significance of artillery on land and at sea. At the same time, mass remained a key element on the battlefield, with most of the mass provided by infantry, as it still is.

This was the dominant arm on the Napoleonic battlefield; although that did not mean that there was only one form of infantry and infantry conflict. Thus, in Britain in particular there was growing interest in light infantry, in part due on the example of conflict in North America, notably the American War of Independence (1775–83), although there were also significant examples elsewhere, particularly, for Britain, the prevalence of skirmishing tactics and small-unit raids in the Caribbean.[2] Light infantry fought in open order as opposed to infantry-of-the-line, also sometimes called heavy infantry, who fought shoulder to shoulder. In 1803, Major General John Moore was appointed commander of a new brigade at Shorncliffe Camp in Kent, which was designed to serve as the basis for a permanent light infantry force. Particular emphasis was placed upon marksmanship. Moore's force was to become the Light Brigade and, subsequently, the Light Division. The cause of light infantry was supported by Frederick, Duke of York, George III's second son, who was Commander-in-Chief of the army from 1795 to 1809 and 1811 to 1827.

The disciplined firepower of the British infantry played a major part in the Duke of Wellington's victories, of which the most important in the Peninsular War were Vimeiro (1808), Talavera (1809), Bussaco (1810), Salamanca (1812), and Vitoria (1813). Nevertheless, this firepower was not necessarily immobile, but, rather, often used as a prelude to a bayonet charge. Wellington ably executed a form of fire-and-movement tactics, balancing the well-drilled line with the extensive use of light infantry, the conservatism of an emphasis on linear firepower formations with a greater role for manoeuvrability. At Albuera (1811), however, a battle in which Wellington was not in command, John Colborne's brigade of infantry suffered 60 per cent casualties when charged on its flank.

As an instance of attack, Bladensburg near Washington in 1814 saw a British force, outnumbered, and heavily outgunned, attack an inexperienced American militia force about 6,500 strong. Major General Robert Ross, the British commander, referred to the Americans 'yielding to the irresistible attack of the bayonet and the well-directed discharge of rockets, got into confusion and fled'. The young Peter Bowlby, an ensign in the 4th Regiment of Food, recorded:

> 'The weather was dreadfully hot.... As soon as the leading regiment, the 85th, cleared this [wood], they extended to the right and

> advanced in light infantry order over a tolerably open country, the 4th Regiment doing the same to the left.... On approaching the wood I received a shot in the shin which splintered the bone but did not break it. I tied a handkerchief round it and marched with the regiment to Washington.'[3]

At Waterloo, Captain John Garland of the 73rd Regiment recalled being in a square with the 30th:

> 'About half past 6 or 7 o'clock the Duke of Wellington rode up and spoke.... He desired me to tell Colonel Harris to form line, but should we be attacked by the cuirassiers [heavy cavalry] to reform square.'[4]

Wellington was not alone. Moore noted of the victory over the French at Aboukir in Egypt in 1801: 'We have beat them without cavalry and inferior in artillery.'[5] Of the battle of Mandara in Egypt, three regiments served to drive off French cavalry and infantry attacks, Major Hudson Lowe recording that the French:

> 'offered a powerful resistance at every step we approached but our troops continued to advance, returned their fire with the most decisive effect.... Nothing could be more admirable than the steadiness and discipline of our troops on this occasion. Every movement was performed with more regularity and precision than I have ever seen practised at any review or field day, though the men were dropping in the ranks under the hottest fire of the enemy's grape and musquetry.'[6]

Against Wellington, the French also had inadequate battlefield tactics, relying on crude attacks in dense columns which provided easy targets for the British, as at Vimeiro, Talavera, Bussaco and Waterloo. Wellington was also very active in counterattacks, and the well-timed bayonet charge, launched when the French were disorganised by their approach march and by British fire, was as effective as the volley. Medical records on casualties, and other sources, suggest that the bayonet was essentially a psychological weapon in most Napoleonic engagements. Firepower caused more casualties and was therefore crucial to the decision of the battle. However, the bayonet charge permitted exploitation of the advantage.

Such a charge, preceded by a volley, had become a standard British tactic from the late 1750s, used with effect in the War of American Independence; and, with his fine grasp of timing and eye for terrain, Wellington brought the system to a high-pitch of effectiveness. At Salamanca, Wellington rapidly and effectively switched from defense to attack, and the offensive was also key to British victories at Vitoria and Toulouse (1814). Casualties were often heavy: more than a quarter of the British force at Talavera.

Wellington described Waterloo in which defensive firepower was crucial, as a 'pounding match.' The British there used lines and squares, whereas their French counterparts focused on columns, as did the Prussians. The French use of the column became formulaic, Wellington noting after Waterloo that Napoleon 'just moved forward in the old style, in columns.'[7] The Prussians adopted the attack column as well as light infantry training, both reflecting the impact of the French example.[8] At Waterloo, the British pursuit was 'in columns of battalions.'[9]

Yet, as with naval battle (including the British at Trafalgar), alongside the focus on grand moves, there could also be caution and indecisiveness. Thus, a French officer in d'Erlon's corps at Waterloo, described the French advance on the east of the battlefield at the close of the battle when the Imperial Guard attacked further west:

> 'We again descended into the hollow to renew our attack on the plateau where we have been already so roughly handled. We there found our old antagonists so much weakened as ourselves, so ere long the attack resolved itself into a desultory skirmishing fight.'

Such conflict was more common than often implied,[10] including during the world wars. Yet, a clear impression of infantry activity was created, both by the established general focus on battles and as a result of the extensive memoir literature. For example, the genre of Napoleonic war memoirs that developed in the 1820s and 1830s, providing opportunities and problems for veterans, was, after a decline in interest in the 1850s and 1860s, changed toward the end of the century as Napoleonic nostalgia gripped a larger generation of readers. More generally, soldiers' tales were recast, as notions of style and content changed, and conventions were remoulded.[11] Yet the focus on battle continues strong. So also with subsequent accounts of the two world wars.[12]

Light infantry was not important in the attritional battles that increasingly characterised the Napoleonic Wars, for example Wagram (1809), Borodino (1812), and Leipzig (1813), but played a major role in increasing trans-oceanic effectiveness. The latter was far from easy for the infantry, both because of the strain of long sea voyages in crowded and unhealthy circumstances, and due to the nature of contested landings, as for example when capturing Louisbourg from the French in 1757. When British troops approached the Egyptian coast in a landing contested by the French in 1801:

> 'the enemy commenced their attack upon us with round shot and shell which as we approached nearer was changed into the hottest discharges imaginable of grape, canister and musquetry without our being able to make any return. In spite of this destructive opposition the boats still advanced'[13]

and, indeed, the landing was successful. However, six years later, a British attack on Spanish-ruled Buenos Aires met strong resistance in the barricaded streets and failed with heavy casualties, leading to a humiliating surrender.

The infantry depended on supplies, which, in the Peninsular War, meant support from Britain's maritime capacity and links as well as making certain that the Commissariat was effective, which was called 'Tracing the biscuit,' a reference to the 'hard tack' eaten by the troops.[14] Yet, the situation still faced major differences, as recorded in the complaints of Lieutenant-Colonel Guard who was in command of the important garrison at Almeida in Portugal in 1808–9. Shortages of food, clothing and shoes led British troops to pillage.[15]

Looking ahead to more recent difficulties for infantry, the major problems of staging attacks in towns, much seen in the 2000s, 2010s and 2020s, were amply demonstrated in 1807, not only at Buenos Aires, but also at Rosetta in Egypt where British infantry took heavy casualties from snipers in the narrow streets of the town and in retreating. Infantry street fighting rewarded detailed knowledge of the terrain, rather than general firepower, and also placed a premium on small-unit effectiveness for which the training of the parade ground and the linear tactics of the battleground were little preparation. There was also an attritional character to urban fighting, one captured by Colonel Hudson Lowe in describing a Russian attack on French forces during the battle of Leipzig in 1813:

> 'under cover of a most formidable fire from about fifty pieces of artillery ... the foremost battalions dispersing in small parties, and pushing the enemy at every point where the ground best admitted ... the enemy firing from the houses (and streets which had been barricaded and filled with obstructions of every kind) and making at every corner and at every house a most obstinate resistance ... the dead and the dying absolutely obstructed the passage in the gates and streets.'[16]

The Franco-Prussian conflict over the village of Placenoit on the eastern part of the Waterloo battlefield was very similar.

So also for the different problems posed by storming fortified positions which in many respects continued to be very similar to those of Antiquity; and very different to the possibilities that were to be created by heavier bombardment later in the century by more powerful explosives and artillery, followed in the twentieth century by air power. In 1807, the forces of the British East India Company attempted to storm Kamona:

> 'Out of 300 of the 17th Regiment which headed the storm, 145 are either killed or wounded. No men could behave more nobly than both Europeans and sepoys, but no courage, no bravery could surmount the obstacles thrown in their way. The ditch was filled with bags of powder covered over with straw. The enemy awaited until our men had advanced within shot point blank. They then opened a most tremendous fire. Our men coolly advanced to the breach. Immediately the enemy set fire to the straw ... as fast as our men mounted [ladders], they were either shot or scorched with powder bags thrown on them.'[17]

The casualties were such that the attack was called off, and the British turned to a month-long bombardment while the defenders withdrew. In contrast, the fort of Chumeer had been taken by storming earlier that year. The 17th Regiment of Foot served in India from 1804 to 1823, a practice, made necessary by the cost and time of movement, which helped to provide infantry with relevant experience and a degree of immunity to local diseases. At the same time, such lengthy postings underlined the extent to which troops were separated from their home communities.

Infantry was challenged by asymmetrical tactics and strategies, as in the popular opposition to Napoleonic rule and the parallels in the Balkans and, from the 1810s, Spanish America, conflicts in which banditry was to the fore.[18] In the Latin American Wars of Independence, which were civil wars, there was a destructiveness to warfare that affected soldiers and civilians. Recruitment was enforced with violence and the threat of violence, desertion punished savagely, frequently with executions, and supplies raised through force. There was much burning and destruction, in order both to deny resources and to punish. A shortage of arms ensured that weapons other than firearms were used, as with the rebels in Mexico in the early 1810s who made much use of bows, clubs and knives.

So also for more 'conventional' conflicts. Thus, a British infantry officer recorded of the battle of Chillianwala (1849) in the 2nd Anglo-Sikh War: '...every bush you passed out rushed a Sikh and tried to cut you down. Of course we never thought of looking into every bush we passed and thus they got in our rear.' He also noted the 'fearful' havoc caused by the Sikh cannon.[19] Earlier, in 1826, an unidentified British soldier noted of fighting at Bharatpur:

> 'Our infantry were much galled at first from the heavy fire from the numerous columns of Rajputs, but at length our troops found that the bayonets were the speediest remedy.... Those Rajputs fought with great gallantry ... if they can find no other resource when in the agonies of death they will spit and grin at a European ... preferred death sooner than they would accept a drink of water from one of us ... refusing quarter though subdued.... Their principal weapon was the matchlock ... no bayonet.... The heaviest of their men carried battle axes.'[20]

The Māori of New Zealand were also to reveal deficiencies in the methods of the British, although the latter could find it difficult to recognise the tactical sophistication of Māori warfare[21] which, in part, arose from a fine understanding of the local environment. A 'spear revolution' has been discerned in Zambia,[22] while in Australia, the Aborigines employed spears against the muskets of British settlers and troops, and learned new tactical methods in order to lessen the dangers posed by the muskets, not least guerrilla warfare that included raids on farmhouses.[23] In West Africa, the Yoruba had cavalry but emphasised infantry which largely used swords, spears, bows and clubs.[24] The Ganda of East Africa focused on spears not guns, while the Masai also used spearmen, their socketed blades proving better than the lighter spears of opponents. The Ngoni focused on short stabbing spears, as did the Zulu who also had age-related military units as a means to training and cohesion.

At the same time, as earlier for the Chinese in Myanmar and Vietnam and for the Ottomans in Arabia, operating in a different environment posed the major problem for Western troops, notably disease, climate (especially heat and humidity), terrain, vegetation, and supplies. Reporting on a punitive expedition in East Bengal in 1850, Lieutenant-Colonel Lister wrote: 'It is not their muskets or other offensive weapons that are to be dreaded, but … the facilities which their jungles afford, both in materials and position, for throwing obstacles in the way of an advance or retreat.'[25]

Despite difficulties, notably but not only in unfamiliar environments, regular infantry could prove effective against irregulars, as with the Austrian defeat of the outnumbered Neapolitan *Carbonari* at Rieti in 1821. The decision to face infantry regulars exposed the irregulars to unsuitable circumstances, as they were best prepared for guerrilla operations. This was an instance of the value of training, but required an opposition fighting as required. There were more serious problems, however, when the setting was urban, as Paris and Brussels in 1830 showed the difficulties regulars faced in street fighting: barricades and windows provided cover. Whatever the setting, the successful use of infantry generally required taking the initiative, although the extent to which that was the tactical or the operative initiative varied. The formations chosen tended to reflect particular circumstances but also the generalship on offer. Thus, in successfully invading central Mexico in 1847 and winning repeated victories, Winfield Scott took the initiative in strategic, operational and tactical terms. Rather than relying on lines of infantry, Scott advocated looser formations, especially clouds of skirmishers, which anticipated Prussian tactical developments later in the century. Scott also showed that his infantry could be readily used to turn flanks, as in the victory at Cerro Gordo.

The battles in Europe in this period showed that densely-packed column attacks and bayonet tactics were still viable as with the Austrian victories over King Charles Albert of Piedmont at Custoza (1848), Santa Lucia (1848), and Novara (1849). Austrian veterans proved highly effective.

Infantry conflict meanwhile was transformed by the continued incremental developments in firearms. This could take time, and face opposition. It is easy to neglect the latter or treat it as anachronistic, but the reasons given against innovations often reflect an informed concern that challenge ideas of a teleological progress in infantry weaponry. Thus, in 1849, Sir Charles Napier, the Commander-in-Chief in India, explained his preference for muskets to the Governor General: 'As an old rifleman myself I cannot be supposed to have any prejudice against the rifle, but as a weapon of war … it is inferior to the musket.' Noting that the rifle took longer to load, Napier continued:

> 'Secondly, it does not range much farther, but if it does (which I doubt) the musket ranges quite as far as any man should fire, for those long shots waste powder and rarely kill anybody.
>
> Third, after much firing the barrel becomes foul; and the firing slackens when it is required to be heaviest.
>
> Fourth, it is not so *handy* as a musket and bayonet; the length is important especially against cavalry.
>
> Fifthly, the bore has been increased to the same calibre as that of the musket, because of the very great inconvenience of having two kinds of ammunition to carry … the supposed great merit of the rifle is the thread or groove which acts on balls having no "windage" that is to say balls which fit tight … now the small smooth ball reduces the rifle to a level with the musket in point of firing.'

Napier continued to argue that the musket/bayonet combination was more effective than the rifle at close quarters and that the rifle was at a disadvantage because it was heavier. It was also more expensive.[26]

Napier's memorandum is valuable (and the comparable ones today will be of value to future historians) because it reflected the experience of a commander who had seen active service in the Peninsular War and the War of 1812, and had conquered the region of Sindh in 1843. Napier also indicated what was believed important in a period of firepower that was coming to a close. The lack of emphasis on range and the stress, instead, on an ability to use the weapon at close quarters were both rapidly to become dated. Instead, new parameters for assessing the capability of individual weapons were soon to be in place, although, in practice, close quarters effectiveness remains important.

Rifling a gun barrel to improve range and accuracy was an idea of the Middle Ages that became readily practical only with subsequent metallurgical progress. Thus, again, the dates of inventions can be misleading. Conception, production and application occurred as very different episodes in the case of rifling. Separately, although, in Britain, Alexander Forsyth patented the use of fulminates of mercury in place of gunpowder as a primer for firearms in 1807, the initial impact of the place of gunpowder as a primer for firearms of mercury, was limited, and the mass-produced metal percussion cap dates from 1822. There was a dramatic reduction of misfires as a result, which led to a great increase in firepower.

The introduction of the percussion rifle and the Minié bullet, both in the 1840s and, subsequently, of breech-loading cartridge rifles were all significant. Nevertheless, the extent to which invention was not the same as successful application was indicated by Johann von Dreyse's *Zündnadelgewehr* or 'needle' rifle, invented in 1835. Named after its needle-shaped firing pin, which penetrated the base of the chamber in order to detonate the propellant, a radically different means for ignition to matchlock or flintlock, this breech-loading, bolt-action, Prussian rifle had an unprecedently high rate of fire, four to seven times a minute, which indeed led to Russian reluctance in using it, because there were concerns about the supply of cartridges.[27] Although the Prussians equipped their troops with the 'needle' rifle in 1841, it was not used in combat until 1849 when it was employed, with great effect, by the Prussians against revolutionaries in Baden and Hesse.

Early versions suffered from design faults, including a brittle firing-pin, a bolt-action that was liable to jam, and a weak seal around the screw-breech, causing an escape of gas that reduced the propellant force, while the rifle's range was also relatively short. These faults discouraged any borrowing of Dreyse's breech-loading technology, and the Austrians, British and French preferred then to continue to rely on muzzle-loading, rifled muskets. The Prussians, nevertheless, used these 'needle' rifles to deadly effect against Denmark in 1864 and Austria in 1866.

Replacing the musket ball, meanwhile, the Minié bullet proved a more rapid adoption in infantry warfare. Captain Claude-Etienne Minié's cylindro-conoidal lead bullet (1848) expanded when fired, to create a tight seal within the rifle, thus obtaining a high velocity. The bullet contained an iron plug in its base and was cast with a diameter slightly smaller than that of the gun bore, so that, when fitted in the muzzle, it slid easily down the bore. When the gun was fired, the charge pushed the iron plug into the base of the bullet, causing it to expand and grip the rifling of the bore, and ensuring that it was fired on an accurate trajectory.

Minié bullets fired by percussion-lock rifles offered a much greater accuracy than balls from smooth-bore muskets, especially at longer ranges, and were a deadly pairing. The combination of ease of loading, which ensured rapid fire, with accuracy was a major advance that encouraged the large-scale use of rifled small arms. A later form of the Minié bullet had a hollow base, which had the same effect of expanding when the charge went off and of sealing the bore, which did away with the need for the iron plug.

The charge was fired by an external percussion cap, and this system married up the reliability of fire of the latter with the greater accuracy of the Minié bullet. The Minié rifle was adopted by the British army in 1851 as the Enfield rifle which was followed by the Pattern 1853 Enfield. The effective range of infantry firepower increased and the casualty rates inflicted on close-packed infantry rose dramatically.

In 1854, in the Crimean War, an Anglo-French force forced a contested passage of the River Alma in part because the defending Russians lacked rifles. Later that year, at the battle of Inkerman, attacking Russian columns seeking to close to bayonet point took heavy casualties from the British with their Enfield rifles, and were defeated.[28] Also that year, during the battle of Balaklava, a key totemic image of infantry warfare was created when the journalist William Howard Russell described the British infantry who successfully resisted a cavalry advance as a 'thin red streak tipped with steel.' This report was memorialised in Robert Gibb's painting *The Thin Red Line* (1881), although that made the engagement more dramatic than was the case: the painting brought the Russians too near the 93rd Highlanders for the latter began firing their rifles at about 600 yards.

At the same time, despite the use of Minié-style rifles, tactics did not change at once. Instead, they were similar to those under Napoleon I, with dense deployments and column formations. As a result, casualties were heavy when the French and Austrians clashed at Solferino and Magenta in Italy in 1859, in part because these battles became attritional. Yet, as an instructive instance of how firepower could face limitations, French infantry advances with the bayonet were successful against poorly-trained and badly-led Austrian infantry, who were unable to draw much benefit from their technically advanced (although still muzzle-loading) rifles. The Austrians had not been adequately trained in range-finding and sighting and, as a consequence, the French were able to close and use their bayonets. The plight of the wounded at Solferino inspired the formation of what became the International Red Cross.

The net effect of the developments in infantry firearms was very substantial changes in precision, mobility and speed of use. This potential for infantry was given force by the greater and more predictable production of munitions that flowed from the more streamlined and systematised manufacturing process that was characteristic of nineteenth-century factory manufacturing. It was possible to mass-produce rifling, sliding bolts, magazine springs, and chain-feeds to a high standard, and also to provide the large quantities of ammunition required. Effective mass production offered a substantial advantage over craft-manufactured firearms, however good the latter were on an individual basis. There was also a feed-back system from infantry in training and in the field. Thus, in 1848–9, British officers commanding regiments with rifle companies reported to the Secretary of the Military Board on the best form of rifle ammunition.[29]

The overall result was a degree of change for infantry far greater in pace and scope than that over the previous century. This was not only the case in the West. For example, whereas earlier muzzle-loaders were not appropriate in East Africa, breech-loaders were far more so because they did not require rigidly disciplined and closely packed bodies of troops, and were thus far more compatible socially and culturally with African modes of warfare.[30] Yet, as a reminder of variety, the successful forces in the *jihad* (holy war) launched by Usuman dan Fodio and the Fulani against the Hausa states in modern northern Nigeria in 1804 initially had no firearms and were essentially mobile infantry forces, principally archers, able to use their firepower to defeat the cavalry of the established powers, as at the battle of Tabkin Kwotto in 1804.

As with other changes in weaponry, the extent of increased firepower for many forces posed tactical, operational and organisational issues, either from the onset or because these limitations were found through combat, as a classic instance of Clausewitzian friction. The essential changes were still impressive. The Model 1855, the standard infantry weapon in use in the American army in 1861, fired the Minié bullet and had a muzzle velocity of 950 feet per second. By 1865, some of the Union army also had repeating rifles. Due to defensive firepower, massed infantry frontal attacks on prepared positions became more costly and unsuccessful in the American Civil War (1861–5), as the Union, in particular, discovered at Second Manassas (1862) and Fredericksburg (1862), and the Confederates at Corinth (1862), Stones River (1862–3), Gettysburg (1863) and Franklin (1864). Most of the casualties inflicted resulted from long-range, accurately-aimed defensive fire from behind entrenchments. Bayonets and rifled muskets were increasingly supplemented by, or even downplayed, in favour of field fortifications and artillery, although the potential offered by firepower was only realised to a limited extent. The leading role of muzzle- rather than breech-loading rifles ensured that Napoleonic-style loading routines predominated in the American Civil War, and, as with the Napoleonic Wars, volley fire was accompanied by massing troops in the open in order to increase the weight of the fire. A preference for linear formations made it harder to retain unit coherence in the advance, to envelop opposing forces, and to switch from firepower to shock attacks.

As a result of the heavy losses that could be caused, there were attempts to lessen exposure to losses on the battlefield. Attacking in columns, not lines, which Union forces increasingly did in the Civil War in 1864 and 1865, was designed to reduce the target for defensive firepower and to increase the speed and mass of attack. The effectiveness of the defence, in turn, was enhanced by the manoeuvrability of riflemen within the relatively compact battlefields, which permitted the ready presentation of new defensive fronts, although that required adequate intelligence and skilled generalship.

However, the increased range of rifled muskets was not fully exploited during the Civil War due to a reliance on holding fire so as to have greater effect at shorter range, and also to the consequences of advances through wooded terrain which provided cover. Separately, a failure to advance to a bayonet assault and, instead, the halting of advances in order to engage in close-range firefights, led to a failure to press home attacks, a failure that often caused indecisive combat. It also proved difficult to secure adequate concentration and co-operation on the battlefield. The parabolic arc of bullet trajectories ensured the need for a training that, however, was very weak in the 1860s, and it was not the accuracy or range of the rifle, but rather the volume of fire, that caused high casualties. Partly as a result, linear tactical systems were not obsolete, not least because rifles were not used sufficiently frequently to make a key difference.[31]

In general, it was difficult to assimilate new military techniques, and notably so if large numbers were involved, which was particularly the case with infantry. Yet this was a more necessary process due both to conscription and to changes in weaponry. The greater deadliness of firepower resulted in a need for more infantry in order to sustain operations, as did the extent to which battles were fought over a broad front, a facet apparent from the Napoleonic Wars, for example at Leipzig and Vitoria in 1813, but not at Borodino (1812). In battle, the manoeuvrability of infantry played a major role, ensuring for example at Sadowa (1866) that the Austrian positions were caught in the flank by the Prussians. Prussian companies, which had been trained to move independently, albeit within the confines of a plan, proved more flexible than the massed Austrian columns. The Austrians were armed with the muzzle-loading Lorenz rifle of 1854. This had effective ballistics, but their battalion columns offered too large a target.

Prussia's victory in 1866 led other powers to adopt or seek to match its weaponry, infantry methods and tactical formations which were now seen as better. Breech-loading rifles were now regarded as far better than the slower muzzle-loaders; but, within the type, there could be improvement, which, more generally, has always been the case with weaponry. Thus, in 1866, the French adopted the *chassepot* rifle which had a more gas-tight breech and a far greater range than the Prussian 'needle' rifle. The latter no longer represented cutting-edge military technology, a situation of rapid superseding that more generally was to characterise modern infantry weaponry, and one that looks toward the present. The *chassepot* showed its value against Prussian frontal attacks in 1870, as a result of which German losses were far higher than at the hands of the Austrians in 1866. The *chassepot*'s rounds had a tendency to tumble through the body, smashing bones, tearing tissue, and blowing exit holes bigger than the entry wound: German casualties mentioned the 'razor pain' of the French bullet. As a consequence of these casualties, Wilhelm I did not initially accept that Gravelotte was a German victory, although, it had, in fact, severed France from its principal army.

Many soldiers, however, preferred the Dreyse rifle to the *chassepot* as it was more soldier-proof. This was always a key dynamic in workable weaponry and tactics. In 1866, the British 1853 Enfield was replaced by the Snider-Enfield, a breech-loader. In turn, that was replaced by the Martini-Henry which was in service from 1871.

The Prussian tactic of concentrating strength on the skirmishing line, and adopting more extended formations that were less dense than columns or lines, and thus less exposed to fire, commanded attention. In an essay of 1864, 'Remarks on the Influence of Improved Rifles on the Attack,' Moltke had decried closely-packed frontal assaults. Furthermore, in marked contrast to the battles of 1859, in which the Prussians had not participated, reliance on more effective firepower also cut the frequency with which units clashed in hand-to-hand fighting, and ensured there was less need for the bayonet. This led Charles Ardant du Picq, a French officer who had acquired practice in light infantry operations in the Crimean War but was killed in 1870, to argue, in his posthumously published *Études sur le combat* (1880), that shock action had become redundant unless it was methodically prepared by appropriate firepower and carried out in open formation. His stress on unit cohesion, morale and discipline was designed to provide an explanation for how best to win in the face of effective firepower on both sides.[32]

Prussian effectiveness included the operation of the infantry at the micro-level, a practice that was far harder to copy than weaponry, and one that helped establish differences in effectiveness and, therefore, capability. Thanks both to an ethos of commitment and to training, there was an emphasis on a professionalism on the part of officers, NCOs, and soldiers that was more consistent than in the French army.

More particularly, the Prussians trained officers to take their own decisions at all levels within the constraints of the command plan. This was important as defensive firepower, by encouraging a lower density battlefield with spread-out units and dispersed formations, accentuated problems of command and communication, which put a premium on coordination and morale. The use of *Aufträgs*, orders that explained the situation and goal of a force, and left a degree of flexibility to the local commanders, was particularly important, ensuring a dynamic interaction, mediated by training, between hierarchy and devolved decision-making which facilitated small-unit operations supporting and harmonising with those of large forces. An emphasis on mass, whether to deliver firepower or striking power, linked the battles of Antiquity to those of the mid-nineteenth century, such as Solferino, but the situation thereafter changed, as mass was diffused in lower-density formations.

Tactical and organisational differences had consequences, as with the Franco-Prussian war of 1870–1 in which the French preference for tight defensive formations increased their vulnerability to firepower, while the Prussians stressed an open-order deployment, which reduced vulnerability, and the related small-unit fire tactics. In contrast to their formations in 1870–1, the French, in their annual manoeuvres in 1898, had, as their infantry fighting line, 'swarms of skirmishers … dressing and closed formations are no longer permissible.'[33] A stress on extended order and on initiative in battle was to be seen in the American Infantry Drill Regulations of 1891. Already, in a work adopted in 1867 for the instruction of the American military, in his *Infantry Tactics … Adapted to American Topography and Improved Firearms* (1866), Brevet Major-General Emory Upton, a Civil War veteran who had been Commandant of Cadets at West Point, abandoned the square and advocated attacks in column rather than lines. In 1873, the War Office approved his revised edition, the Preface declaring:

> 'While attacks in masses have been abandoned, a preponderance of men and of fire, in the future as in the past, will have to be relied upon to carry positions which are beyond the power of skirmishers.… The introduction of the breech-loader has changed none of the principles

> of grand tactics; and, while it has given a great impetus to the employment of skirmishers, which is to be encouraged, experience will prove that the safety of an army cannot be intrusted to men in open order with whom it is difficult to communicate.'

Conscription and changes in weaponry were both significant in the late nineteenth century and as an aspect of institutional professionalism that became particularly important to infantry, and not only in the West. Thus, in Japan in 1877, in the domain of Satsuma, a substantial *samurai* force, armed with swords and matchlock muskets, was brought into combat with the new mass army of conscript peasants. In what was in some respects a repeat of the Ottoman and Napoleonic defeats of the Mamluks of Egypt in 1517 and 1798 respectively, individual military prowess and bravery succumbed to the organised, disciplined force of an army that, on an individual basis, was less proficient. Civil wars regularly posed (and continue to pose) issues in obtaining weaponry, as an important part of the process by which rebel forces had to be recruited, equipped and trained.

The results, however, were far from fixed, which underlines the danger with assuming a certain outcome. Thus, in China, the Taiping Rebellion of 1850–64 saw the creation of very large rebel armies that were extensively armed with handheld slashing and stabbing weapons and had fewer firearms than their regular opponents who eventually defeated the rebels. In contrast, in the American Civil War, there was an ability on the rebel Confederate part to field armies with considerable numbers of firearms. Infantry predominated again, but the Civil War was more similar to the regular combat of forces in Europe, for example the Wars of German Unification, than to the civil wars in China and Japan. In part, the American situation was different due to the peacetime personal ownership of firearms, and therefore familiarity with their use. This provided a context for infantry preparation and mobilisation very different to the infantries of societies that lacked peacetime weaponry. If modern infantry weaponry and tactics do not require years of training and experience, and this was certainly true of the mass formation tactics of the mid-nineteenth century, it was still the case that training helped in using the range of weapons successfully.

In the development of infantry as a more effective arm, conscription was a crucial process as it broke down the division, still then seen in

Abyssinia, China, Madagascar, Persia and Turkey, between a small regular army and very differently armed levies that were often tribal or clan-based in character. This contrast was significant not only for armaments but also for command practices. Thus, the development of the Abyssinian (Ethiopian) army produced a large force nearly half of whom were armed with modern weapons, but the military culture and political context were different to those in Europe.[34] Abyssinia had used Western weaponry from the sixteenth century when it was provided by Portugal, but the extent to which this weaponry was diffused was far less than in the late nineteenth century and, prior to that, there was more of an add-on character to the use of such infantry.

Hostility to this process of change was frequently violent, as there was no other means to express it. This was seen in the Ottoman case.[35] More generally, opposition to conscription was a major theme in resistance to empires in the early nineteenth century, for example to Napoleonic rule and also to Ottoman control. As such conscription ended previous, more nuanced, patterns of control and mutual benefit. It was a product of necessity, as by Selim III (r. 1789–1808) and Mahmud II (r. 1808–39), a necessity driven by international competition.[36]

In the nineteenth century, even in the case of relatively small regular armies, there were significant changes in the infantry, as with the Egyptian army, which had modern Remington rifles by the 1870s, and, earlier in the century, with the use of European weaponry by the Sikhs. In the 1870s, the Ottomans adopted the breech-loading Peabody-Martini rifle, a highly-effective weapon. More generally, Western firearms were sought for the infantry, but could be difficult to supply and maintain. At the Jiangnan arsenal in China, founded in 1865, Remington rifles were manufactured, but they were of poorer quality than those obtainable in the West.

Toward the close of the nineteenth century, single-shot breech-loaders, such as the French Gras and the British Martini-Henry, were replaced by more effective magazine rifles such as the model 1886 Lebel, the Mauser in 1889, the Lee-Metford, and the Kropatschek. Approved in 1888, the Lee-Metford was a small-bore magazine rifle fired by smokeless powder, sending a bullet at a muzzle velocity of 2,000 feet per second over a range of 3,000 yards. The small bore meant lighter ammunition and therefore an ability to carry more rounds. This was important because spring-action mechanisms fed cartridges at a rapid rate. Meanwhile, smokeless powder ensured that the field of vision was not blocked and that it was harder for opponents to discern the source of fire. Smokeless propellants also caused less fouling, and therefore fewer jams. Moreover, refinements in the manufacture of cartridges reduced jamming. The development of the spitzer or boat-tail bullet provided a smaller, more aerodynamically-stable, and longer-range, bullet.

Infantry were both beneficiaries and victims of the sophisticated weapons that had a greater number of components and characteristics. As a result, the development toward effectiveness was complex, but, at the same time, the nature of modern industrial society made it possible. In order to make a significant impact, the bolt-action required the invention of fixed ammunition (the bullet fixed in a metal cartridge so that the round becomes the key armament) in the 1850s and 1860s, smokeless nitrocellulose (not gunpowder) propellants, and the box magazine. The invention of Poudre B in 1884, ballistic, by Alfred Nobel in 1887, and cordite in 1888, was important, and the power of the new repeating rifles of the 1880s was demonstrated by Western forces operating in China in 1900.

Firepower helped Western forces in their imperial conflicts. Invading Abyssinia (Ethiopia) in 1867, the British rifles, whether muzzle-loading or breech-loaders, were more effective than the Abyssinian matchlocks and smooth-bore shotguns. At Amoaful in 1874, during the Third Anglo-Ashanti (Asante) War, a much larger Asante force was defeated by an advancing British square led by the 42nd Regiment firing its breech-loading rifles repeatedly into the surrounding vegetation. The British were much less successful when outnumbered by attacking Zulus at Isandlwana in 1879. The Zulus enveloped the British flanks and destroyed the British force, but, thanks to the British Martini-Henry rifles, Zulu casualties were very high, while the Zulus referred to the British as cowards because they would not fight hand-to-hand. In later battles, notably Ulundi in 1879, heavy defensive infantry fire from British prepared positions stopped the Zulu attack. As an instance of the racial politics of infantry service, the Natal Native Contingent had White officers and was largely used for labour: only one rifle was issued to every tenth man, and he was only given ten cartridges.[37]

The Second Afghan War (1878–80) proved more difficult, not least because the Afghans were armed with British Enfield rifles which contributed to the British defeat at Maiwand (1880). So also in smaller-scale clashes. Of a British sortie from the invested city of Kandahar against the village of Deh Khoja:

> 'we began by shelling the place. There was no reply so 800 of our infantry advanced to the attack when at once a galling fire was opened on them from loop holes round the village. Our men rushed on and entered the village on the south side but only to find it filled with armed men firing from the windows, doors and roofs. It was a hopeless task ... had to return in hot haste under the same heavy fire.'[38]

In contrast, at Omdurman in 1898, Lee-Metford magazine rifles helped bring a crushing British victory over the Mahdists of Sudan. Earlier, the Mahdists saw spearmen as fundamental, although they also had an infantry force armed with Western rifles, the *jihadiyya*, which played a crucial role in their destruction of an Egyptian army at Shaykan in 1883. Egyptian failures tend to be overlooked as a result of the focus on Omdurman, but that presents a misleading guide to the difficulties of the task and the major effort involved. It is also necessary to note battles such as El Teb (1884), Hashin (1885), Tofrek (1885) and Tokar (1891), in which British forces defeated the Mahdists. In 1906, in South Bali, the two *raga* families ritually purified themselves for death and fought their final battle (*puputan*): armed only with daggers and lances, they were all slaughtered as they advanced in the face of Dutch firepower, killing their own wounded as they did so.

Column advances in general, proved the means most suited, both operationally and tactically, for imperial forces in a variety of terrains and contexts, whereas conventional methods were inappropriate. The emphasis on mobile columns was seen for example in French campaigning, including by Bugeaud in Algeria in the 1840s, Faidherbe in Senegal in the 1850s and 1860s, and Gallieni in Indo-China and Madagascar in the 1890s. The relatively close-packed nature of column formations contrasted with increased interest in looser formations on the Western battlefields, but this reflected a different ratio between firepower and shock on the part of non-Western opponents. Column advances continued to be used after the First World War.

In the face of ambushes, columns needed to be capable of all-round defence. A German column ambushed at Lugalo in East Africa by the Hehe tribe in 1891 lost most of the 300-strong force. Under attack, hollow squares were often formed as by the British at El Teb in 1884 and by the Portuguese against the Gaza in southern Mozambique in 1895, for example at the battle of Coolela, in which the Portuguese used machine guns and Kropatschek magazine rifles. Bush fighting in Africa gave a new lease of life to the square formation and to volley firing. However, lightly-armed mobile forces could only achieve so much in Africa, and large numbers of regulars supplied with modern weaponry were required in some circumstances.[39]

The impact of firepower, however, was affected by vegetation, as with German columns ambushed, for example by Herero in South-West Africa in 1904. It was also useful in some terrains, such as southern Africa and Somaliland, to have mounted infantry who provided both mobility and firepower.[40] The use of infantry in colonial warfare developed in terms of a doctrine of small wars, most notably with Charles Callwell's *Small Wars: Their Principles and Practice* which went through three editions in 1896, 1899 and 1906 and drew on significant literature on the subject, which very much represented a different infantry strand to that in Europe.[41]

The destruction of crops and food stores was advocated by Callwell who argued that tactics favoured the regular army whereas logistical factors helped their opponents, and that, therefore the need of the regulars was to fight, not manoeuvre, and their main problem was that of making and supplying the advance. Problems of supply encouraged frontal assaults.

In the Spanish-American War of 1898, the German Mauser rifle used by the Spaniards proved particularly effective. The American regulars had the Krag-Jorgensen rifle, but the volunteers were armed with the old, black-powder, traditional Springfield. The (Second) Boer War of 1899–1902 also revealed the consequences. Already, a British officer at the Battle of Majuba Hill in the First Boer War (1881) had emphasised the skill of Boer firepower, recording the problems caused by 'bullets from an enemy we could not see … the Boer fire so completely dominated ours.'[42] The British were defeated with their commander killed. In 1899–1902, superior Boer marksmanship and the utilisation of the range of their Mauser rifles, a process helped by the atmospheric conditions of the *veldt*, enabled the Boers to inflict heavy casualties, including on British artillerymen. Furthermore, providing cover against and for fire, the Boers made effective use of trenches. A letter signed 'Colonel' published in *The Times* on 27 December 1899 noted:

> 'The modern method of fortifications, introduced with the breech-loading rifle, is based upon the practical indestructibility by modern artillery fire of properly designed earthworks, and the improbability of an attacking force being able to rush a properly prepared position defended by a sufficient number of troops armed with the breech-loading rifle. This improbability became impossibility, now that the magazine rifle is substituted for the breechloader, until the defences shall have been seriously injured by artillery fire.'

In response, the British developed an appropriate use of cover and infantry advances in rushes, coordinated with the artillery. Those British troops who had seen action in the great tribal rising of 1897 who then fought the Boers were familiar with many of the challenges. The learning curve in the Boer War included deployment on extended fronts rather than focus on a column advance on one axis, an approach that could readily be thwarted by Boer firepower. Uniform was camouflaged, with red replaced by khaki (Urdu for dust-coloured) as its primary colour, even for insignia of rank, which Boer marksmen were keen to notice. At the same time, there was much tension over tactics. Colin Ballard of the 9th Foot, preferred charging the Boers to 'firing at them at 5000 yards range.'[43]

The lessons of the war and an understanding of the defensive strength of trenches already affected the Belgian manoeuvres in 1900,[44] while Ian Hamilton suggested to the Royal Commission on the War in South Africa the value of equipping soldiers with entrenching tools, and also wheeled shields for infantry. In 1901, British Intelligence reported: 'Russia has lost no time in realising that infantry is unlikely to be employed in the future without its own proportion of guns with it.'[45] The British experience in South Africa with camouflaged uniforms helped lead the German army to abandon Prussian blue for field grey in 1910.

Not every army, however, took on the lessons of the recent wars. In part, the drill, discipline and tactics adopted to maximise and make best use of infantry firepower could become institutionalised and persist beyond their point of value, as with the continued use of volley fire such that, in 1898, the Spaniards fired modern rifles, Mausers, but in volley on command. Ian Hamilton, then General Officer Commanding Southern Command in Britain, in his observations on the Austrian manoeuvres in 1906, thought the infantry 'evinced but small appreciation of the power of modern artillery or rifles, or of the necessity these new factors involve for quick movement and concealment.'[46] In 1909, then Adjutant General, he observed the manoeuvres of the Saxon army, part of the German forces. Noting that 'the spirit of the offensive [was] sedulously fostered,' he wrote:

> 'the Germans are ever preaching fire effect, but here we find fire effect prematurely discarded in favour of that primitive arme blanche [shock action] which is the negation of modern armaments … not a single entrenchment worthy the name was ever even attempted.'

Hamilton also felt the attacks were on too narrow a front and that the compact forces would be vulnerable to defensive fire, although he noted the German use of machine guns.[47] At peace, apart from for colonial operations, since 1871, German troops were not familiar with the intensity of battle or the dynamics of attack under enemy fire, but military exercises provided some preparation for aspects of the stressful wartime environment.[48]

In the Russo-Japanese War of 1904–5, the defensive advantages (and resulting costs for attackers) resulting from the new, breech-loading, smokeless, quick-firing firearms attracted attention. Colonel Waters, of the British Military Mission with the Russian army, observed, in his report on the 1904 Manchurian campaign, 'Fire is now, or should be, the all-important factor in a battle.'[49] Arguing that the Russian reliance on close-order formations and shock attack was foolish, and that firepower could beat off the bayonet, Waters also commented that the manpower available affected tactical best practice:

> 'Frontal attacks were a very conspicuous feature of both sides during the late campaign in Manchuria. In some instances they could have been advantageously omitted, and flank attacks made in their stead, but when armies, each numbering say a couple of hundred thousand

combatants, cover the whole of the ground available for a battlefield, as on the Shaho, frontal attacks cannot be avoided.'[50]

Infantry also remained exposed to classic supply issues, as with the loss of nearly 6,000 Russian troops from beriberi as a result of vitamin B1 deficiency.

However, there was a firm conviction within army General Staffs that the élan of infantry advances, supported by artillery, would overcome infantry benefiting from trenches, barbed wire and automatic weaponry. The sceptical *Times* responded to the British field manoeuvres of 1903, in which victory was won by an attack culminating in an assault on artillery positions, by asking 'At what precise point will this principle of attack become applicable under modern conditions?'[51] The British army responded to the Boer War by emphasising shooting by individual soldiers, and training accordingly, but drill books, such as *Combined Training, 1905* continued to emphasise the offensive, so that fire action was to remain secondary to the movement of troops, and the firing line was expected to advance.[52]

Yet there was no one form of infantry offensive. That was the lesson taken also from the Balkan War of 1912–13: as with the Russo-Japanese War, the attacker could win, which was certainly necessary if territory was to be seized. In defeating the Turks in battle in October 1912, the Bulgarians benefited from disciplined infantry with good morale who attacked, boldly making good use of bayonets, although this did not help them against prepared positions the following month. The description of battles in the newspapers of the period put an emphasis on frontal attacks and the use of bayonets as a way to demonstrate bravery.[53] The experience gained in the Balkan Wars was to be helpful for some in the First World War, for example for the Serbs successfully opposing Austrian invasion in 1914.[54]

At the same time, alongside the emphasis on the combined arms combat of infantry and artillery, it was clear to perceptive observers that open-order advances were necessary, while volley firing was being abandoned in favour of individual fire.[55] Already, in 1877–8, when the Russians sought to emulate the Germans, launching frontal attacks, they lost heavily to entrenched Turkish riflemen, particularly at Plevna, which, instead, fell finally to siege. In the battle of Second Plevna, Russian casualties amounted to 23 per cent of their rank and file.[56] The Russians failed to appreciate the limitations of direct infantry attacks, but this preference, in part, reflected Russian logistical limitations and the need to maintain the initiative in order to prevent counter-attacks. In the War of the Pacific, there was also frontal assaults, for example by the Chileans successfully of the Peruvian port of Arica in 1880, in part because, in what was a conflict of rapid advances, there was no time to bring up heavy artillery in order to attack fortified positions. Infantry losses in the War of the Pacific were a consequence of a lack of supporting artillery and of the degree to which the opposing infantry made effective use of their rifles. Arica fell in part because the Chilean force was considerably larger.

Alongside failures in perception and difficulties in application across the world, it is striking how far change proved possible. In part, this was a reflection of the importance of war to the states of the period, and in part to the relative ease of obtaining weapons and of training troops in their use. Lengthy training was not necessary in order to ensure that rifles were employed in lethal fashion.

The proposed use and training of infantry in part reflected an emphasis on morale that arose irrespective of improved technology, and, in part, was a response to it in supposedly providing a crucial capability gap between similarly armed forces. Thus, attacking appeared to be the most appropriate way to encourage and hold the enthusiasm of the troops and to provide a way to overcome the defensive. This was linked to a belief in the moral value of the bayonet as encouraging an offensive spirit.

At the same time, raising large numbers of infantry created or exacerbated serious issues of supply, training and command. Numbers alone could not suffice: it was the way in which men were trained and integrated into existing military structures that was crucial, as the Prussians showed. Problems were not readily apparent in peacetime, but war repeatedly showed that bulk did not equal mass, nor movement manoeuvre, and that it could be difficult to retain and sustain the initiative.

Infantry continued to mean very different characteristics, circumstances and contexts, but it was the general outcome because it was the solution to most military requirements. This led the way toward the First World War (1914–18), but, even had there not been such a conflict with its infantry-focus in trench warfare, there would still have been an infantry dominance, albeit in probably pursuing a different tactical means of combat.

It is possible to propose a dichotomy between Western forces engaged in infantry-dominated symmetrical conflict by regular troops within the West, and such forces taking part in non-symmetrical conflict with non-Western opponents. However, that would be an inappropriate summary of a continuum of contexts, not least in terms of non-Western forces. Moreover, there was conflict with irregulars within the West, in Europe, Latin America and the American Civil War.[57] Guerrilla warfare in the latter was largely irregular warfare by regulars, particularly engaged in raiding activities. In the Franco-Prussian War (1870–1), *francs-tireurs*, French civilians, fought back only to be treated brutally, not least with the shooting of captives and suspects, taking of hostages, mutilation of prisoners, and destruction of towns and villages. In part, this reflected German frustration at the difficulty of protecting increasingly lengthy supply routes, as well as the problems posed by hostile citizen volunteers who did not wear uniforms and were impossible to identify once they had discarded their rifles. In response, the Germans adopted a social typology that prefigured those of the following century, treating every 'blue smock,' the customary clothes of the French worker, as a potential guerrilla.

In practice, German casualties as a result of this warfare were modest, but the idea of such violence threatened not only to introduce a level of 'friction' and uncertainty that the Germans did not want operationally, but also to usher in a chaos that they could not accept psychologically. The use by regulars of violence against civilians suspected of opposition, in order to ensure that the regulars had a monopoly of force, was not new, but it entered a deadlier cycle, when it was seen by the Germans as necessary and became an automatic response. Infantry were to the forefront in such activity.

In Latin American conflict, there was more irregular warfare, with the infantry of both sides often employed with scant concern about casualties. The execution of prisoners was frequent, in part designed to intimidate in a situation in which it was difficult to prevail. Raids and ambushes also played a major role in Latin American conflicts, whether international or civil wars, with the prevention of access to opponents' supplies important. Due to force-space ratios and the difficulty of sustaining forces, there was an emphasis on rapid advances. Restraints on violence were lessened. In March 1882, in the War of the Pacific, after Chilean troops destroyed the Peruvian village of Nahiumpuqio, slaughtering its inhabitants, they were attacked by guerrillas at nearby Tongos, and the heads of the troops killed were displayed on pikes. This was very different in scale to the suppression of the radical Paris Commune in 1871 by French regular troops, but there was a comparable anti-societal violence that very much looked toward the present day.

The care for troops in this period varied by country and circumstances, but, on the whole, was less to the fore than in the following century. This was particularly apparent when campaigning at a distance, as for the British in the Crimean War in 1854–6, notably with the horrific conditions in the winter siege of Sevastopol in 1854–5, especially the lack of adequate food, clean water, shelter and clothing. These helped to lead to very heavy losses from disease, to which hunger and the winter contributed. During the war as a whole, whereas about 3,000 British troops were killed in action, 19,000 died of disease, exposure or infected wounds. At the same time, the infantry benefited, as so often, from improvement during the conflict, with better medical provisions and logistics helping the army's health.

The control of soldiers was often brutal, and notably so with conscription, especially when it was introduced where hitherto absent, as in America in 1862–3. Sam Watkins, who served in the Confederate army, wrote later of the Confederate Congress's Conscription Act of 1862: 'From this time until the end of the war a soldier was simply a machine, a conscript. It was mighty rough on rebels [Confederates]. We cursed the war.' He had already noted that soldiers were 'deserting by the thousands.' In 1863, a British military observer wrote of the Army of Tennessee, in which Watkins served, that the commander had the reputation for 'shooting freely for insubordination.' Many were also shot for desertion, while in 1864 Joseph Johnson, then the commander, was regarded as having even more soldiers shot.

The low repute of modern infantry service, 'the poor bloody infantry,' in part dates to the world wars, but was also set by the widespread unpopularity of conscription in the late nineteenth century. In part, this was a reaction to the demands of new states, not least in conquered and annexed areas, as with Saxons in the Prussian army in 1815, many of whom deserted, and to the Italian government after it seized control in southern Italy in 1860. In 1866, conscription for the war with Austria excluded that region. Austria faced similar problems once it annexed Bosnia.

Separately, there was opposition across entire countries. Thus, there was widespread evasion and desertion in Argentina, especially in 1865–70 in response to conscription for the War of the Triple Alliance against Paraguay. This encouraged political opposition, one of the classic ways in which, instead of war strengthening the state, as is often argued, it in fact greatly weakens it. In the case of Argentina, this evasion in 1865–70 led to serious manpower problems and to a reliance on Brazil, Argentina's ally. Brazil itself did not turn to conscription until 1916. Prior to that, the emphasis was on coercion and control, but in the shape of the army, notably the infantry, as an essentially penal institution. Issues of class and race were both significant in this situation, with the poor and non-whites most likely to serve in the infantry.[58] In France, political and social divisions in part focused on the army, with the left opposing the longer term of conscript service sought by conservatives.[59]

Conscription was difficult as well as contentious, not only because it directly related to personal freedom, but also as it was a way to define society and to contest these definitions. In large part, this was a matter of those included in the scope of conscription. The regulations established age criteria, but also those of inclusion or exclusion on grounds of nationality, religion and ethnicity. For instance, the position of Jews within society was redefined. In large part, the definitions were also those of control in society, as the male population was brought under military discipline and in a very hierarchical context.

The experience of infantry is usually seen in terms of battle, but it is worth remembering the range of experience involved, notably the extent to which most infantry service did not involve conflict. Thus, Gustavus Otto, a German immigrant who enlisted in 1848, complained about the severity of the Wisconsin winter and about the drudgery of garrisons having to obtain their own firewood, water and hay:

> 'we were plagued much with the hardest labour … we had to procure from a distance of 2 miles wood, hay, and water, where one's life was not safe one minute, not to slip and fall down with the wood, which we had to throw down from the bluffs.'[60]

This situation, as well as the difficulties of civilian life, notably exposure to the elements by those who worked on the land, made it easier to cope with the often difficult circumstances of campaigning. Thus, the American soldiers who fought in the Black Hawk War of 1832 faced bad food, marches, sleeping in mud and rain, and vicious mosquitoes.[61]

Whatever complaints about food or the stress on manly struggle and suffering, the reality for much of the infantry was disease. Most survived, but disease in the American Civil War (1861–5), which did not pose the challenges of service in the Tropics, still claimed the lives of about twice as many troops as combat. Poor sanitation was a terrible problem and it exacerbated the impact of such conditions as dysentery. The reality of military service was matched by that of parlous conditions for the wounded. This was a reflection not simply of the nature of contemporary medicine and surgery, but also of the lack of surgeons, doctors and adequate facilities.[62]

Disease was a significant aspect of the more general proximity of death in military service. A high rate of accidents was also important. Linked to these factors came a willingness to kill, including among civilian volunteers only recently enlisted, as in the American Civil War. This reflected the role of duty, wartime politicisation, a familiarity with arms, and the frequency of the peacetime slaughter of animals. At the same time, attitudes to the taking of prisoners varied greatly by culture, political setting and military circumstances.[63] Thus, the Peruvian use of mines in defending Arica in 1880 led to the Chilean slaughter of prisoners.

While cavalry continued to have an heroic appeal, infantry increasingly dominated the visual representation of war. That was at a time when conflict was taking on new meaning in states, whether or not democratic or authoritarian in their political system, that sought to popularise military service as an exemplary form of citizenship. The very emphasis on infantry encouraged this approach, as did the extent to which large-scale conflict generally relied on an expansion of the military, meaning infantry, whether through volunteers, militia or conscripts.[64]

The First World War inevitably ends this chapter, as the destination point for developments prior to 1914. Yet the 1910s also saw civil war in China and Mexico, and it would be misleading to see the First World War (which itself was far from homogenous in fighting methods) as the sole definition of conflict in the decade. Again, this raises questions about how best to characterise infantry requirements and capabilities, and also to assess military developments over the previous decades.

Chapter 8

Twentieth Century

> 'At about 8.00 am there was a heavy bombardment on the battalion on our left, against whom they advanced in waves presenting excellent targets for cross-fire.... This attack quietened down about noon, and at this the battalion on our right was attacked, heavily shelled and machine-gunned and withdrew, but No. 2 Company at once restored the situation by a gallant charge, some going through up to their waists in water.'
>
> Lieutenant-Colonel Percy Worrall on the successful defence against the German Lys offensive, Western Front, 1918.[1]

Infantry (and artillery) were to the fore in the First World War (1914–18), with cavalry pushed to the background in a final settlement of the longstanding tension between the two arms. The plight of the infantry is the theme that emerges most clearly and frequently from accounts and presentations of the war, and, not least, its vulnerability to artillery and machine guns. However, despite the obvious danger of heavy casualties if throwing infantry against defensive positions, the combatants believed that they would be more successful if they took the initiative, thus utilising the potential of both infantry and artillery. The attacker could choose when, where and with what numbers to attack, and could amass forces accordingly, those countering the advantages the defenders enjoyed, and restoring mobility to the infantry. Moreover, mounting offensives offered the possibility of gaining strategic advantages, however defined.

In practice, repeated attacks from late 1914 revealed the difficulties of breaking through an opposing front line, as opposed to breaking into it, costly as the latter certainly was. The standard message form on maps used by British field units included 'Am held up by a) M.G. [Machine Gun] b) [barbed] wire at ....'[2] Defences-in-depth increased the requirements for defenders and also for the number of attackers, and helped ensure an attritional character to the infantry conflict, one that focused on artillery but was not limited to it. The available manpower provided by conscription on a demographic base that had massively increased over the last century, and the ease with which populations were controlled prior to the Russian Revolution of 1917, made it possible to hold the front line with strength and to provide reserves. Continuous trench lines packed with infantry offered both defensive mass but also plentiful targets for bombardments. The lethality of weaponry was increased by the use of poison gas from 1915, although most casualties were caused by artillery and, secondarily, machine guns.

Trench warfare is frequently held up for much of the blame for the heavy losses of infantry. Yet, had the campaigns been waged in a different manner – for example, albeit within the context of limited mobility for the infantry, been more manoeuvrist and less static, there is no reason to assume that casualties would have been lower. Instead, in the open, infantry would have been more exposed to both offensive and defensive fire, as in the campaigning in 1914 and 1918, the two most 'mobile' years of the war on the Western Front, and, indeed, many Second World War operations, for example the Anglo-American advance from Normandy to the Rhine in 1944–5. In practice, trenches served to protect infantry, as well as to stabilize the line.

There was the new challenge, at least at this scale, of shell shock. This was a new phenomenon of infantry conflict as a whole, affecting morale and expanding the understanding and definition of 'nervous illness,' but confronting them with far-larger numbers. The evaluation of mental shock became an issue addressed by new institutional practices; but, unsurprisingly, not rising to the challenge.[3] The stress of war saw fear and stress presenting in terms of physical conditions, while there were also psychological conditions including depression and post-traumatic stress disorder.[4] Shell-shock induced a powerful sense of hopelessness not only in the individuals who suffered but also by and in a medical system that could not cope with the number of cases nor properly understand them, and that was affected by more general governmental financial constraints. Writing in the late 1920s, Private Stanley Green referred to men sobbing after the pressure of fighting, to the stunned nature of survivors, to the 1927 suicide of a comrade who could not cope, to his own mind still being fixed on the war and how 'today thousands of men rave and wear out their war-ridden minds in the padded cells of our asylums.'[5] Nevertheless, shell shock was not the fate of the majority of soldiers. Indeed, the morale of much of the British army seems to have been pretty good throughout, and that also appears to have been the case with the German army until the summer of 1918.

Field fortifications had long been a feature on battlefields, and entrenchment was scarcely new, but the danger from artillery in the First World War very much ensured that entrenchments played the major role in field fortifications. By November 1914, there was a stalemate on what had become a fixed Western Front and 'the chief need ... for infantry and as many of them as possible,' so that cavalry units were dismounted and sent into the trenches.[6] This prefigured pressures on numbers in subsequent conflicts, including the Second World War and the Russo-Ukrainian War of 2022-. As Lieutenant Colonel Alan Thomson, a British artillery officer, noted in Gallipoli in 1915, troops were never more vulnerable than before trenches could be dug.[7] Trenches were vulnerable to plunging shell fire as well as mortars and grenades, but the men who moved above ground were far more exposed to machine guns and artillery. The war fitted into a continuum in which, as small arms and artillery became more powerful during the nineteenth century, so the role of trenches for protection increased.

Aside from entrenchment, but also for protection, there were major changes to uniforms, which were already being altered prior to the outbreak of the war in order to make troops less conspicuous. The Germans had adopted field grey and the French decided on horizon blue, but the French troops who went into combat in 1914 wore bright red trousers. However, these were swiftly covered with blue overalls and, by the end of 1915, French troops had blue uniforms as well as Adrian helmets which provided some protection against head wounds.

In early 1915, it was widely believed that the stalemate of the winter reflected the exhaustion of men and supplies in the previous autumn's campaigning, and that it would be possible, with fresh men and munitions, to restart a war of manoeuvre. It was not generally appreciated that stalemate and trench warfare reflected the nature of war once both sides had committed large numbers of infantry and lacked the ability to accomplish a breakthrough. In addition, the strength of the German defensive positions was not understood. The high losses reflected not so much the futility of war, or of this war, as was subsequently claimed by critics, but, rather, the determination of the world's leading industrial powers to continue hostilities almost at any cost. More specifically, casualties were high because of the willingness to attack, combined with the advantage weapons technology gave the defence and the value of defence in moderate depth, given the constraints on offensive warfare and the numbers of troops available for the defence. The different (lower) force-space ratio on the far-more-extensive Eastern Front provided more opportunities for the offensive.

The circumstances of trench life varied, in particular with surface geology and weather: in some soils, it was easy to dig deep in order to gain cover, and in others, for example the stony soils of Champagne, it was not. Moreover, some soils and terrains were free-draining, and others were not. The British frequently found trenches in the soil in Flanders and nearby areas of northern France, such as the Somme Valley, difficult to keep dry. Lieutenant Aubrey Harris of the Manchester Regiment noted: 'We've been up and down in the mud two feet deep and water deeper still.... Working parties are trying to mend the trenches, they are all falling in.' He was killed in action in September 1916, aged 22. At Ypres, troops were 'up to the waist in slug [sludge] and water.'[8]

Wet weather increased exposure to vermin and to trench conditions such as trench foot, a form of foot damage due to moisture and limited blood circulation, and frostbite. Damp and cold ensured that soldiers and officers were keen to obtain warm clothing, notably gloves, boots, socks and drawers. Letters from the Western Front commented frequently on such weather, as well as on the dread created by a forthcoming winter. Indeed, the constraints of the season and the weather affected conflict so that, despite description in terms of industrial and/or total warfare, the war was not fought in the relentless manner of an industrial machine which is never allowed to halt. Instead, operations were limited in the winter. The rain could also be a problem in the summer, Captain Roland Garvin of the South Lancashire Regiment complaining in August 1915, 'the trenches became a mere glutinous mass underfoot.'[9] He was killed aged 20 in 1916. Many of these issues were to recur in the Second World War and the Korean War.

At the same time, units were rotated out of the front line, while, in the latter, in part due to a system of live and let live,[10] there were long periods without attacks; although these periods could still be hazardous as a result of shell fire, sniping and raids, especially night raids to gain information and grasp the initiative. Exposure to sniping encapsulated the randomness of fate that so many soldiers recorded. The First Battalion of the London Rifle Brigade noted in its War Diary for one day: 'Practically no sniping all day,' but recorded heavy shelling the next two.[11]

Medical care varied, being far better for the British infantry than the Russian and Italian. Improvements reflected the range, needs and possibilities, notably the scale of the casualties, the significance for morale of the care, the ideas focused on the citizenry under arms, and the need to return as many of the wounded as possible to the Front.[12]

Both medical care and food supplies were better than those that many of the soldiers had experienced in civilian life, although this was far less true of the 'housing' offered in trench systems. Edward Southcomb, a young officer who did not survive the war on the Western Front, was troubled by incessant rain in April 1917, so that 'all round my tent is a regular mud swamp,' but he was warm and, at times, the accommodation seemed very good. The following month, he noted 'The last two days I am in a topping billet, very clean and comfy and some pretty French lasses.' Food for this officer was reasonable:

> 'Our rations *generally* consist of bacon, meat, bread, margarine, tea, sugar, marmalade, and vegetables the latter are very scarce. There is always heaps of "bully beef" [corned beef, salt-cured brisket of beef, ie not fresh beef]'[13]

although he had not seen potatoes for three weeks. Ordinary British troops ate less well, but, thanks to the development of a logistics capability able to support a static front line, there was generally enough food, although shortages and grievances rose while ration scales fell, in part in response to harvest and transport problems. There was some resentment of the better treatment of officers.[14] There was far less food for combatants on the Balkan fronts. In the Russian army, soldiers received 2½ pounds of bread daily, which was better than peasants at home, and contributed to morale, but troops were anxious about how their families were coping.[15]

After the failure of a major attack at Neuve Chapelle in 1915, Private Stanley Green commented on the stunned nature of the surviving attackers: the operation proved very different to the 'visions of thrilling charges and hand to hand combat' he and others had anticipated.[16] Later that year, at Loos, another British attack failed. Captain G.D. Robert of the 8th Devons described a covering of smoke and gas that 'produced a very passable imitation of a bad London fog.' There was savage German fire from artillery, machine guns and rifles, and casualties, as he noted:

> 'were at once very heavy and before reaching the first German trench all but two officers were either killed or wounded.... 750 men went over the parapet and about 130 came back ... though of course many of the wounded were very slightly hurt and gassed and have since rejoined.'[17]

Frontal attacks were the conventional tactical form, for example also used across the Atlantic in the Mexican Revolution. In Western Europe, where the ratio of troops and firepower to space was far higher than in Mexico, such methods were much more costly. In September 1914, Maurice Hankey, Secretary to the Committee of Imperial Defence, wrote about 'the absolute disregard of human life by the Germans in the recent fighting. Time after time prepared positions have been captured on land in frontal attack by sheer weight of numbers notwithstanding terrible losses.'[18] Sir Horace Smith-Dorrien, the commander of the British Second Army, reported heavy German casualties when attacking at Ypres in April 1915: 'Artillery observing officers claim to have mown them down over and over again during the day.'[19]

Bombardment by artillery was a particular cause of casualties, Captain Hugh Orr-Ewing, a British Medical Officer, writing to his fiancée from the battle of Loos in 1915:

> 'I lit a cigarette and tried to pretend I wasn't frightened to death. And just then a man ran by with his arm nearly off. I was so afraid he would bleed to death that I lost my fear for a minute or two and followed him, stood in the trench and dressed him. Lewis, my corporal, was cowering down by my side in a small scoop. I would not let him come out, as I told him one of us was enough at a time, when suddenly a shell exploded on him and blew him to pieces, knocked me over and broke the leg of a stretcher bearer who was two yards

further off than I was. I do not know why I wasn't killed. My nerve went and I would have bolted only I heard the poor beggar hit in the leg calling for me so I groped my way to him and dressed him. I have never been so shaken… Found Lloyd of A Company – his servant had had one of his legs blown off – I got down and dressed him, how I don't know, and was absolutely literally sick from shock, then dressed two others and then had a very stiff brandy then I am afraid I broke down.'[20]

The fighting at Gallipoli that year also rapidly became static, with the tiny, exposed Allied positions made even grimmer by the heat, dysentery and, eventually, typhoid. Lieutenant General Sir William Birdwood, the commander of the Austrian and New Zealand force, reported that he was 'practically reduced to a state of siege' in the face of repeated Turkish attacks, following later: 'It seems quite ridiculous that we should be within ten yards of each other, and yet I am unable to get into their trenches.'[21] From the perspective of the Allied infantry, they were bearing the burden of strategic risk and operational inadequacies; but from their opponents' perspective, this was an infantry triumph, that of the Turks.

The attritional nature of conflict was captured in the War Diary of the London Rifle Brigade which claimed for 1 July 1916, the first day of the deadly Somme offensive: 'It seems probable that although the actual attack was unsuccessful and was very costly, we killed a large number of Germans but undoubtedly the attack failed.'[22] British losses were very heavy.

Infantry tactics developed in order to overcome the strength of the defence and to reflect the experience gained so far. The improvement of coordination with artillery was significant and was publicly discussed as a way to reduce infantry losses; rather than as a substitute for infantry. Artillery cannot hold ground. Thus, *The Times* on 13 April 1917 noted:

'The chief lesson learnt is that against strong defensive positions the pace of a sustained attack is the pace of the heavy artillery. To attempt to force the pace is to neglect the searching preparation which alone can make assaults in force successful without overwhelming sacrifice … time is given for the guns to get into position and to prepare the way for the infantry, then the strength of the defensive lines

> crumbles to chaos.... The role of the guns must be taken up again, and when they have played their part again, then the storming lines will go forward.'

Separately, infantry tactics devised for overcoming strong posts offered more mobile firepower. Indeed, the British had by 1917 the all-arms infantrymen, skilled with rifle, bayonet, Lewis gun (an effective light machine gun), and hand and rifle grenade, and accustomed to working in cooperation with artillery and mortars, notably the Stokes light mortar. In an instance of a broader pattern, British grenade and mortar tactics came from experience, which was taught in infantry schools set up from mid-1915 onward. The report of operations by the British Fifty-Sixth Division in January 1917 noted a frequent use of Lewis Guns, Stokes Mortars, and rifle grenades. A battalion report of September 1918 commented that a company advanced under considerable machine gun fire by dribbling men across open spaces under covering fire from massed company Lewis guns.[23]

Meanwhile, what were to be called storm-trooper techniques or infiltration tactics had been developed by the Germans, and notably so in raids against the French from October 1915. These storm-trooper techniques, for which the Germans get the credit because of the term *Stosstruppen* (storm troopers), relied on carefully planned surprise assaults employing infiltration and focusing on opponents' strong points in order to destroy the cohesion of their defence. Captain Reginald Benson, a British liaison officer with the French, wrote a memorandum in July 1917 about German attacks in the Chemin des Dames: 'surprise attacks usually at day-break or dusk: assaulting infantry keep well up with the [creeping barrage] ... Stosstrupps ... They consist of bombers, pioneers carrying flame-projectors, wire-cutters, and artillery liaison officers.' Benson reported that such units had been used ably since the beginning of the year, but that they drained the best men from the infantry,[24] as indeed does any system of specialisation as with later panzer grenadiers, commandoes, and parachute units. Indeed, the misleading idea that 'ordinary' or 'bog standard' infantry units are second-base 'rump' developed in part due to this practice, although it was also a consequence of the earlier focus on cavalry. Such storm-trooper units affected the structures of infantry forces. Instead of being made up solely of ordinary infantry battalions or regiments, they were now combined with special formations, including, for example, machine guns and mortars.

For the Germans, these storm-trooper tactics were those of specialists and, in the winter of 1917–18, an attempt was made to train German units so as to inculcate the need for appropriate action by individual soldiers. Training was now done near the front line, which was not only easier but also very much underlined the significance of experience, as well as the way in which the latter was far from constant.

Stanley Green of the 17th London Regiment recorded of the opening of the German Somme offensive on 21 March 1918: 'with a preliminary bombardment of gas which covered the ground in mist and swamped our clothes … in overwhelming force … as the shelling increased, the phone lines naturally were broken.' His unit retreated 'in indescribable confusion' and Green was struck by the pace of the German attack:

> 'the mobile artillery that kept up with Jerry's front line … by means of motor tractors … those pincers of storm troops … hitting every time with uncanny skill those parts of our line most thinly held and creeping round in enfilading and enflanking movements that we could not stop.'[25]

The British and the French developed similar tactics at much the same time, with Captain André Laffargue possibly launching the idea in print in August 1915 in his pamphlet *Étude sur l'attaque dans la période actuelle de la guerre* (*Study of the Attack in the Current Period of the War*), which called for mobile firepower and infiltration. An English version was published that December. The British infantry gained a lot of tactical experience from raids, which often encouraged infiltration and artillery-box barrages, as well as mortars and machine guns operating in fire-suppression roles, before these tactics became widespread among the infantry as a whole during larger-scale operations. The Canadians developed raid-like tactics for major operations in 1916–17. The British made the tactics widespread across the British Expeditionary Force, on a pattern also seen in the Second World War, and training took place near the front line as a way to incorporate field experience.

These tactics had considerable success, notably for the Germans in the spring of 1918, but could not overcome defence-in-depth. To do so required well-applied artillery bombardment. which was a key means of helping infantry fulfil its potential. In place of generalised firepower, there was by then systematic coordination, reflecting precise control of both infantry and massive artillery support, plus improved communications between the two, not least in order to provide prompt artillery support for the infantry. Artillery was crucial for the Allied infantry advances in late 1918, as for the British in the Battle of the River Selle in late October: '...a fine barrage ... men ... kept up well under the barrage.... The five minutes' bombardment demanded by the CO undoubtedly saved the battalion many lives and won for them an almost impregnable position.'[26] So also for the field artillery:

> 'the Infantry always knew the guns were close behind and ready to help them when required ... the keenness and push of the officers in charge of the forward sections allotted to my attacking battalions each day ... my battalions are full of praise for the shooting of your gunners.'[27]

German intelligence reports noted that the Americans, who entered the war on the Allied side in 1917, were less cautious than the French who preferred to advance only after very extensive artillery preparations.[28] The Americans faced the issues of insufficient experience and an inappropriate doctrine conditioning experience as well as influencing American commanders.[29] General John Pershing, the commander of the American Expeditionary Force, proved flawed not least at the tactical level with his commitment to aimed rifle fire and rapid advance without sufficient preparation.

The key to converting a break-in into a breakthrough was Allied artillery that neutralised the German ability to mount counterattacks, a factor also seen in the Second World War. And the key to breaking in was infiltration rather than wave assaults. Infantry infiltration, taking advantage of skilfully applied artillery firepower, neutralised the German defences-in-depth, whereas sheer firepower alone could not do that. In doing so, the Allied learning curve in offensive battle beat that of the Germans in defensive battle. Trench warfare had evolved into deep battle, with important help from aerial reconnaissance. Infantry were key to the Allied solution in 1918, not an also-ran to tanks, and frequently advanced when there were few or no tanks present. Allied infantry backed by artillery benefited in 1918 from the German inability to mount the counterattacks necessary to limit manoeuvre warfare.[30]

It is all-too-easy to present the development of infantry doctrine, tactics and weaponry in terms of a clear pattern of development based on obvious best practice, but this was not the case; no more than it was for other episodes of infantry development. Thus, automatic rifles, around from the end of the nineteenth century, were not viewed with great favour during the First World War, and notably not by the British. This was due to their being unreliable, a key problem for infantry weaponry when in the face of the enemy, and also heavy, not least due to their need for a bigger magazine. In contrast, the British reorganised their infantry tactics around the Lewis gun. The commanders of infantry battalions were largely competent regular officers, and poor commanders were removed.[31]

At the same time, German resistance led to heavy casualties and posed serious problems, as for the first battalion of the Devonshire Regiment in August 1918:

> '[30 August] The advance was extremely difficult owing to the open nature of the country and the strength of the enemy resistance ... small parties pushed on to Beugny, where they were met by intense rifle and machine gun fire ... made it necessary to withdraw...
> [31 August] hostile machine-guns fired immediately on any movement.'[32]

Brigadier General Thomas Blamey of the Australian army recorded that near Peronne on 2 September the attack was met by 'hurricane machine gun fire.'[33] Switching to a war of movement left the infantry exposed away from the relative safety of the trenches. Furthermore, the Italian attack on the Austrian positions near Mount Grappa on 24 October was a dismal demonstration that warfighting did not necessarily improve: linear advances into Austrian firepower led to no gains and nearly 25,000 casualties.

A degree of consensualism was seen in infantry service in the First World War. In part, there was enthusiasm, comradeship, and patriotic nationalism that greatly encouraged service, as did pre-war training and reserve systems, wartime training, and a sense of doing their 'bit' and emulating their ancestors.[34] Morale could hold up well, as with the multinational Egyptian Expeditionary Force deployed by the British in the harsh environment of Sinai and Palestine.[35] However, the threat of coercion also played a role. The number of deserters shot was small, but the constant threat of execution was a constraint. Furthermore, the nature of the campaigning made desertion difficult.

Yet in 1917–18 there was serious demoralisation, first in the French and Russian armies and then, in 1918, in the Austrian and German ones. The response among the French army to the heavy losses in the Nivelle offensive in 1917 was a form of passive mutiny which ensured that, for the remainder of that year and in early 1918, the French army refrained from offensive operations. This was an infantry pressure that greatly affected strategy.

The developmental account of this century, from infantry conflict as the characteristic of the deadly stasis of trench warfare in the First World War, to the subsequent regaining of mobility, notably by the use of the tank, is overly simplistic. This is not least in misunderstanding, by overestimating, the capabilities and impact of the tank, and also from failing to appreciate the degree to which the development of artillery-infantry coordination represented the key means to regain mobility in the last stages of the First World War; the tank then, moreover, was an infantry-support weapon. The infantry was crucial in this coordination, but not in any static fashion. Indeed, the development of more flexible attack and defence doctrines was rapid, such that, it can be claimed, that by the start of 1917 'the whole shape of modern infantry tactics had been settled.'[36] Wartime experience forced a rethinking of the attack as a way to overcome static warfare, with a reconceptualisation of combined-arms operations and the extension of mission command down the command chain.[37]

The coordination necessary to defend large trench complexes suggested the means to break them, which, in turn, helped lead to the development of the capabilities that eventually led armies out of the trenches. This was because the size of the armies, the proliferation of new weapons and the extent of entrenchment forced leaders to start thinking about the co-ordination in time and space of fire, manoeuvre, obstacles, reserve positions and so on, largely sight unseen, and accomplishing such coordination by topographic maps, aerial photography, electronic communications, and a common knowledge of the time of day. These were essential, first in the defence, but also provided the elementary skills and infrastructure that allowed offensive ideas to grow. Thus, the Germans evolved from a decentralised defence in depth to a similarly offensive capability. The Allies similarly displayed a process of development. The coordination of manoeuvre with artillery was very important, and this explained the significance of maps, watches and telephones. Much synchronisation had to take place to carry an army through an enemy's defences.

Already, earlier in the war, the difference in troop density on the Eastern Front created tactical opportunities for the attacker. Indeed, for the infantry, our image of the war would be different if the Eastern Front received equivalent scholarly attention to the Western. The Eastern Front showed that tactical problems did not preclude operational and strategic mobility. Moreover, the key problems in Eastern Europe were operational and strategic, notably where best to allocate troops and mount offensives. Focus on the 'Face of Battle' does not answer this issue.

The presence of continuous front lines served as a prime requirement for infantry but also a constraint on it. These lines, and the related density and effectiveness of the defensive pushed further the already strong emphasis on infantry as opposed to cavalry. Manoeuvre warfare came to have a different meaning in terms of a breakthrough of defences rather than an outflanking of them. At the same time, there were areas where there were not the complete front lines of that type, notably in the campaigns centred on the attempts to conquer Germany's African colonies. These saw a manoeuvrist practice that drew on imperial methods of column advance and South African Boer experience with mobility.[38] There were elements of this in the American tradition, but it proved seriously inappropriate on the Western Front in 1918.

In a 1920 memorandum, 'Explanation of the theory of the application of the essential principles of strategy to infantry tactics,' Basil Liddell Hart, a British infantry officer turned commentator, wrote:

> 'The improvements in weapons and the wide extensions enforced by them have created new conditions in the infantry fight. It has developed into what may be termed group combats; the defenders realising that a self-contained group based on a tactical point is more effective than a trench line, the breaking of which results in the whole line falling back; the attackers countering this method

> of defence by endeavouring to penetrate between the centres of resistance and turn their flanks.'[39]

Liddell Hart's proposed use of both infantry and armour emphasised manoeuvre and an 'indirect approach,' not frontal attacks and attrition. Infantry was becoming more manoeuvrist in part due to the availability of motor transport, but also due to the ethos of campaigning that became so insistent in and from 1918.

Artillery-infantry coordination, however, could have a less benign side. Thus, in October 1919, Captain John Kennedy, an artillery liaison officer with the British Military Mission to South Russia, wrote of the White Russian forces, to which he was attached, that the infantry did not like to advance in front of the artillery, while a lack of protection meant that the latter only fired at extreme range.[40] Kennedy was unimpressed. In practice, both sides in the Russian Civil War (1918–21) tended to rely on frontal attacks by infantry that were designed to break a thin enemy line and force withdrawal. These could include the storming of prepared positions because the artillery necessary to suppress defences was in limited supply and, anyway, of restricted use for fast-moving operations over large areas. Reporting on the linked Soviet-Polish struggle in 1920, Major General Sir Percy Rawcliffe noted the new context, but, in doing so emphasised the role of tasking:

> 'The tide of battle has surged backwards and forwards more in response to psychological and emotional factors than to the result of hard blows on either side, and the possibilities of manoeuvre once more reached a pitch of development that has not been seen in Europe since the days of Napoleon.
>
> Coming so quickly on the heels of the long stagnation, which was the feature of the war on the Western Front, the antithesis is all the more striking.'[41]

It is significant that the days of Napoleon were the basis for judgment.

The postwar infantry drew on the experience, weaponry and doctrine of the recent world war. No post-1918 Western infantry went back to the pre-war ways, and this was not only the case for the European powers. A British intelligence report of 1919 noted that 'Dervish rushing tactics' in British Somaliland, as with the successful attack on the British at Dul Madoba in 1913, tactics that looked back to anti-imperial techniques of the nineteenth century, had been superseded by a stress on the defence:

> 'The large increase in the number of rifles in the Mullah's[42] possession and the consequent discard of the spear... We may expect the Dervishes to take up defensive positions which they will defend stubbornly behind cover without exposing themselves. We must be ready to carry out attacks against most difficult positions and up narrow and steep-sided valleys, to employ covering fire and frequently to capture the heights or the key to the position before it will be possible to make any headway. It will also be necessary to employ artillery, firing high explosive-shell, if the various Dervish strongholds are to be captured without very heavy casualties. In short, whereas in the past the training of troops in Somaliland could, in the main, be carried out with a view to meeting one form of savage warfare, namely the Dervish rush in bush country, troops must now be trained to readily adapt themselves to a more varied form of fighting which will, in some degree, resemble hill warfare in India.'[43]

Infantry, more generally, was equipped and trained in the 1920s to fight a flexible battle with a range of weapons. One of the fundamental lessons of the world war had been that of the need for preparation and the value of training, which was regularly updated and reiterated. It was by this means that every British infantryman had become proficient during the war with rifle, bayonet, hand and rifle grenades, and the Lewis gun. Tactical doctrine was adapted to take advantage of these developments.

Yet, these changes also entailed cost, and that at a time of great concern about expenditure. In the 1920s, this led to interest in the idea of machines as a way to deliver increased capability at lower cost. The preference on the part of many commentators was for an élite, well-equipped force, with the emphasis for the army on mechanisation, particularly with tanks. That option clashed with the constraints on tactics and operations requiring large numbers of troops, posed by a smaller army as well as with institutional preferences for continuity and size in the army. In the case of many governments, numbers were seen as necessary for the maintenance of control in colonies, which for Britain and France expanded to an unprecedented extent, and, if appropriate, for control at home. The emphasis on numbers was also in order to match the armies of other powers. There was the strong preference for the very idea of a large army, which was equated with the impression at least of national strength. This was a tendency much strengthened by the recent world war.

The range of postwar military commitments in 1919–23 was formidable, and notably so for Britain, France, America, Japan, Italy, and Canada. Fifteen states were involved in the Russian Civil War, while there was also the need to defend new territorial gains, including new trans-oceanic imperial acquisitions. Most of this was done by infantry. Moreover, alongside the use of aircraft, for example by the British in Somalia, the conflicts of those years offered an ironic counterpoint to the emphasis on new technology. Thus, the Romanian suppression of Hungarian Communism, the Polish defeat of Soviet invasion, and the Turkish crushing of the Greeks in Asia Minor, were all essentially infantry conflicts. Mechanisation played a very modest role.

So also for the major powers, as in the unsuccessful British resistance to Irish insurgents in 1919–21, both insurgency and resistance focusing on infantry. This resistance was unsuccessful in large part for political reasons, as the political costs of a continued presence were judged unacceptable. As with so many counterinsurgency conflicts, the military analysis was far more problematic, with neither side having won in terms of ending the capacity of the other to take steps and contest control. The insurgency in Ireland, and the civil war in 1922–3 that followed the departure of British forces from the South, were each in part affected by the presence of veterans. This was an after-effect of the First World War, although conscription in Ireland was far more limited than elsewhere in the United Kingdom.

More generally, however, this world war brought the military experience of conscription into the reality of hazardous service and total war. That created a large group of men who had the relevant background for paramilitary action, which was an important feature of the interwar years. Most of these men had served in the infantry, and their politics in these years was therefore an aspect of the history of infantry, and most clearly so when there was a military or paramilitary dimension.

The clash between numbers and weaponry as priorities became apparent in Italy. General Antonino DiGiorgio, the War Minister, favoured a small army with modern weapons, providing firepower, mobility and offensive capacity; but the military leadership argued that this choice would weaken Italy, while the cost was also a major problem. In 1925, the Fascist dictator, Benito Mussolini, came out against Di Giorgio's proposals as he also wanted a large army, in part as a show of force. Di Giorgio resigned.[44]

In Japan, the Imperial Way faction in the army pressed for an emphasis on manpower and the military spirit, rather than on machines. The call was for 'flesh before steel,' and their belief that Japanese manpower had inherent and unique qualities that made them effective, or what others had called 'human bullets'. In 1928, the army's strategic manual was rewritten accordingly. In the early 1930s, the emphasis, under General Araki Sadao, was on the Imperial Way approach.[45]

At war with China from 1937, the Japanese emphasis on 'spirit' included a stress on the use of bayonets and swords in attacks. As the army was shaped for war on Continental Asia, the artillery was reduced, because it hampered mobility, another case of terrain shaping force structure. Brutalized training contributed to Japanese fighting determination, as did self-preservation, comradeship and racism, all linked to militarism.[46] In the event, despite major territorial gains in 1937–8, this emphasis did not suffice, with the determination of Chinese resistance combined with the deficiencies of the Japanese army which included severe logistical problems leading to malnutrition and contributing to disease. Japanese propaganda films made much of the role of tanks, but this was a misrepresentation of an army that was very heavily reliant on infantry. So also for its Chinese opponent, and the consequences for both were seen in the determination to control railway lines and junctions.

The German army did not match the claims made for it by propagandists who emphasised tanks. Much of its doctrine in the 1920s and 1930s related to infantry rather than tanks, with the concept of delaying resistance increasingly prominent,[47] and the mechanisation of its infantry was limited. Indeed, the notion that tanks should be used primarily in an infantry support role had major advocates including among German generals, into the early stages of the Second World War. This was very different to what would later be presented as *Blitzkrieg*.

Soviet planners argued that they could, and must, have both mass (infantry) and mechanisation,[48] but, in practice, for the Soviet Union and other states, there were repeated tendencies if not choices. States that rejected conscription, notably Britain and America, did not tend to focus on numbers, and, instead, emphasised equipment, morale and alliances as compensation for manpower. This was easier for these two powers as they were wealthy and had advanced industrial economies. In some respects, the focus on mechanisation was an extension, with these powers, of their already strong interest in navies. In the latter, the tendency from the introduction of steam technology in the early nineteenth century, had been for a greater emphasis on the ship as machine. France had conscription, but stressed fortifications, notably the Maginot Line, as a way to cope with the greater numbers in Germany. So also with the French interest in armour.

At the same time, there was an overlap between choices, in that machines could help provide a mobility that made infantry more valuable. Indeed, there was a more general complementary dimension across the questions of force structure. Thus, visiting France in 1935, Sir Archibald Montgomery-Massingberd, the Chief of the British Imperial General Staff, saw the idea of fortifications as providing not only protection but also a support for operational mobility: 'Here again the underlying idea of economy in men so as to set free as many troops as possible for the mobile army.'[49]

The British, however, continued to face the need to match force structure to tasking; and infantry was seen as particularly suited to the mixed-environment, counter-insurgency, tasks of colonial warfare. In 1934, the Defence Requirements Sub-Committee of the Committee of Imperial Defence reported:

> 'The complete mechanisation of the army is not today, or in the near future, a possible or desirable measure. It would demand a highly-specialised army trained and equipped for one contingency only, viz. war in a European theatre and on ground suitable for its employment.'

The Sub-Committee argued that imperial tasks cannot 'be met by the creation of a highly specialised "robot" army at home, ie. tanks, but also concluded that the infantry needed anti-tank guns and mechanised first-line transport.'[50]

The French also needed infantry for colonial struggles, much of it locally raised, as in opposing the Druze rebellion in Syria in the mid 1920s. French military control of Syria and Lebanon substantially rested on the *Armée du Levant*, 70,000 strong in 1921, a force largely composed of colonial troops from Africa, and on local military and police forces: the *Troupes Spéciales du Levant*, 14,000 strong in 1935, and the *Gendarmerie*. These were infantry, but the key element was the proportion of local minority groups, such as Christians, that could be relied upon in the event of clashes with the remainder of the population.[51] The conflict often involved anti-societal violence. The French crushed nationalist uprisings in Vietnam in 1930–1 in part by the intimidation and counter-logistics of killing livestock, village burnings and crop destruction.[52]

The conflicts of the 1930s, notably the struggle between government and Communists in China in the early 1930s, unsurprisingly did not reveal an ease in implementing recent ideas about war, notably motorisation. The largest war of the century in South America, the Chaco War of 1932–5 between Bolivia and Paraguay, saw infantry movement 'ankle deep in the dust and suffering torture from thirst and dust.'[53]

While the First World War is seen as an infantry conflict, this is certainly not the case with the perception of the Second World War, even though the numbers of infantry in the latter were far greater than those of other combat army units. Furthermore, mechanised and even armoured units included many infantry. As with the First World War, but far more so, there has been a tendency for the Second World War not only to underrate the role of infantry, but also to ignore the extent to which training played an important role, and therefore could help differentiate between infantry units.

There was a great need for training, not only to match the nature of the fighting but also to deal with the major expansion of numbers. Thus, the German army, from 1.1 million strong at the start of 1939, reached 5.76 million in June 1940, an expansion, mostly in infantry, that worried German commanders, and with training and experience problems that were to be matched by the British and Americans. Indeed, when the Soviet Union was invaded in June 1941, much of the German infantry was not fully combat-ready, in part due to a lack of sufficient training. Equally, as part of the more general problem of assessing judgment, what not fully combat-ready means is far from fixed. Moreover, it is unsurprising that most[54] infantries can be seen in that light as also with the other branches of the army.

In 1939, the Germans benefited in invading Poland from the advantages of armour over infantry but, in part, this was because of strategy, namely the Poles defending the full extent of their borders, rather than concentrating in the heart of Poland to provide defence in depth and to respond to German thrusts separately. The difficulties for the Poles of losing control of the tempo of operations was seen in the general lack of strong and sustained counterattacks, and this enabled the German armour to advance ahead of the marching infantry and with exposed flanks.

In contrast, with the Soviet invasion of Finland later that year, the unsuitability of terrain and climate for armour gave more of the initiative to the Finnish infantry, some moving on skis. The Finns found Soviet tanks vulnerable to Molotov cocktails. In response, in May 1940, the Supreme Military Soviet issued Order No. 120 which called for better training, more fluid infantry tactics, and better all-arms coordination. The lack of winter wear was closely linked to numerous Soviet casualties from frostbite, and also affected morale. The shortage of lorries restricted deliveries of food, fuel and ammunition, while the death or disabling of horses due to the cold also hit transport. Rations were limited, cooking difficult, and the Soviets relied on hardtack biscuits. No water was provided, and the use of melted and boiled snow was linked to illness.

In 1940, the French suffered from a very poor overall strategy, but also from an infantry-focused doctrine which saw tanks essentially as mobile artillery support for infantry. The Germans benefited not only from the armoured tip of their army, but also from well-trained regular infantry divisions. At the same time, there were also numerous German reserve divisions with less impressive training and morale. *Panzergrenadiers* (mechanised infantry) were only a minority of the infantry, but, in turn, were affected by fuel shortages, as also happened with the invasions of Poland and, in 1941, the Soviet Union.[55] To provide mobility and save on fuel, the Germans made extensive use of bicycles, manufacturing types able to carry fully-equipped soldiers; but these bicycles were dependent on roads and provided no protection against enemy fire.[56] In contrast, the British and American infantry were far more mechanised, although terrain remained a key issue, with artillery-infantry co-operation even more important where it was poor for armour, as in successful British operations against the Italians in northern Ethiopia in 1941.

On the Eastern Front, as before, German propaganda focused on tanks but infantry support was important for countering Soviet anti-tank guns. These offered a modern equivalent to the destructive use of infantry, particularly infantry firing from behind field entrenchments, against cavalry advances in the sixteenth century. Where it occurred, the mechanisation of infantry only partly addressed the gap between armour and supporting infantry, for there were many differences in the pace of conflict, not least as infantry dismounted to fight.

On the Eastern Front, infantry was crucial to both sides, but had to face a brutal environment, not least due to the temperatures, lack of cover, and treatment of prisoners.[57] As J.F.C. Fuller pointed out in the *Evening Standard* of 2 August 1941, the Soviet army, unlike its French counterpart, fought on when broken into fragments, leading to 'an unexpected change from field to, what may be called, morcellated siege warfare.' This was a major problem for the Germans, for the Soviet ability to create defence in depth proved effective once the initial shock and surprise of the German attack had been absorbed. The Soviet response ensured that the German timetable for victory was totally derailed, and the serious deficiencies in the German army became clear, as did the improvised solutions they gave rise to in combat conditions.

As an instance of the problems of classification, anti-tank guns were an important infantry tool as much as a key artillery weapon. Fuller, a noted advocate for tanks, had already claimed, in the *War Weekly* of 10 November 1939, that 'because of the enormous numbers of anti-tank weapons which today will be met within attacks on narrow and strongly fortified fronts, the tank, originally designed to storm parapets and trenches, has ceased to be an effective siege warfare weapon.' Thus it could not be a substitute for an attacking infantry.

Training conditioned men both to machines, notably their weapons and those of others, both within their army and those of opponents. Training also conditioned men to the machine, at once complex and simple, that is the army. Training, moreover, enabled troops to assimilate new tactical thinking and to convey an instructive response; provided experience of the unit in, and with, which troops would fight; and gave a psychological form of empowerment, providing an understanding of what was to happen as troops became 'combat-wise.' Infantry were exposed to live firing in training as well as to night operations.

Training proved a way to familiarise recruits with their tasks, but this did not necessarily lead them to appreciate their conditions of service nor the ethos of an hierarchical institution, nor the extent to which their task was dangerous, with infantry casualty rates particularly high not least because the infantry manned the front line, indeed were the front line.[58] In contrast, élite formations, notably armour, did not generally encounter such sustained combat, although casualties in combat could be very heavy as they were, even more, for airborne troops, a major development in infantry. As well as specific skills, it was necessary in training to overcome the civilising effects of peacetime and to prepare troops for killing. Bayonet drill was a classic instance, even though bayonets were rarely used for that end, other than by the Japanese.[59] Indeed, close combat frequently found other parts of the gun or weapons used for bludgeoning. Much of the discussion of combat emphasized hand-to-hand combat and thus the prowess, skills and masculinity involved.

Morale very much varied in its institutional practice, not least with a variable reliance on coercion to ensure combat behaviour. Thus, the Soviets used executions in large numbers in order to ensure an environment of terror and automatic obedience. Over 150,000 death sentences were issued to Soviet soldiers, generally in a very arbitrary fashion, and many others were shot in the field. The treatment of German soldiers deemed lacking in zeal became increasingly violent in 1944–5, while, in contrast, American and British soldiers were executed in very low numbers and not in this arbitrary fashion.

The importance of morale to infantry conduct was captured by General Claude Auchinleck in his explanation of total British failure in Norway in 1940 in the face of the German invasion. German aerial superiority was seen as affecting infantry morale, as it certainly did, but, in addition, there was:

> 'the lack of training of the men as soldiers and a lack of adaptability which induced in them a feeling of inferiority as compared with the enemy.... their flanks and rear were continually threatened ... our men for the most part seemed distressingly young, not so much in years as in self-reliance and manliness generally.'[60]

In practice, Auchinleck lacked sympathy for new recruits, preferring experienced regulars, while there were also in the Norway operations serious flaws in planning and command.[61] At any rate, a sense of German superiority fostered by recent successes was also detrimentally to affect British army performance in North Africa in early 1942. In turn, a change in the situation contributed to success there later in the year,[62] although British victory at El Alamein, in the face of a determined defence, was still hard-fought.[63] German determination remained high in 1944–5 despite the war clearly going against Germany. The importance of training and morale are generally underplayed by later commentators due to the customary emphasis on weaponry.

Infantry training was far more complex than when going into the First World War, in part due to the nature, range and challenge of combined-armed operations. In addition, the management of troops in close-order formations, whether lines, squares, or columns, was replaced, in the 'empty battlefield,' by more dispersed formations. Due to defensive firepower, infantry attacks were not generally in massed formations, although these were seen with the Japanese, as on the island of Guadalcanal in late 1942, and with the Soviets. In each case, high casualties were taken as a result.

When formations were more dispersed, officers could not readily give orders, and individual soldiers as well as non-commissioned officers now had to make their own choices. That troops were more educated, better read, and less familiar than in the past with the rural experiences of coping with weather, understanding terrain, and seeing death in the case of animals, was also significant in affecting training and the experience of combat. At the same time, training itself was not enough. It was necessary to consider the framework of training. In the case of the Canadians, the tactical role of junior NCOs was neglected prior to 1944 due to an inherited culture of focusing on commissioned officers.[64] At the same time, these men were crucial to the ability of infantry units to implement instructions.[65] This, indeed, was a key factor that helped determine differences both between units and also between particular levels of command.[66]

The importance of leadership and training was repeatedly argued by officers. Troy Middleton, who commanded the American Eighth Corps in its bloody and rather unsuccessful offensive against the Germans in the western Cotentin on 3–22 July 1944, wrote to Lieutenant General Omar Bradley, his superior, on 23 July:

> 'Our men do not close on and follow our own artillery fire. Men do not use their own fire to help them forward, there should and must be more marching fire. Men permit themselves to become pinned down under hostile fire, thereby adding to our losses. There is entirely too much bunching of troops. When in danger, there is a tendency to gather together.... Infantrymen do not shoot enough... Our infantry rely too much on our artillery.'[67]

William DePuy wrote of his time as an officer in Normandy:

> 'I certainly came away with a feeling that only a small percentage of the soldiers did almost all the fighting. If you just left them alone then some 10 per cent of the soldiers were the ones who actually took the initiative, moved, fired their rifles, threw hand grenades and so on. The other 90 per cent would defend themselves if they had to, but would not do the other things unless an officer or a sergeant directly would do it, in which case they usually would do it. I learned that you couldn't depend on them doing things simply because there was a plan to do it, or because of some generalised order to do it, and this included the junior officers. You had to say, "do this," "do that," "now fire there," "now do this" and "now move there." You would always end up with three or four men doing all the work. Unfortunately, the rest contributed to the casualties. And, to this very day, I'd rather have a 40-man company than a 220-man company, if I could pick the 40 men. I'd pick sergeants and officers and a few natural fighters if I could.'

Far more than in the previous world war, there was also the case of unfamiliar environments. Whereas Europe had dominated land fighting in the First World War (albeit with important campaigning in the Middle East and sub-Saharan Africa), the experience of North Africa was significant in 1940–3 and (far more) of the Pacific and South-East Asia in 1941–5. The latter entailed infantry combat in very unfamiliar circumstances, for example the damp, deep, thickly forested valleys of New Guinea and the India-Burma (Myanmar) border. Thomas Blamey, the Australian commander in New Guinea, wrote thence in 1942: 'The wastage in tropical warfare in undeveloped areas is immense … at least one-third of our force at Milne Bay is already infected with malaria.'[68]

Indeed, it was only during the twentieth century that infantry death rates from disease came down significantly.[69] In part, the use of native troops in the Tropics addressed this issue, and notably so in Africa. The British force sent against Kano in what became northern Nigeria in 1902 was essentially one of White officers and 800 African troops. There was also the necessity to train and prepare forces for operations in the Tropics. Blamey, who took personal command of the Allied operations in September 1942, produced a report on them in July 1943, in which he argued that 'the chief reason for our success in this campaign was that our ground troops proved to be better led, better equipped and better trained than those of the enemy and were man for man better fighters.' In his report, Blamey drew attention to the role of resources, arguing that air support in particular was crucial, but his stress on the difficulty of the terrain underlined an emphasis on human resilience and effort:

> 'Throughout the region the tangled undergrowth, broken ground and ever prevailing damp made movement off the track difficult and arduous in the extreme… Beyond Nauro the track is inches deep in mud while whole leeches abound everywhere.'[70]

A subsequent report, by Blamey's protégé, Major General Stanley Savige, on the operations of the 3rd Australian Division which Savige had commanded in the Salamaua area of New Guinea in 1943, again emphasised air support, but also underlined the need for physical fitness on the part of the troops and for very good junior officers and NCOs. The stress was on greater Australian effectiveness in fighting on the ground, and on the role of training and determination in achieving this:

> 'All companies must retain their mobility and endeavouring to infiltrate between the companies…. Standing, reconnaissance and fighting patrols must be constantly active…. At least three days food, water and ammunition must be placed in each perimeter. It is inevitable that, when attacked by large and determined forces, perimeters will be surrounded, but defenders must hold out. In every instance where this was done the enemy were beaten off and

> the defenders were relieved… On occasions when withdrawals were attempted the casualties suffered were heavy … the rules of hygiene and sanitation and anti-malarial precautions must be strictly observed at all times, no matter how hard the fighting, or how weary the troops…. Patrolling must be aggressive and continuous and is the key to success in the jungle…. A high standard of training is necessary.'

In contrast, the Japanese were reported as sticking to simple and inflexible tactics, as disliking moving in small patrols, and as lacking accuracy with small arms.[71]

Training was particularly necessary because of the rapid expansion of forces, as well as the unfamiliarity and complexity of campaigning. Blamey observed in December 1942:

> 'I had hoped that our strategical plans would have been crowned with complete and rapid success in the tactical field. It was completely successful strategically in as much as we brought an American division on to Buna and an Australian division on to Gona simultaneously But in the tactical field … it was a very sorry story … the American troops cannot be classified as attack troops … from the moment they met opposition set down and have hardly gone forward a yard … the American forces, which have been expanded even more rapidly than our own were in the first years of the war, will not attain any high standard of training or war spirit for very many months to come.'[72]

British infantry familiar with the arid, high, mountainous environment on the North-West Frontier of British India (modern Pakistan), found the jungles of Malaya and Burma very difficult when faced by attacking Japanese forces in 1941–2. The British (very much understood as including imperial units notably Australian and Indian) infantry did not prove fit-for-purpose in this context, a situation exposed by the Japanese, most of whom were infantry. Rapidly-advancing Japanese troops, many using bicycles, displayed greater flexibility in taking advantage of opportunities and outmanoeuvred British defensive positions. The ability of a primarily infantry force to gain the initiative and deprive the defender of the opportunity to recover their equipoise was clearly demonstrated in both

Malaya and Burma. Concentrating on infantry operations, not mechanised warfare, the Japanese army showed its superiority over Western forces in these operations. Allied deficiencies reflected their role as all-purpose fighting troops rather than being trained for tropical warfare. The Japanese weaponry was robust and, in part due to the lightness of their supply 'tail,' their forces were fast-moving. Field Marshal Sir William Slim recorded of the Japanese, whom he unsuccessfully resisted in Burma in 1942, the problem for infantry defenders posed by fighting blind:

> 'It is no exaggeration to say that we had practically no useful or reliable information of enemy strength, movements, or intentions. Our first intimation of a Japanese move was usually the stream of red tracer bullets and the animal yells that announced their arrival on our flank or rear.... Our British, India, and Gurkha troops were a match for the Japanese in a stand-up fight, but, invariably, this being tied to a road proved our undoing.'[73]

Training, which involves environmental preparation, was inadequate, but there was also for the British the classic problem of not controlling the flow of the battle, a situation that poses problems for infantry. Fighting in Burma remained difficult throughout the war, Lieutenant General Sir Henry Pownall writing in 1944:

> 'It is bound to be a slow business, I fear. That jungle is so infernally thick you literally cannot see ten yards into it, and to winkle out concealed Japs, one by one (and they have to be killed to the last man) is the devil of a business.'[74]

The unsuccessful Japanese invasion of north-east India in 1944, however, showed a simplicity of determined offensive tactics that was wasteful of troops as well as a poor logistical system that greatly weakened their troops. The British, in contrast, benefited from air-dropped supplies. Japanese tactics were no longer adequate against better-trained forces under British command, their training resulting in higher unit quality. A fundamental change in British training reflected a rigorous evaluation of what had gone wrong both when the Japanese attacked in 1942 and, subsequently, in the First Arakan campaign in Burma. A full complement of basic training followed by jungle training, with a standardisation of training across the army in order to produce a consistent doctrine, had been insisted upon by the Infantry Committee report of June 1943. A more aggressive fighting style had been inculcated: mentally overcoming the jungle, patrolling no-man's land to deny it to the Japanese, seeking out Japanese concentrations, and responding to their infiltration tactics by using all-round defences.

Malaria Forward Treatment Units provided structured regimes for prevention and treatment, including the introduction of more effective drugs, especially penicillin and mepacrine.[75] As usual, morale was a key part of the equation. Food supplies improved, and, in place of dehydrated meat and tinned-food, animals were transported live from central India from late 1943.[76] The low morale seen in 1942, in particular in Malaya and Singapore, had been replaced by a determination that was more impressive given the difficulties posed by terrain and climate. A conviction that the Japanese could be defeated was an important counter to Japanese morale. However, in the subsequent advance into Burma, diseases such as scrub typhus were a major problem.

Infantry armaments in this world war took forward the developments of the First World War, as with rocket grenades. American infantry companies were armed with automatic and semi-automatic rifles and reliable light machine guns, bazookas, mortars and grenades. Light machine guns of the German MG 34 and German MG 42 type were very important to the infantry firefight in the European Theatre of Operations because they were different to others in combining belted ammunition, air-cooling, recoil operation and a quick barrel change mechanism. Assault rifles with a range of about 400 yards were extensively used in combat by the Germans. They also developed the handheld *Panzerfaust* rocket launcher, and the Americans the Bazooka antitank rocket first employed in 1942. Infantry, moreover, benefited from the availability of combat engineers, as with American attacks on Japanese Pacific positions, attacks in which flamethrowers and satchel charges played a major role.[77] Other armies also made extensive use of such engineers.

Flamethrowers illustrated the incremental nature of infantry weaponry, but also the way in which it could be greatly changed. The use of a pressurised system to provide flamethrowers, employed by Byzantium as a form of artillery in the ninth and tenth centuries, was reinvented in the

1910s, but the specifications rapidly improved. The one- and two-man flamethrowers of the First World War, as well as the wheeled and static models, were not mobile in the fashion of backpack models of the 1930s and 1940s, and were also severely hampered by being capable of only short-range bursts. Flamethrowers were more effective in the Second World War thanks to the invention of thickening agents that allowed the fuel to be projected a reasonable distance without being consumed in the process. Thickened fuels, especially napalm (petrol thickened with *nap*hthalic and *pal*mitic acids) also stuck to the target. Napalm is a lethal weapon that not only kills by burning but also causes asphyxiation due to the oxygen being consumed.

Fighting could be very deadly, with the daily average British loss rates higher in Normandy in 1944 than at Passchendaele in 1917. In light of these losses as well as manpower shortages, 'do not send a man where you could send a bomb or shell' became the watchword. The American infantry also suffered from a relative lack of divisions that, in turn, ensured a shortage of reserve divisions. The resulting duration of combat without a break for individual units in 1944–5 created serious difficulties. This was an aspect of the often complex relationship between experience, training and casualty rates. Thus, the Soviet army benefited from a growth in combat experience, but, to do so at the tactical rather than just operational and strategic levels, had to ensure that sufficient troops survived.

For the powers involved in the European theatre, there was no uniformity in circumstances of operation, but, instead, troops had to adapt to the environments provided by the terrain and the task. Thus, in Italy there were seemingly intractable defensive positions to overcome, such as German-held Monte Cassino for the Allies,[78] as well as areas of rapid advance. Attacking defending positions, put a premium on the infantry. Moreover, the infantry was less vulnerable to air attack than was armour, a situation that remains the case today. The role of armour and of cover from hostile air attack was seen with the German offensive in December 1944 in what became the Battle of the Bulge, a tank-led assault under the cover of cloud. However, that bitter struggle also showed how a defence could be centred on infantry and artillery, as the Americans slowed and stopped the German advance, notably on the flanks of the advance and also at Bastogne. The (American) 1965 film emphasised resistance to

German armour, but in practice much of the attacking force was infantry and short of supplies, equipment and mobility.

There was a lack of the latter due to a shortage of armoured personnel carriers (called infantry fighting vehicles today). The Germans had the excellent Sd Kf3 251 but in insufficient quantity, and the British in 1944 improvised by taking the artillery piece from a Priest mobile howitzer. The Americans came closest to solving this problem.

As far as fighting to the death was concerned, there were major variations in ratios of prisoners to fatalities. The Japanese were least willing to surrender and many of those who were captured were wounded. The Army Field Service Order of 1941 that forbade being captured was in accordance with strong currents in Japanese public culture. Although there were signs of lower morale as defeats accumulated – for example, in Burma – the willingness of the Japanese to fight on meant that the destruction of their forces was the key objective for the Allies. This fed into both the character of Allied warmaking, in order to further the securing of what was seen as a uniquely difficult unconditional surrender, as well as into the Japanese leadership's attempt to leave no space for such a solution.

The importance of defensive positions to infantry warfare, qualifying the impact of resources notably bombing, was seen in the American conquest of the islands of Iwo Jim and Okinawa in early 1945. The Japanese had created a dense network of underground fortifications, and this not only vitiated the effects of American firepower, but also made an American fighting advance on foot difficult, not least because the network provided the Japanese with a myriad of interconnected firing positions. Much of the fighting was at close quarters, centred on infantry but including combat engineers, tanks and artillery.

The fighting on these islands indicated the continued determination of Axis forces, one also seen with the Germans in 1944–5. Indeed, the Allied successes on all European fronts in the third quarter of 1944 did not lead to the surrender of Germany as might have been expected after success in the battle of Normandy. In part, as with Japan but not in the case of Germany's Balkan allies, there was a process of renewed determination, to a degree fatalistic, but also ideological.[79] The Allies approaching German frontiers in late 1944 helped stiffen the resistance, although that did not happen with Germany's European allies.

Most of the twentieth century came after the world wars, and conflicts in 1946–99 saw much use of infantry, and by leading powers, notably America in Korea and Vietnam, as well as by others. Yet, investment was greatly directed to air power, and, for the major powers, also to nuclear weaponry and missiles. American practice was of particular significance as America was the leading military power and a leading supplier of weaponry, doctrine, advice and training. The Korean War of 1950–3 involved trenches, infantry assaults and fire fights. America's principal rival in this war, China, very much relied on infantry. The combat in this conflict was reminiscent in many respects of the First World War. In contrast, America's rival in Europe, the Soviet Union, put its emphasis within the army on armour.

The largest wars in scale in the late twentieth century, notably the Chinese Civil War of 1946–9, and the Iran-Iraq War of 1980–8, were very much infantry conflicts; and the latter saw much in the way of a continuous front line, trenches and frontal assaults. However, the role of infantry in the post-1945 wars does not tend to attract attention. Thus, the sequence of Israeli-Arab wars that began in 1948, and the India-Pakistan wars that began in 1947, are generally discussed in terms of armour and airpower. Yet, infantry was very important in all these conflicts, and notably so in holding positions. Although mechanisation, often of an improvised form, was significant, the Israeli-Arab War of 1948–9 was very much an infantry conflict. In the 1956, 1967, 1973 and 1982 Arab-Israeli wars, armour was more significant, as was air power, but infantry was necessary, to support and consolidate tank advances, to hold defensive positions, and also for conflict both with infantry and armour. The use of hand-held anti-aircraft and anti-tank missiles gave an important capability to infantry, as used, for example by the Egyptians in resisting Israeli counter-attacks east of the Suez Canal in 1973. This success represented an important bridging of infantry and artillery, one that looked toward the (different) later deployment in the early 2020s of individually-controlled drones. In 1973, the Egyptians inflicted heavy casualties.

In the 1960s, armies became increasingly motorised and mechanised as the character of infantry changed. This permitted the development of infantry doctrine that focused on rapid mobility, rather than on advances on foot or essentially static position warfare. Already, when there was less motorisation, the ability of infantry to take the initiative, advance and manoeuvre was important to success, as in the Greek Civil War of 1946–9 when, in 1948, the Greek army replaced a policy of static defence by that of a systematic clearance of Communist guerrilla forces out of particular areas.

The design, commissioning, training for and use of vehicles were all important. In the early 1960s, the Americans developed the M113 armoured personnel carrier, while, in 1967, the Soviet army introduced the high-speed *Boevaya Mashina Pekhoty* infantry vehicle capable of carrying eight men as well as a crew of three, protected by an air filtration system, and armed with a gun, a machine gun, an anti-tank guided missile, and rifle ports. This was designed to give bite to the expansion in the number of Soviet motor vehicle divisions.[80]

Infantries which had a less regular structure, let alone doctrine, also used mechanisation, as with the 'Toyota War' between Chad and Libya in 1987. In this, Chadian troops in Toyota pickup trucks equipped with anti-tank guided missiles were able to outmanoeuvre Soviet-supplied Libyan tanks inflicting heavy casualties, which prefigured Ukrainian successes against Russian invaders in 2022. The widespread change in the infantry with mechanisation, a change pushed further with the NATO manoeuvrist doctrines of the 1970s and 1980s, was linked to an improvement in logistics, with horses replaced by lorries.

Meanwhile, weaponry was changing. The use of sub-machine guns was an important aspect of a weapons culture that put great pressure on logistics and that saw only limited significance for aiming. The accuracy of individual single-shot fire that had been so important in 1914, and notably by the British in resisting the advancing Germans in Belgium at the battle of Mons, became far less significant as weaponry took on spray characteristics. These left infantry differently vulnerable. More generally, the increased variety and range of weaponry meant that infantry vulnerabilities had considerably increased. At the individual level, modern high-velocity rifle bullets cause different sorts of wounds because of their higher impact energies. They leave a track through the body and set up hydrostatic effects on body fluids in the area of the track. Furthermore, unlike spherical bullets, conical bullets can yaw and tumble, which causes worse wounds than bullets that strike point first and aligned on their trajectory.

There were also the vulnerabilities arising from the intensity of service in the field, and the intractabilities of counterinsurgency warfare. Thus, the Vietnam War for the Americans became not a heroic struggle akin to what was described in action magazines, but a conflict without clear adversaries or front lines, and one of deadly booby traps and a resort again to ambushes; and, in response, counter-insurgency techniques. At the same time, as in other insurgency conflicts, there were also aspects of conventional warfare with the linked firefights. American disillusionment contributed to some atrocities as well as to disobedience, although most American soldiers did their duty, many very bravely so, and in very difficult circumstances.

Other counterinsurgency struggles also posed major problems for the infantry of regular forces, which tended very much to be the branch in the front line, as for the British in the 1950s in Malaya, Kenya and Cyprus, and the French in Algeria in the late 1950s and early 1960s, even if the nature of the front changed, for example with the extensive use of helicopters. These were an important aspect of the mechanisation already referred to, a mechanisation that appeared militarily relevant, an answer to a doctrinal emphasis on armour and/or air power, politically necessary as a way to secure funds, and a way to cut troop numbers. Nevertheless, feet on the ground were regarded as significant.

The emphasis in most discussion of counterinsurgency is on Western attempts to suppress anti-imperial 'national liberation' struggles, but this is an overly limited approach, thematically, geographically, and chronologically. Thus, newly independent states, including India, Indonesia, Pakistan, Myanmar, Iraq, Syria and Nigeria, sought to overcome regional autonomy if not separatism. These struggles involved a high level of anti-societal violence. In the Biafran War of 1967–70, an anti-separatist war in Nigeria, blockade contributed to the starvation of the Igbo people, against whom the victorious Nigerians directed much destruction. On both sides, conscription was chaotic and intimidatory, desertion treated viciously, and the war essentially an episode of armed violence that continued after the struggle ended.[81]

The emphasis in post-1945 military history can be on combined operations, as with armour or air power, but the bulk, for example, of the 250,000 Soviet troops who invaded Czechoslovakia in 1968 were infantry, as also with the troops deployed to Northern Ireland by the British from 1969. Infantry was required to take and hold positions in these cases. More generally, infantry purposes were very different across the ranges of war to policing and, differently, offensive to defensive. As an instance of war, the careful integration of infantry with artillery support in firefights was crucial to the success of the British forces in defeating the Argentinians on the Falkland Islands in 1982, and that in the absence of control of the air. Good morale, bravely executed attacks, and an ability to maintain the initiative, destroyed the Argentinian will to fight on even though they still had plentiful troops. Yet the Argentinians lacked combat-readiness in part due to the poor training of both conscripts and officers, and the lack of an understanding of the operational requirements of modern infantry conflict, specifically small-unit cohesion.

In the Yugoslav conflicts of the 1990s, the bulk of the military on all sides was infantry, and, in part due to the terrain contested, the conflict was very much infantry in character. In Yugoslavia, many of the soldiers were irregulars. So, even more, with some of the conflicts in sub-Saharan Africa. In many countries there, for example Angola, Ethiopia, Ivory Coast, Congo, Somalia, Sudan, and Mozambique, civil wars were to the fore. The nature of infantry in Sierra Leone and Liberia in the 1990s included drugged teenagers and outright looters who had little, if any, idea of the cause they were fighting for, except for their personal gains. There were no defined chains of command, but, rather, militia characterised by apparently arbitrary violence.[82]

In contrast, for more regular forces, a major transition in most infantries came from the key lessening of conscription, notably in the 1960s and 1970s. This ensured that far fewer men had experience of infantry service, but also transformed the contexts, political, social, military and financial, for infantry recruitment, discipline, training, weaponry, and force-structure including the reserves. In Britain, conscription was phased out in 1957–63, in part in order to reduce costs, while in France, where discontent with national service grew in the late 1960s, conscription was cut to a year in 1970. For France, conscription and a large army had played a role in the attempts to maintain imperial control in the 1950s and early 1960s, while also deploying an army as part of NATO commitments in Germany. The situation changed with France leaving Algeria in 1962, and with a growing commitment to nuclear weaponry to provide national defence.

In the Soviet Union, conscription was cut from three to two years in 1967, although, in place of a system in which many had not had to serve, more men were drafted, which led to an increase in desertion and in going absent without leave. In America, on the other hand, President Richard Nixon ended the draft in order to quieten popular anxieties about the Vietnam War and improve his prospects for re-election, leading, from 1973, to an all-volunteer force. In contrast, the absence of such a move helped cause revolution in Portugal in 1974 as the strain of conscription had lessened support for the counter-insurgency wars in its African colonies (Angloa, Mozambique, Guinea-Bissau), ensuring that these were abandoned in 1975 in a major shift that was not a product of specific events in the field.

The move into or out of conscription in the twentieth century was not a new development, but part of a variety that can be seen across history. It did not correspond to a pattern, cyclical or otherwise, but, rather, was a response to particular circumstances. The world wars, the Cold War, and the end of the Cold War, all proved significant instances. Conscription, however, continued for security and/or ideological reasons in some countries, such as Israel and Switzerland respectively. This looked toward the situation in the early twenty-first century, with a pressure in the 2020s for the return or extension of conscription in some countries, for example Taiwan, which extended conscription in 2022, the Baltic States, Sweden and Finland.

A major change over the century for the infantry was the improvement in medical care. This was strongly marked in Western armies. Thus, in the First World War, the British, French and German armies proved particularly successful in returning troops to the front line, in part because they provided the thorough care that was eased by relatively static front lines, good transport links, and an understanding of hygiene.

During the Second World War, there were again major differences between armies, with the Chinese and Japanese wounded suffering most, and the Russians more than the Germans. The Americans and British injured in particular benefited from new treatments and drugs, notably active immunisation against tetanus, sulphonamide drugs, and penicillin. In contrast, the Germans lacked antibiotics, so that many of their wounded suffered from severe sepsis. Yet at the same time, the use made of resources was important. For example, the significance of administrative advances was particularly the case with the British system for blood transfusion established after the foundation of the Army Blood Transfusion Service in 1938. In contrast, the German collection and storage of blood in forward areas was inadequate.

The British showed a capacity to learn during the Second World War, leading to a marked improvement in the provision of their medical care. Defeat in the early years of the war led to many problems, not least of all because the level of care available in the field was affected by the disruption attendant on defeat and rapid retreat. These early campaigns, however, provided some valuable experience. It became apparent that blood transfusion apparatus needed to be available in all forward units, and not just in specialist ones. The early campaigns also indicated that larger field hospitals were of limited use in mobile warfare, and this led to a later emphasis on field ambulances and mobile specialist units. By 1944, most British casualties were receiving treatment within hours of wounding.

An important aspect of care was provided by the growing awareness of Post-Traumatic Stress Disorder, with novel diagnoses and treatments, but, in turn, major cultural differences between and within armies. These differences reflected both attitudes within the military, notably to honour and cowardice, and also in society as a whole.[83]

The end of the Cold War in 1989–91 led to talk of a defence dividend as military preparedness was transformed away from 'high intensity conflict' to a 'low intensity' alternative that would be less frequent because of the decline and/or change in strength of the rival sponsoring power. Infantry would no longer primarily be required to man the frontline of the Cold War, America, as a consequence, providing large trans-oceanic garrisons in Western Europe and South Korea; but rather increasingly to be part of an expeditionary profile, as was dramatically demonstrated against Iraq in 1991 in driving its forces from Kuwait.

The applicability of the specific doctrines and particular changes of the period were to be debated;[84] but the net impact was a move away from infantry, a move that owed much to the emphasis on aircraft and armour in the transformative notions of a 'Revolution in Military Affairs' much trumpeted in America in the 1990s. This doctrine and practice left scant room for infantry, but, despite the influence of the American model, the agenda was different for most states. This owed much to the role of maintaining internal control, which was the priority for most governments. As a consequence of the occupation of Iraq in 2003, the American military was to face the same task.

Chapter 9

Twenty-First Century

'…the trenches nearby, which form a crescent around Donetsk. The autumn rains meant we were knee deep in mud. It could have been Flanders in 1916 apart from one thing: the drones…. The day before one had flown into the trench and dropped a grenade. I asked them which sound was worse – the whizz and crash of the shelling or the mosquito buzz of a drone? "The drones," one former miner said. "They kill or maim three or four men a day in these trenches. My nerves are shot to pieces."'

Ukraine, 2024.[1]

'a violent confrontation with numerous weapons, tomahawks, axes, knives, clubs.'

The description by Michael Murphy, the Northern Territory's Police Commissioner, of about 150 people in an Aboriginal town camp at Alice Springs, Australia in March 2024.[2]

In terms of highly-mechanised warfare, it might seem that the infantry has been relegated to support and backup roles due to changes in technology and operational methods. This was certainly the implication of the so-called 'Revolution in Military Affairs' (RMA), followed by its successor, 'Transformation,' which dominated American attention at the beginning of the millennium.

Breaking out in 2022, the Russo-Ukrainian war led to a further foregrounding of the role of technology, notably air power, with the emphasis in particular on drones. Alongside long-range drones able to hit targets 600 miles away, has come the frequent use of shorter range drones on the nearby battlefield, as with the fighting over the town of Avdiivka in November 2022-February 2023, fighting which saw drones allegedly responsible by the end of that struggle for about a third of the casualties compared to a far lower rate when it started.

Moreover, discussion of the future of war and concerning specific possible conflicts such as China-Taiwan, focus on the missile and air dimensions. From these perspectives, infantry appeared slow, inflexible, of limited kinetic capability, and a force that would not sway the battle. This appeared to exemplify the comments made by General William E. DePuy, who had been a junior officer in the American 90th Infantry Division in Normandy in 1944 and went on in 1973–7 to be first Commander of the United States Army Training and Doctrine Command:

> '…I honestly concluded at the end of World War II, when I soberly considered what I had accomplished, that I had moved the forward observers of the artillery across France and Germany. In other words, my battalion was the means by which Field Artillery forward observers were moved to the next piece of high ground. Once you had a forward observer on a piece of ground, he could call up five to ten battalions of artillery and that meant you had moved combat power to the next observation point – more combat power than the light infantry could dispose of. Now, you needed infantry to do that. You needed the infantry to protect them, but the combat power came from this other source, and I think that trend has accelerated ever since. I think the infantry has the dirtiest job of them all. But, if you want to be rigorously analytical about what you're really trying to do, it's trying to move combat power forward to destroy the enemy, and the combat power that you are moving forward has been, in the past, mostly artillery, and that is even more true today.'[3]

Yet the Russo-Ukrainian war also saw a return to lengthy operations, largely static fronts, intense artillery fire fights and bombardments, and high casualties. There was talk of a glaciation of conflict and, in particular, focus on a return to trench conflict and to massed attacks, notably by the Ukrainians in 2023 and the Russians in 2024. Thus, the Ukrainian lines east of Kupiansk saw trenches protected by barbed wire, minefields, and anti-tank obstacles, with soldiers in underground bunkers. This situation led to scepticism about the idea of a 'Revolution in Military Affairs,'[4] scepticism matching earlier and current caution about the concept and its application, both in recent years and more generally.

At the same time, whether revolution or not, there is change, not least the increased surveillance by opponents and longer-range munitions. As a result, infantry is likely to face higher casualties, not only in battle, but also before encountering the enemy.[5] Battle will be imposed on infantry rather than vice versa. All of these elements encouraged discussion of the need for larger armies and even the return of an element of conscription. The latter was a marked reversal of the move against conscription in the late twentieth century, a move in part linked to the decline of a reliance on infantry. Now, conscription is seen as the way to deliver far more infantry, although the nature of much of the population scarcely matches the physical fitness and endurance that are seen as necessary for combat and became important in training in the twentieth century.[6]

To make up numbers, there was a reliance on reservists, the American military in Iraq and Afghanistan being composed in part by National Guard and Reservists. This raised questions about the understanding of soldiering by both public and troops, and, by extension, given the bulk of the task, the nature of infantry. So also for other militaries faced by this shift. Separately, unless direct governmental control is maintained, such a shift can be an aspect of a privatisation, as with the employment of military contractors, or at least delegation of tasks, as with the Chinese shift to militia for internal control, notably in the late eighteenth century,[7] and the equivalent for other states.

Across the world, the varied combat-zones on land is such that infantry, as the means to control territory, is still crucial. This is also true on the battlefield. In 1939, Sir John Dill, commander of the British I Corps in France, complained about the 'incalculable' harm done by Basil Liddell Hart, the tank advocate, writing:

> 'Thanks largely to Liddell-Hart's advice battalions were cut down. The argument was that it is fire power, not man power that is wanted on the battlefield. That may be true up to a point but at night, in fog, and when the enemy uses smoke one must have men on the ground.'[8]

Moreover, but separately, on a longstanding pattern, there is much about conflict that scarcely conforms to the idea of a regular or conventional combat that can be readily mastered in terms of a turn to new technological or organisational systems. Both terrain and opponent were key elements. In 1738, Edward Trelawny, Governor of the British colony of Jamaica, reported on operations against the Maroons, runaway, or, in some cases, freed, slaves, who controlled much of the interior of the island:

> 'The service here is not like that in Flanders [Belgium] or any part of Europe. Here the great difficulty is not to beat, but to see the enemy ... in short, nothing can be done in strict conformity to usual military preparations, and according to a regular manner; bushfighting as they call it being a thing particular by itself.'[9]

In 1924, Field Marshal Frederick, 10th Earl of Cavan, the Chief of the British Imperial General Staff, observed: 'So much of our work has to be done in uncivilized parts of the world that it is a mistake to pin faith to a type of unit largely dependent on civilized conditions, good roads and open country.'[10]

The varied environmental situation, with its multiple requirements for infantry, has been taken further in recent years by the emphasis on urban terrain as the battleground of greater relative significance.[11] This was scarcely new, and the Second World War saw lengthy struggles in Shanghai (1937), Stalingrad (1942–3), Warsaw (1944), and Manila (1945), as well as cities that, in contrast, fell with relatively little conflict within them, such as Brussels and Paris (for both, 1940 and 1944). The period since 1990 has seen intensive urban conflict of very different forms, notably in Mogadishu, Grozny, Mosul, Mariupol and Gaza. In each, there was a reliance on other forms of warfare including artillery, armour and air power, the last extending to helicopters as in Mogadishu. Yet, infantry was the key element in controlling and contesting urban terrain. This has increased the human cost of operating there, and also made it easier for non-regulars to impose heavy demands on regular forces driving them out, as with the ISIS resistance to American-backed Iraqi regulars in Mosul, and Hamas resisting the Israelis in Gaza in 2023–5, a conflict that extended to extensive underground operations. Hamas took heavier losses than the Israelis, but the casualties suffered by the latter proved a major blow. Moreover, whereas the tradition and doctrine of the Israeli army was predicated on rapid manoeuvrist warfare, the urban terrain of the Gaza Strip meant delay, a delay that led to a loss of Israeli momentum and initiative that proved to have serious political consequences.

The range of environments posed issues for infantry, from training to experience, logistics to morale. At the same time, technological contexts were changing rapidly and were so varied that the appropriate term is contexts not context. In large part, there were advantages for well-prepared forces. Thus, new information platforms ensured that messages about needs could be transformed more rapidly than hitherto. Logistics were eased by the use of lightweight substances, for both content and packaging. Thus, in Afghanistan in the 2000s, CamelBak, an American company that, among other products, makes military-grade equipment, came up with a 'Lumber Reservoir Carry Pack,' with a feeder tube that could be sucked on while walking, and a cloth outer covering to prevent excessive sweating by the wearer.

Irrespective of the environment, it is unclear how infantry will be redefined in a future in which large numbers of individually-controlled drones are being manufactured. So also with the extent to which the overlap between regulars and irregulars may extend in the future in some contexts to encompass even more of the latter. How far they are assessed as infantry may change if personal mobility alters, for example with electric bicycles, but most will still fight on foot. In this respect and others, the definition of infantry remains loose, if not uncertain, not least how troops moved into combat. The emphasis on mobility seen with the concept of the strike brigade has been linked to infantry being made more mobile, with vehicles protected notably against ambushes and mines, as in the American Stryker, the Russian R-15 IFV series, and the French VBCI. Separately, there is also an enhancement but also continuation of infantry weapons systems, notably with the plentiful use of rocket-propelled grenades.

There will then in the future be the extension provided by the use of implanted characteristics, genetic engineering, and even robots, which, again, are likely to be primarily infantry. This may not, however, seem a helpful topic as a last stage of a discussion of infantry that has repeatedly warned about the need to handle ideas of modernisation with care. Furthermore, the cost of developing and operating such infantry may well be very high, and, as with other weapons systems, there will be anti-systems, including electronic interference, which is already a factor for drones. In general, the least expensive method that is fit-for-purpose is the one that will gain and retain traction, and, in a world with over eight billion people, that is likely to be a continuation of the present means of raising infantry.

Looked at differently, drones and robots represent a possible fusion, one that can be discussed as one of the developments in the wider envelopment of Artificial Intelligence (AI). Rather than the latter bypassing infantry in concept or practice, it may be that it offers enhancements both to the existing type of soldiers who can be provided with far more up-to-date information, and to the future soldiery that may develop. At the same time, guided-firing systems of greater sophistication make infantry more vulnerable. Yet this is a situation shared with all other branches of the military, while these guided-firing systems are both expensive to use, maintain and supply, and subject to interference.

Thus, far from being a second-rank, second-rate, and, indeed, anachronistic form of the military, the infantry continues to offer considerable flexibility, albeit within a situation of great hazard. The potential, furthermore, remains great: the global population rose from three billion in 1960 to eight billion in 2023, and may reach ten billion by mid-century, and that provides plenty of manpower, regular or irregular, for the organised use of force by means of fighting as infantry. Moreover, to seize and occupy territory held by opposing infantry, however defined, it is infantry that is the best means, even if other arms provide ways to kill. In essence, the range of infantry is a key element, and also the very different tactics and weaponry that can be used. It is also important to focus on the cost as infantry can be the cheapest means available, which is important as most conflicts are fought by poor states and communities lacking sophisticated arms. Conversely, many states already suffer from a declining population, notably in the younger cohorts, and this may affect support for conscription or, indeed, a reliance on large infantry forces. The issue helped explain the Ukrainian reluctance in 2022–4 to conscript men under 27.

As a prescient prefigurement of the current situation with taskings and the asymmetrical nature of goals which can greatly complicate infantry combat, the General Staff of the British War Office pressed the government in 1920 not to send troops in order to ensure Armenian independence from the Turks. Aside from outlining specific difficulties facing such a mission, the General Staff warned that:

> 'the resulting operations would partake of the nature of guerrilla warfare, which is a method of fighting above all things to be avoided. The whole spirit of the art of conducting small wars is to strive for the attainment of decisive methods, the very essence of partisan warfare from the point of view of the enemy being to avoid definite engagements. Consequently, it usually happens that many more men are required than were originally estimated, and that warfare of this nature continues for years.'[12]

In the event, no troops were sent, and, indeed, the British in 1923 withdrew their forces from Constantinople (Istanbul) in the face of a resurgent Turkey.

Moreover, public history offers a focus on groups not classically included within the scope of infantry. Thus, in Colombia, in the village of San Basilio de Palenque, is a modern statue to Benkos Biohó, an African born in the Bissagos Islands of modern Guinea-Bissau, who was enslaved, escaping in 1599 from Cartagena into the nearby marshes and coming with other Maroons, or escaped slaves to dominate the nearby Montes de María. The Spaniards failed to defeat them, and, although Biohó was seized in 1619 when a peace was treacherously broken, the Maroons continued their defiance. So also in Brazil, Cuba, Jamaica, Saint-Domingue, Surinam, and other slave societies, while in the 1790s and 1800s there were widespread slave risings. This was an aspect of the reliance on slave soldiers, an aspect that is now more widely noted, and that could potentially overlap with other aspects of imperial soldiery.[13]

The point about the potential for guerrilla warfare extends to the role of infantry in a policing that can be violent. Large-scale criminality excited public concern and governmental attention in a number of countries in the 2010s, focusing in particular on cities such as Brussels, Kingston (Jamaica), Marseille, Naples and Palermo, with infantry acting as a support, and therefore substitute, for the police. This feature remains the case in the 2020s, with National Guard troops deployed on the New York subway in March 2024 in response to a series of murders; and is likely to become more widespread, not least in response to economic circumstances. So also for protection against terrorism, as in France in 2015, again a situation that has continued and is likely to become more intense.

Infantry, separately, dominates the non-conflict use of the military. In Britain, for example, infantry was deployed in the 2000s to replace striking firefighters and to help deal with 'mad cow' disease, and in 2012 provided security for the Olympic Games in London. This is a reminder of the role of infantry as the arm of the state, and also of the range of security challenges to the modern state.

In light of the last, the treatment of infantry as a force for international war is of only limited use. That point was taken further in 2023 when lawlessness threatened to overtake Ecuador and, even more, in 2024 Haiti, where 'pretty much every neighbourhood was putting up makeshift barricades and manning them with armed men.'[14] Soldiers and footsoldiers are terms used to describe gang-members, as in Marbella in Spain. Indeed, the relationship between civil and international tasks has become more clearly germane as states have buckled under the pressure of population growth, economic difficulties, public concerns, and criminality. The modern technology on display in the Russo-Ukraine war that began in 2022 appeared less relevant from this perspective.

The extent to which this situation will pertain in the future is unclear. It is certainly not addressed by endless references to drones and other aspects of new military technology. Indeed, the continuities also present in the Russo-Ukrainian War were part of a pattern, as with the rapid move of the Iran-Iraq war of 1980–8 from mobility to trench warfare. The draft report of 30 Corps, part of the British Eighth Army, drawn up in November 1942 after its victory in Egypt at El Alamein over a German-Italian force, noted:

> 'The operations proved the general soundness of our principles of training for war, some of which had been neglected during previous fighting in the desert. In all forms of warfare, new methods should never disregard basic principles. The operations involved a reversion, with the difference due to the developments in weapons, to the static warfare of the war of 1914–18. This reversion should not be regarded as an isolated exception unlikely to recur.... Our organisations and

weapons must remain suitable both for mobile and periodical static operations.'[15]

The comments from the Russo-Ukrainian war captured aspects of the experience, but were also snapshots of a grinding reality. Thus, one article on the Ukrainian effort in early 2024 reported:

> 'Lemur, an infantryman…. "F... awful. We can barely hold the line, let alone move forward We are losing so many people, there are so many bodies we can't even bring them all back."'
>
> 'Russia still fielding prisoners as their first line of frontline fighters, taking vast casualties. Ilya, an infantry commander: "That is not how we fight. My job is to bring back my soldiers alive, not in pieces and not in coffins."'
>
> 'Kostiantyn… battalion commander… "we cannot win this war with drones alone… It is so much harder to take back a town. There are buildings, there are basements to fight from. And attack is much much harder than defence."'[16]

The last point reflected a continuity in infantry warfare that is affected by changes in weaponry but not trumped by them. In practical terms, offsetting the force-equals-mass-times-acceleration equation of a physical shock, defence became inherently stronger once firepower was an option because it is harder to move and fire (not least if aiming) than it is to rest on the defensive and fire, not least if the defence benefits from the supporting effects of positioning and protective entrenchments.

Accounts of the present lead at once to speculation about the future, which is seen as a way to gaining advantage in the becoming present. In particular, the role of infantry as opposed to drones has become a duality in discussion. In practice, the first has a strategic capacity that the latter lacks: infantry is far more than a tool. It is not just a presence, highly significant as that is, but an identity, one important to nations, for they set the parameters of the service. At the same time, while many states, notably if under threat, continued to have a close identification with the military, there was a concern in many, especially America but also for example Britain and Japan, that military life was increasingly divorced from society,[17] and particularly so for infantry who lacked the glamour of special forces, armour, and airpower.

The unwillingness, in America and other societies, to accept conscription or even be at ease with discussion about it (whatever the criteria for this conscription), was, and remains, a reflection of the redefinitions of civil culture and collective obligation that occurred and were sustained during and after the Cold War. In large part, this situation encouraged belief, instead, in a focus on advanced technology and specialist forces, which was an aspect of the degree to which infantry is defined by politics. The reluctance to tolerate conscription also encouraged, if not ensured, either a desire on the part of governments to avoid conflict, as in modern Germany, or led to an embrace of the military option without a due acceptance of the constraints posed by troop numbers and much else, as for America in Iraq in 2003.[18] In part, the latter is an aspect of the operationalisation of strategy that can be so significant in modern planning. There is also, as an instance of the primacy of politics, the decision that only one war can be fought at a given time, which is a major constraint as far as American commitments are involved.

The role of nations in the recruitment, direction, support and legitimation of infantry service looks to the relationships between public and private providers of infantry. The private provision of protection and violence may be by delegation from the state, but also despite or, indeed, in defiance of it. All are revivals of earlier practices and thus reminders of the degree to which a developmental model of the history of infantry, focused on state provision, is flawed. The significance of America as a military model, not least the drive for interoperability with allies, is such that the American employment of private military contractors is of particular importance. In part, this use is a response to price structures and to the more general nature of privatisation as both organisational method and goal, but, more generally, the use also reflects particular political contexts, notably the authority and strength of the state, and the power and role of the police.[19] Contractors were focused on support functions, with the regular military retaining control of higher-end capabilities, both due to their lethality and as a result of their maintenance requirements. The role of contractors meant that military conduct became even more varied than it might otherwise have been, and also affected accountability and effectiveness. There was a reversal of the standard state-army equation.

So also with the composition of regular forces themselves. Thus, the idea of infantry as a modern development looking toward the Anglo-American practice in the Second World War of conscription-provided, fire-power strong, and heavy logistical backing,[20] appears problematic as a result of a subsequent preference on the part of both powers for smaller and lighter forces combined with more precise air support. How far the current conflicts may encourage, instead, an emphasis on greater numbers of infantry, and indeed the the Second World War practice, is unclear, although probable in Russia; but the definitions and practices of infantry conduct and context are scarcely fixed. Nor is it clear what will be the model that is most influential in the assessment of current infantry and the probable development of future infantry. The perception of success, indeed fame was, is, and will, be a key element in the willingness to look to foreign models, ready digestibility being a crucial element of reputation.[21]

The availability of state of the art weaponry and other assistance, notably training, is also very important in disseminating models for military behaviour. At the same time, the applicability of the examples from other powers (and other periods) involves controversy and subjective evaluations, as well as the discussions and major differences bound up in task-based assessments of current and future needs. These cannot be divorced from the realm of military politics within and between countries. For the post-Cold War period, America was the dominant model for other militaries; but this is likely to be less the case in the future. In part this reflects the compromising across parts of the world of America's political reputation as well as its relative decline, but the latter is made more relevant by the likely rise of other models, notably that of China which is seeking to be a significant influence, especially in Africa. The future relationship between states as models for emulation, however, is far from fixed.

As with the Cold War, America's opponents will provide examples in doctrine and weaponry that reflect not just rivalry but also an apparently more relevant set of taskings, for example as far as the violent subjugation of domestic dissent is concerned. The relevance of this for infantry is readily apparent, as it is that dimension of activity that commands most attention in certain parts of the world, for example the *sahel* states of sub-Saharan Africa.

It might appear strange to end a chapter on the future of infantry by referring to states such as Niger, Mali, Burkina Faso, and the Central African Republic, states whose armies currently look to Russia, but may increasingly turn to China. Yet it is in these states, as well as more prominent neighbours and near-neighbours such as Nigeria and Sudan, that militaries centred on infantry and conflict involving them is to the fore. In many states, domestic control is the prime purpose of the military and therefore of the infantry. The latter can be motorised and, as in Syria in the 2010s, joined by armour, air, and all branches of the military; but infantry is to the fore, not least in the militias that are so significant, as in Syria and Congo, leading, in 2024, to the overthrow of the Syrian government. America has relatively little to offer in this role, and, indeed, its military is focused on state-to-state conflict. The mistake would be to assume that that defines the subject.

Chapter 10

Conclusions

'I sent for all officers, W.O.s [warrant officers] c.s.m.s [company sergeant majors] and sergeants to our apology of a mess and explained the dire necessity of stopping the Germans and told them that it must be "so far and no further" and then asked everyone present to take a solemn oath that whenever I gave the order to stand, they would stand, and then to sign their names … we kept our word and never gave way.… There must have been few who really expected to survive and stop the German advance which had made steady progress for eight days as reports of the incoming tide were ominous.'
Lieutenant Colonel Percy Worrall, Western Front, April 1918.[1]

'As an average infantryman, one of the first questions that you ask is "Which way is the front?" So that you know if the worst comes to the worst which way you can go to get out of the bloody place. In this sort of situation, which is a typical urban "battlefront," it's all around you.'

British soldier recalling Athens in December 1944,
when British troops were sent, with success,
to help contain the Greek Communist movement.[2]

If Ukraine, Gaza, Ethiopia, the *Sahel*, Congo, Myanmar and Haiti in recent years prove anything, it is that conventional war will only disappear when mankind does. Moreover, infantry remains the backbone of conventional war, which is why combat effectiveness and infantry leadership remain crucial. These reflect specific factors but also raise questions about the combination of nature and nurture. Social developments and sociocultural understandings of mankind shape the perception of war and of how best to fight. Thus, Herodotus referred to Cyrus's warning in his discussion of the Persians, that 'soft lands breed soft men,' 'civilization' weakening combat effectiveness by sapping endurance and challenging determination. The old Turkish word for man and warrior was the same, and the peoples of the Eurasian steppe were so effective, in both combat and in terms of leadership, because they understood that life was war. In the West, there was this understanding during Antiquity, with work attributed to Hesiod, a Greek poet of *c.*750-*c.*650 BCE, noting the triumph of violence and the degree to which life was a struggle, in the medieval era and into the early twentieth century.[3] Resolve is a key element. This understanding has since been largely lost, affecting both combat effectiveness and leadership. This led to concern about Western resilience at the time of the Russo-Ukrainian war as expressed for example in an interview Emmanuel Macron gave the *Economist* on 2 May 2024.

This was a general cultural point, one of considerable validity and better addressed in Eastern Europe, under the shadow of Russian aggressiveness, than in Western Europe. The general cultural point echoed earlier concern in and after 1940 about what had led to the collapse of Western Europe in the face of German power. These cultural points play a major role in issues of combat effectiveness. It may appear inappropriate to adopt a perspective that can be criticised as declinism, but issues of morale and determination are crucial to combat effectiveness, and thereby permit leadership.

Infantry combat provides the best basis for considering this issue across time. As a subject. it might not have the appeal of cavalry, armour or air power, but infantry is more fundamental as a longstanding means of military power, one that is pertinent, indeed effective, in a range of contexts. Infantry is also important as the central subject for the raising of forces, and for most of the world across most of history. Often crucial in combat, infantry has also served many non-combat roles, notably as the arm of government. As a result, the achievements of infantry can be central to political history and nation-building,[4] not least with infantry playing the key role in many of the battles that were important to identity, and thereby cultural integrity, past and/or present, such as Thermopylae (480 BCE) for Greece, Gallipoli (1915) for Australia and New Zealand, Verdun (1916) for France, and Vimy (1917) for Canada.[5] So also for many battles that have a mythic character such as those around the siege of Troy. Most of those buried in military cemeteries were infantry, and this continues to be the case.

This topic has no single chronology and it is necessary to be cautious about adopting or proposing any relationship between (the movable criteria of) governmental sophistication and raising infantry. Yet such ideas are longstanding, and infantry has been crucial to them. In 1776, the Scottish economist Adam Smith offered, in his *Inquiry into the Nature and Causes of the Wealth of Nations* (which was to prove the foundational work for modern economics), an analysis of the sociology of warfare in which he adopted the standard Western stadial (stages) approach, and contrasted nations of hunters and shepherds with the 'more advanced state of society', in which industry was important. He provided an alternative to the suggestion made by Herodotus.

These advanced societies were seen by Smith as providing a hierarchy of military organisation and sophistication in which 'a well-regulated standing army' was vital to the defence of civilisation. Firearms, Smith claimed, were crucial in the onset of military modernity and as a measure of military capability:

> 'Before the invention of fire-arms, that army was superior in which the soldiers had, each individually, the greatest skill in dexterity in the use of their arms … since the invention … strength and agility of body, or even extraordinary dexterity and skill in the use of arms, though they are far from being of no consequence, are, however, of less consequence… In modern war the great expense of fire-arms gives an evident advantage to the nation which can best afford that expense; and consequently, to an opulent and civilised, over a poor and barbarous nation. In ancient times the opulent and civilised found it difficult to defend themselves against the poor and barbarous nations. In modern times the poor and barbarous find it difficult to defend themselves against the opulent and civilised.'[6]

Although exaggerating the military advantages of the 'opulent and civilised', Smith, like his British contemporaries the famous historians Edward Gibbon and William Robertson, had captured an important development. He also drew attention to the question of why there were different 'types' of society and military systems, and what the consequences were.

Systems of conscription required not just what can be termed consent or collective willpower, but also administrative capability, and at the local level across states. So also with supplying and paying such forces, however much the burden might be pushed out onto the population in the campaign zone, not least when campaigning in foreign territory. Yet, if infantry can require the state, or at least an element of government, so, even more, do fortifications, navies, air forces, and mechanised units.

Indeed, infantry is the most varied outcome, as it can be produced by sophisticated states but also by governments of limited resource and dependence on non-governmental actors,[7] indeed by non-state actors and those actively seeking to resist the state. This is true across history, and there is no reason to assume that the situation will be different in the future.

The range of contexts and taskings for infantry make comparisons difficult. For example, an instructive comparison of the motivation of American soldiers in the 1860s and 1940s, one that could be readily repeated for other countries, has drawn attention to major changes in American society, not least of which was a decline in 'dense organic relationships,' with the argument that its presence in the 1860s ensured that soldiers were able to perform courageously, despite little training, because of their identities as autonomous free men and, in many cases, proprietors of society in the sense of landowners, while, in the 1940s, the weakness of such male identities ensured a need for basic training and the emotional bonding of unit cohesion if troops were to perform.[8] There was also considerable debate about the extent to which many American conscripts in subsequent conflicts did not shoot when instructed to do so.

However, indicating the difficulties with such an assessment of infantry, there are problems with all comparisons, not least, in this case, differences between fighting at home, as in the American Civil War, and abroad, as well as the extent to which the infantry got the worse of the pick of American conscripts in the Second World War because of a policy of directing better-grade recruits to the air force and navy. The relationship between volunteering and conscription was also different in the two conflicts.

Nevertheless, the suggestion that the social changes linked to modernisation made it more difficult to inculcate morale and battle motivation, raises instructive questions about the context for twentieth-century infantry, with 'industrial war,' in this approach a reflection of need as well as opportunity. DePuy was part of a trend in analysis suggesting that many soldiers did not fight with enthusiasm or well. The issue of morale could in part be addressed by enhancing firepower and using technology.

Morale in the context of modern society also raises questions about the direction of influence in creating and sustaining morale and of the content of what is meant by morale, which focus issues about the convergence of motivation, ideology and conditions. Winning and displaying success was an important part of the morale equation. Thus, being on the defensive could create serious problems for militaries hitherto on the offensive and/or parts of expansionist peoples/states; problems structurally and in terms of ethos, and also in specific tactical and operational matters.

Repeatedly, possibilities and expectations for infantry were set by politics, understood in the broadest sense, a situation that will continue. In America, a concept of the citizen-soldier that had rested in militia origins, and led to contractual attitudes encouraging sometimes a lack of discipline and even disobedience,[9] was transformed into a more orderly practice focused, first, on volunteering into the more defined army that followed the Civil War, subsequently into conscription, and then into a voluntary and impressive professionalism.

The changing nature of taskings redefines what the infantry means in practice. Thus, in the 1950s, the American infantry found a new role manning vulnerable front lines in Europe and Korea.[10] This role was very different to the far less vulnerable position for America after the First World War, let alone the hemispheric army of the 1930s. However, the cultural ability to sustain this role appeared compromised from the late 1960s by a societal reaction focused on antipathy to the Vietnam War. At the same time, it is unclear that this was a matter of institutional combat effectiveness as opposed to a failure of political support for a particular conflict.

The political perspective is relevant for many aspects of the history and present of infantry. Thus, the organisational nature of the infantry had a politics of its own. A British observer at the German manoeuvres in September 1897 was impressed by the methodical character of the military means, with infantry systematised in a fashion that captured the nature of a desired military society:

> '.... The complete system of organisation which exists throughout the German army.... Drenched to the skin with rain, deep in mud as were the infantry, no sign of discomfort was noticed, nor word of grumbling heard. All ranks seemed to take the heavy rain and hard work as a matter of course, and as a natural consequence of the day's proceedings ... on many occasions it was observed that companies were kept in columns at effective artillery and even at decisive infantry ranges. The idea is consistently observed that everything should be sacrificed, even human life, to a steady cohesive discipline upon the field of battle.... Each man seemed to know his place and what was expected of him ... almost machine-like discipline.... No effort is spared by means of mechanical drill and precision to prevent confusion, to minimise skulking, and to make the timid firm in the critical moments of an assault ... there was something peculiarly impressive in the slow, methodical, onward movement of a mass of men thus formed, resistless as a rising tide.'

Yet the observer continued by drawing attention to the problems this approach was to pose in the forthcoming world war:

> 'It was, doubtless, very effective in appearance, and against irresolute, half-trained troops should prove very demoralising, but against steady infantry in line, it seemed a question if such a series of spasmodic efforts in attack could possibly succeed.'[11]

Similarly, Captain Holland, a British observer at the German manoeuvres of 1898, commented on 'a system by which losses of smaller units are ignored, provided the main object is gained, the great aim being to train the soldier to carry out his orders regardless of consequences.'[12]

From Gallipoli in 1915, John Monash, an Australian brigade commander, provided an account of a different infantry in a difficult campaign, an account that presented the nature of organisation through specialisation that was important to the character of regular armies:

> 'We have got our battle procedure now thoroughly well organised. To a stranger it would probably look like a disturbed ant heap with everybody running a different way but the thing is really a triumph

> of organisation. There are orderlies carrying messages, staff officers with orders, lines of ammunition carriers, water carriers, bomb carriers, stretcher bearers, burial parties, sandbag parties, periscope hands, pioneers, quartermaster's parties, and reinforcing troops, running about all over the place, apparently in confusion but yet everything works as smoothly as on a peace parade, although the air is thick with clamour and bullets and bursting shells, and bombs and flares.'[13]

Infantry also captures in its history the role of many other histories and, indeed, historiographies. Thus, condescension by Western commentators could be highly misleading, as remains the case. Foreign observers often prepared to focus on the allegedly inherent national characteristics of combatants, which led to an unwillingness to draw lessons, for example from Turkish losses at the Shipka Pass in 1877.[14] Criticism of the Ottomans was longstanding, as in 1806, when Colonel John Hely-Hutchinson claimed that Turkish forces were 'not capable of resisting any European troops' and their infantry an 'armed mob' who were 'worth nothing' if lacking cover; and, in 1854, when Sir James Graham, the First Lord of the Admiralty, opposing a campaign in Bulgaria, wrote of Britain's allies: 'the Turks, who except in position and behind entrenchments will be found no true support.'[15]

The Gallipoli operation in 1915 was affected by the Allies' flawed assessment of Turkish fighting quality and skill. The *Notes on the Turkish Army* published by the British army that March were misleading:

> 'The Turkish army, which suffered to a very great extent both in men and material during the last Balkans wars [1912–13], have since then been reorganised, and …undergone a severe course of training under the supervision of German officers…. Although a great improvement has taken place during the last two years, it cannot truthfully be said that Turkish troops are even now in any way equal, except in courage, to those of the Balkan states with whom they were lately at war.'

This misunderstanding of Turkish troops helped lead to disastrous tactical errors in a greatly flawed and totally unsuccessful campaign.[16]

The Allied forces reached Gallipoli by sea, a longstanding practice greatly eased by steamships, while the mobility of infantry on land also was potentially affected by the application of steam, albeit not in this case. In turn, the movement to the battlefield offered by rail was replaced by the movement on the battlefield of the last century as motorisation became more prominent as a theme. Thus, the Internal Security Instructions for India issued by the (British) General Staff Branch in 1937 emphasised the combination of firepower and mobility, and, linked to that, the degree to which it was possible for infantry to take a more offensive stance:

> 'Automatic weapons have rendered easier the defence of keeps, posts, important buildings and bridges etc, from attacks by insurgents. The number of troops employed on defensive duties can be reduced accordingly. The measures taken by troops should be active rather than passive. Patrols and mobile columns are more efficacious than fixed piquets and defensive measures for quelling disturbances.... The number of troops employed on purely defensive measures should be reduced to a minimum, and strong mobile reserves should be formed. The fullest possible use should be made of the mobility conferred by motor and air transport to reduce the number and size of detachments.'[17]

The disruptive as well as enhancing consequences of change in other spheres for the operation and effectiveness of infantry can be assessed alongside the extent to which infantry was a potential consequence of transformation in other spheres or a means for it.

Yet change is not the sole theme. Thus, in its domestic consequences, infantry and the military more generally could be a major means of enforcing reaction; or rather order. Separately, the presence and development of infantry could be 'contained' so that it does not need to lead to governmental or political transformation. For example, in Eastern Europe, it was not firearms but rather:

> 'professional armies and the rise of infantry that were the striking military innovations but they did not overturn society and political regimes. Society was able to restrain their impact inside the loose pockets of the existing social structure. The political regimes

> adapted to the military innovations employing the corporatisation of sovereignty, oligarchic government and military dictatorship.'[18]

This might appear counter-intuitive, not least due to the significance of concepts and practices of recruitment. However, the social politics of recruitment, which focused on infantry, acted to restrict disruption. For example, a challenge to the political order could be latent in mass conscript arms, the nation in arms. Thus, although conscription was reintroduced in France in 1818 by Gouvion St Cyr, the Minister of War, who had been a Napoleonic Marshal, only 40,000 out of the 290,000 eligible men were selected annually (by lot), and it was possible to arrange a substitute by means of payment. The conscripts, who were therefore mostly lower class, served six years in a regular unit, which in practice was reduced to four years.

The general European choice in the late 1810s for smaller armies and, therefore, not a mass infantry, represented the primacy of political and organisational factors in military culture and force structure, not least the avoidance of problems. The emphasis was on training through drill, notably to inculcate and affirm the downward-facing values of the military. Irrespective of technology, this emphasis was also linked to the conviction that trained and experienced troops would be more effective than committed amateurs, both tactically and in other respects.

The volunteer path also faced serious problems, notably in producing sufficient numbers, as it does still today, for example in Britain and America. The infantry was the major issue, and remains so, because it requires the largest numbers and is generally regarded as the least attractive branch of the service. To take America in the early nineteenth century, desertion was especially serious in the 1820s and early 1850s, peacetime periods of economic boom when there were many other opportunities for employment; but it was also a problem at other times. In December 1830, the British envoy drew on the report of the American Secretary of War when he noted that one sixth of the American army had deserted the previous year, a rate that challenged continuity and undermined training.[19] Desertion, in turn, led to distrust of American soldiers by their officers in this period. Combined with poor pay, unacceptable food and accommodation, and boredom, especially in the isolation of frontier postings, this distrust ensured that military service remained unattractive,[20] and thus was an expedient resorted to not only by recent immigrants, but also by those who were distrusted in their communities, possibly as a consequence of criminal activities. Driven by desperation, they were more prepared to make the difficult adjustment to military life.

The avoidance of any sense of an automatic linkage between developments in infantry, or the armed forces more generally, and those in politics and government, is significant because there is all-too-often such a reading: whether from the military to the other sphere, or vice versa. The lack of any such necessity of specific consequence contributes to the great fascination of infantry and to the importance of its history.

At the same time, to return to the point made in the Preface, we are dealing with individuals, and the fortitude expected of them and enforced by fate. The British battle with American Patriots at Princeton in 1776, Captain William Leslie noted as he advanced:

> 'all the bushes, hedges, trees and hollows were lined with riflers … from which they fired at our regiment at a few yards distance…. A few minutes after I joined the advanced guard I was told Sir Alexander Murray was killed and Lieutenant Morgan wounded, my two most intimate friends.'[21]

Murray, a Captain in the 17th Regiment, died aged 21, the last baronet in the family. Leslie was shot dead within four months.

The practice of allocating 'low-quality' men to the infantry was established in a number of militaries in the Second World War and helped reflect and condition attitudes toward them within the military.[22] Given conscription, this also affected wider social attitudes. In reality, both the Second World War and subsequent conflicts, showed that infantry were repeatedly called upon to show quality and frequently displayed the necessary combat effectiveness.

At the end of the European war in 1945, Field Marshal Archibald, 1st Earl Wavell (who had served in the Second Boer War, on the North West Frontier, and in World Wars One and Two), offered a view to the public that still resonates:

> '…the Infantry arm … does not receive either the respect or the treatment to which its importance and its exploits entitle it…. Let

us be clear about three facts. First, all battles and all wars are won in the end by the infantryman. Secondly, the infantryman always bears the brunt. His casualties are heavier, he suffers greater extremes of discomfort and fatigue than the other arms. Thirdly, the art of the infantry is less stereotyped and far harder to acquire in modern war than that of any other arm.... The infantryman has to use initiative and intelligence in almost every step he moves, every action he takes on the battle-field.

'Yet the Infantry in peace or war receives the lowest rates of pay, the drabbest uniforms, sometimes even the least promising of recruits; most important of all, it ranks lowest in the public estimation and prestige. This is all wrong ... the inevitable, enduring, despised, long-suffering Infantry ... bears the danger, the dirt, and the discomfort.'[23]

Notes

Preface

1. T. Ballard, 'Army After-Action Reports, circa 1860s,' *Army History*, 30 (1994), p. 37.
2. F. Krome and G. Loving (eds), Hans Schiller, *Memories of War* (Lawrence KS, 2024).
3. Italy-Abyssinian War Diary, Fuller Papers, New Brunswick, New Jersey, Rutgers University Library, Box 4, pp. 16–17.
4. Thomas Orby Hunter to Henry Pelham, 22 Aug. 1747, New Haven, Beinecke Library, Osborn Shelves, Pelham Box.
5. W.C. Horsley (trans), *The Chronicles of an Old Campaigner* (London, 1904), pp. 184–5.
6. Ligonier to Charles, 2nd Duke of Grafton, 30 Ap. 1743, Bury St Edmunds, West Suffolk CRO., Grafton Corresp., No. 900; Z. P. Bagi, 'The Life of Soldiers during the Long Turkish War', *Hungarian Historical Review*, 4 (2015) pp.384–417.
7. J. Black, *War for America* (Stroud, 1991), p. 100.
8. *Aris's Birmingham Gazette*, 24 Aug. 1761.
9. M. Hardy, '"Be Cheerful in Adversity": Views from the Trenches, 1917–1918,' Buckingham Record Office, *Annual Report and List of Accessions* (1995).
10. 'The British Soldier Then and Now. An Interview with Richard Holmes,' in D.A. Yerxa (ed.), *Recent Themes in Military History* (Charleston, SC., 2008), pp. 86–7. See, more generally, Holmes, *Tommy: The British Soldier on the Western Front, 1914–1918* (London, 2004).
11. See, for example, C. Reardon, *Pickett's Charge in History and Memory* (Chapel Hill, NC, 1997), esp. pp. 2–4; R. Muir, *Salamanca, 1812* (New Haven, Conn., 2001).
12. Birdwood to C. in C. India, 3 Dec. 1915, AWM, 3 DRL/3376, 11/4. The New Army referred to newly-recruited British units.
13. W. Weston to Hugh, 4th Earl Fortescue, 24 July 1915, Exeter, Devon Record Office, 1262/FC 60.
14. A. Ferrill, *The Origins of War: From the Stone Age to Alexander the Great* (London, 1985).

Chapter 1

1. D.E. Graves (ed.), *Merry Hearts Make Light Days: The War of 1812 Journal of Lieutenant John Le Couteur* (Ottawa, 1993), p. 176.
2. Graves, *Red Coats and Grey Jackets: The Battle of Chippawa* (Toronto, 1994).
3. A.R. Millett, *Well Planned and Splendidly Executed: The Battle of Cantigny May 28–31, 1918* (2nd edn, Chicago, Ill., 2013).
4. K. and S. Möbius, *Prussian Army Soldiers and the Seven Years' War: The Psychology of Honour* (London, 2019).
5. B.A. Friedman, *On Tactics: A Theory of Victory in Battle* (Annapolis, MD., 2017).

6. D.R. Haggard, 'The First Invasion of Georgia and the Myth of Westo Power, 1656–1684,' *JMH*, 86 (2022), p. 554.
7. LH. Hamilton 1/3/3, p. 166.
8. E. McGeer, 'Infantry versus Cavalry: The Byzantine Response,' *Revue des Etudes Byzantines*, 46 (1988), pp. 135–45.
9. J. France, 'A Changing Balance: Cavalry and Infantry, 1000–1300,' *Revista de história das ideas*, 30 (2009), pp. 153–77.
10. Pierce's journal, 28 Jan. 1846, BL. IO. MSS. Eur. A 108 f. 14.
11. LH. 4/2/9.
12. LH. Alanbroooke papers, 6/2/37.
13. G. Phillips, *The Anglo-Scots Wars 1513–1550. A Military History* (Woodbridge, 1999).
14. O'Connor to Major-General Sir Percy Hobart, 24 Aug. 1944, LH. O'Connor papers, 5/3/41.
15. S. Hart, *Colossal Cracks: Montgomery's 21st Army Group in Northwest Europe, 1944–45* (Mechanicsburg, Penn., 2007); J. Peaty, *British Army manpower crisis, 1944* (King's College, London, PhD, 2000).
16. J. Buckley, *Monty's Men: The British Army and the Liberation of Europe* (New Haven, Conn., 2013).
17. S. Marble (ed.), *Scraping the Barrel: The Military Use of Substandard Manpower, 1860–1960* (New York, 2012).
18. Brigadier General Thomas Troland, Commander of Army Service Forces, to John Babcock, J.B. Babcock, *Taught to Kill: An American Boy's War from the Ardennes to Berlin* (Washington, 2005), p. 128. See also, J. Reed, 'The Infantry's "Problem of Quality": Classification and Assignment to MOS 745, Rifleman, 1942–1945,' *JMH*, 88 (2024); P. Mansoor, *The GI Offensive in Europe: The Triumph of American Infantry Divisions, 1941–1945* (Lawrence, KS, 1999).
19. O'Connor to Major General Allan Adair, 24 July 1944, LH. O'Connor papers, 5/3/22; J. Peaty, *British Army manpower crisis, 1944* (Kings' College, London, PhD, 2000).
20. E. Zürcher (ed.), *Fighting for a Living: A Comparative History of Military Labour, 1500–2000* (Amsterdam, 2014).
21. D. Chandler, *Atlas of Military Strategy: The Art, Theory and Practice of War, 1618–1878* (London, 1980), pp. 116–17.
22. Graves, *Field of Glory: The Battle of Crysler's Farm, 1813* (Toronto, 1999); R.S. Quimby, *The U.S. Army in the War of 1812: An Operational and Command Study* (East Lansing, Mi., 1997), p. 343.
23. A.D. Gaff, *Bayonets in the Wilderness: Anthony Wayne's Legion in the Old Northwest* (Norman, Ok., 2004).
24. For a useful corrective, M. Arfaioli, 'Bastion of Empire: The Italian *terzo vecchio* of the Army of Flanders (1597–1682),' *JMH*, 85 (2021), pp. 27–50.
25. K. and S. Möbius, 'Fighting in Frederick II's Favourite Musketeer Regiment: A Unique Series of Prussian Soldiers' Letters from the Seven Years War,' in A.S. Burns (ed.), *The Changing Face of Old Regime Warfare* (Warwick, 2022), p. 246.
26. B. and R. Wilkin, *Fighting for Napoleon: French Soldiers' Letters, 1799–1815* (Barnsley, 2015).
27. Fawcett to James Lister, 24 Oct. 1760, Halifax, Calderdale Archives, SH:7/FAW/60.
28. P. Brummett, 'The River Crossing: Breaking Points (Metaphorical and "Real") in Ottoman Mutiny', in J. Hathaway (ed.), *Rebellion, Repression, Reinvention. Mutiny in Comparative Perspective* (Westport, Conn., 2001), pp. 222–3.

29. L.M. Heywood, 'Slavery and its Transformation in the Kingdom of Kongo, 1491–1800', *Journal of African History*, 50 (2009), p. 18.
30. J. Lindegern, 'The "Swedish Military State" 1560–1720', *Scandinavian Journal of History*, 10 (1985), pp. 305–36.
31. Rush to John Adams, 2 Aug. 1813, Philadelphia, Pennsylvania Historical Society, AM. 1352.
32. *Madison Papers*, V, 344; *Clay Papers*, I, 723.
33. Warren to William Shirley, Governor of Massachusetts Bay, 2 Ap. 1746, HL. HM. 9708.
34. F. Maurice, *On the Uses of the Study of War* (London, 1927), p. x.
35. M.H. Fisher (ed.), *The Travels of Dean Mahomet. An Eighteenth-Century Journey Through India* (Berkeley, Calif., 1997), p. 55.
36. Oliver to John Parsons, 30 Dec. 1789, Gloucester, CRO. D214 F1/93.
37. Thomas Waite to Sir Robert Wilmot, Matlock, Derbyshire CRO. D 3155 WH3461.
38. Dundas, memorandum, Oct. 1796, BL. Add. 59280 f. 189–90.
39. C. Moore, 'Is the Church paying reparations on a false premise?,' *Daily Telegraph*, 23 Ap. 2024.
40. R. Burns, 'British Folk Songs of the Great War – Then and Now,' *JMH*, 79 (2015), p. 1066.

Chapter 2

1. NA. WO. 33/1819, p. 50.
2. W.J. Hamblin, *Warfare in the Ancient Near East to 1600 BC* (London, 2006).
3. P. Kern, *Ancient Siege Warfare* (Bloomington, Ind., 1999).
4. R. Drews, 'Catastrophe Revisited' in G. Middleton (ed.), *Collapse and Transformation: The Late Bronze Age and Early Iron Age in the Aegean* (Oxford, 2020), pp. 229–35.
5. I. Shaw, *Ancient Egyptian Warfare. Tactics, Weapons and Ideology of the Pharaohs* (Oxford, 2019).
6. J. Darnell and C. Manassa, *Tutankhamun's Armies: Battle and Conquest during Egypt's Late Eighteenth Century* (Hoboken, NJ, 2007).
7. A.S. Kolberg, 'There is Power in a Cohort: Development of Warfare in Iron Age to Early Medieval Scotland,' *JMH*, 83 (2019), p. 29.
8. J. Crowley, *The Psychology of the Athenian Hoplite: The Culture of Combat in Classical Athens* (Cambridge, 2012); P.A. Rahe, *The Spartan Regime. Its Character, Origins and Grand Strategy* (New Haven, Conn., 2016), p. 82.
9. V.D. Hanson, *The Western Way of War: Infantry Battle in Classical Greece* (Berkeley, Calif., 1994); P. Matyszak, *Sparta: Rise of a Warrior Nation* (Barnsley, 2018); R. Konijnendijk, *Classical Greek Tactics: A Cultural History* (London 2018).
10. P. Krentz, 'Casualties in Hoplite Battles,' *Greek, Roman and Byzantium Studies*, 26 (1985), pp. 13–20.
11. D. Kagan and G.F. Viggiano (eds), *Men of Bronze: Hoplite Warfare in Ancient Greece* (Princeton, NJ, 2013).
12. J. Lee, 'The Classical Greek Experience,' in B. Campbell and L. Tritle (eds), *The Oxford Handbook of Warfare in the Classical World* (Oxford, 2013), p. 154.
13. M.R. Abbas, 'A Survey of the Military Role of the Sherden Warriors in the Egyptian Army during the Ramesside Period,' *Égypte nilotique et méditerranéenne*, 10 (2017), pp. 7–23.
14. K. Roy, *Warfare in pre-British India* (London, 2005).

15. P. Erdkamp (ed.), *The Companion to the Roman Army* (Malden, 2007); J. Tomczak, 'Roman military equipment in the 4th Century BC: pilum, scutum and the introduction of manipular tactics,' *Folia Archeologica*, 29 (2013), pp. 38–65; P. Connolly, 'The reconstruction and use of Roman weaponry in the second century BC,' *Journal of Roman Military Equipment Studies*, 11 (2000), pp. 43–46.
16. T. Dezsö, *The Assyrian Army I: The Structure of the Neo-Assyrian Army. I: Infantry* (Budapest, 2012).
17. A.O. Anders, *Roman Light Infantry and The Art of Combat. The Nature and Experience of Skirmishing and Non-Pitched Battle in Roman Warfare 264 BC – AD 235* (DPhil., Cardiff, 2011), esp. p. 237, and 'Face of Skirmish: The Nature and Experience of Skirmishing and Non-Pitched Battle,' *Historia*, 64 (2015), pp. 263–300..
18. T. McArthur, 'Should Roman Soldiers be Called "Professional" Prior to Augustus?,' *JMH*, 85 (2021), pp. 9–26.
19. M.J. Taylor, *Soldiers and Silver: Mobilizing Resources in the Age of Roman Conquest* (Austin, Tx, 2020)
20. A.K. Goldsworthy, *The Roman Army at War: 100 BC – AD 200* (Oxford, 1996); P. Sabin, 'The Face of Roman Battle,' *Journal of Roman Studies*, 90 (2000), pp. 1–17; S. Koon, *Infantry Combat in Livy's Battle Narratives* (Oxford, 2010); H. Elton, *Understanding Ancient Battle:Combat in the Classical World from the Unit Commander's Perspective* (Barnsley, 2024)
21. J. Armstrong, *War and Society in Early Rome: From Warlords to Generals* (Cambridge, 2016); M.J. Taylor, 'Tactical Reform in the Late Roman Republic: The View from Italy,' *Historia*, 68 (2019), pp. 76–94; G.Brusa, *Le Coorti Nell' Esercito Romano Di Età Repubblicana* (Pisa, 2020); G. Wrighton, The Third Macedonian War (Barnsley, 2023); K. H. Milne, Inside the Roman Legions: The Soldier's Experience 264–107 BCE (Barnsley, 2024)
22. S. James, *Rome and the Sword: How Warriors and Weapons Shaped Roman History* (London, 2011); J. C. N. Coulston, 'Late Roman Military Equipment Culture' in A. Sarantis and N. Christie (ed.) *War and Warfare in Late Antiquity* (Leiden, 2013), pp.463–92.
23. G. Halsall, 'The Western European Kingdoms, 600–1000,' in A. Curry and D.A. Graff (eds), *The Cambridge History of War. II. War and the Medieval World* (Cambridge, 2020), pp. 50–82.
24. R.J. Chacon and R. Mendoza (eds), *Latin American Indigenous Warfare and Ritual Violence* (Tucson, Az, 2007).
25. V. Tiesler and A. Cucina, 'Where Are the Warriors? Cranial Trauma Patterns and Conflict among the Ancient Maya,' in D.L. Martin, R.P. Harrod and V.R. Perez (eds), *Bioarchaeology of Violence* (Gainesville, Fl., 2012), pp. 160–79.

Chapter 3

1. R. Naismith, M.N. Mhaonaigh and E.A. Rowe (eds), *Writing Battles: New Perspectives on Warfare and Memory in Medieval Europe* (London, 2021).
2. E. McGeer, *Sowing the Dragon's Teeth. Byzantine Warfare in the Tenth Century* (Washington, 1995); M.J. Decker, *The Byzantine Art of War* (Yardley, Penn., 2013).
3. V. Lagardère, 'Esquisse de l'organisation militaire des7 Murabitun à époque de Yusuf ibn Tashfin, 430 H/1039 à 500 H/1106,' *Revue de l'Occident musulman et de la Méditerranéan*, 27 (1979), pp. 99–114.
4. J. Gommans, *The Indian Frontier: Horse and Warband in the Making of Empires* (New Delhi, 2018).

5. D.S. and B.S. Bachrach, 'Bruno of Merseburg's Saxon War: A Study in Eleventh-Century German Military History,' *JMH*, 81 (2017), p. 387.
6. M. Prestwich, *A Short History of the Hundred Years War* (London, 2018).
7. M. Haidar, *Medieval Central Asia: Polity, Economy and Military Organisation* (New Delhi, 2004), pp. 264–302.
8. J. France, 'A Changing Balance: Cavalry and Infantry, 1000–1300,' *Revista de história das ideas*, 30 (2009), pp. 153–77.
9. J. France, 'Thirty Years of War – the cities of the Lombard Plain,' in R.G. Khamisy, R.Y. Lewis and V.R. Shotten-Hallel (eds), *Exploring Outremer* (London, 2023), pp. 127–41.
10. B.L. Davies, 'Guliai-gorod, Wagenburg, and Tabor Tactics in 16th-17th Century Muscovy and Eastern Europe,' in Davies (ed.), *Warfare in Eastern Europe, 1500–1800* (Leiden, 2012), pp. 93–108.
11. K. DeVries, *Infantry Warfare in the Early Fourteenth Century: Discipline, Tactics, and Technology* (Woodbridge, 1996); J. Waldman, *Hafted Weapons in Medieval and Renaissance Europe: The Evolution of European Staff Weapons between 1200 and 1650* (Leiden, 2005).
12. K. Roy, *A Global History of Premodern Warfare: Before the Rise of the West* (London, 2022).
13. A. Curry and M. Mercer (eds), *The Battle of Agincourt* (New Haven, Conn., 2015).
14. T. Richardson, *The Tower Armoury in the Fourteenth Century* (Chicago, Ill., 2018).
15. C.J. Rogers, 'The Development of the Longbow in Late Medieval England and Technological Determinism,' *Journal of Medieval History*, 37 (2011), p. 340.
16. T. Pálosfalvi, *From Nicopolis to Mohács: a history of Ottoman-Hungarian Warfare, 1389–1526* (Leiden, 2018), pp. 29–30.
17. A. Borosy, 'The Militia Portalis in Hungary before 1526,' in J.M. Bak and B.K. Király (eds), *From Hunyadi to Rakoczi. War and Society in Late Medieval and Early Modern Hungary* (New York, 1982), pp. 63–80; F.N. Ardelean, 'From Legislation to Practice: Some Aspects of Military Service in Medieval Hungary and Transylvania,' in M. Rady and A. Simon (eds), *Government and Law in Medieval Moldavia, Wallachia and Transylvania* (London, 2013), pp. 29–36.
18. Pálosfalvi, *Nicopolis to Mohács*, pp. 269–71.
19. J. Alm, *European Crossbows: A Survey* (Leeds, 1994).
20. J. France (ed.), *Mercenaries and Paid Men: The Mercenary Identity in the Middle Ages* (Leiden, 2008).
21. C.F. Petry, *Twilight of Majesty: The Reigns of the Mamluk Sultans al-Ashrāf Qaytbay and Qansuh al-Ghawbri in Egypt* (Seattle, Wa, 1993), pp. 62–3.
22. G. Ágoston, 'A Flexible Empire: Authority and its Limits on the Ottoman Frontiers,' in K.H. Karpat and R.W. Zens (eds), *Ottoman Borderlands* (Madison, Wisc, 2003), pp. 26–7.
23. A.R. Bell and A. Curry (eds), *The Soldier Experience in the Fourteenth Century* (Woodbridge, 2011).

Chapter 4

1. A.J. King (ed.), *Muster Books for North and East Hertfordshire 1580–1605* (Hertford, 1996); G. Phillips, 'Longbow and Hackbutt. Weapons Technology and Technology Transfer in Early Modern England,' *Technology and Culture*, 40 (1999), pp. 576–93; N. Probasco, 'The Role of Commoners and Print in Elizabethan England's Acceptance of Firearms,' *JMH*, 76 (2012), pp. 343–72.

2. L. Kaba, 'Archers, Musketeers and Mosquitoes: The Moroccan Invasion of the Sudan and the Songhay Resistance, 1591–1612,' *Journal of African History*, 22 (1981), pp. 457–75.
3. R. Pankhurst, *The Ethiopian Borderlands* (Lawrenceville, NJ, 1997), pp. 287, 281.
4. C. Divall, *Redcoats Against Napoleon: The 30th Regiment During the Revolutionary and Napoleonic Wars* (Barnsley, 2009), p. 168.
5. Stendhal, *The Charterhouse of Parma* (1839; London, 1958), p. 59.
6. Kritovoulus, *History of Mehmed the Conqueror*, trans. C.T. Riggs (Princeton, NJ, 1954), p. 171; R. Irwin, 'Gunpowder and Firearms in the Mamluk Sultanate Reconsidered,' in M. Winter and A. Levanoni (eds), *The Mamluks in Egyptian and Syrian Politics and Society* (Leiden, 2004), pp. 124, 136.
7. G. Ágoston, *Guns for the Sultan: Military Power and the Weapons Industry in the Ottoman Empire* (Cambridge, 2008), p. 26.
8. R. Murphey, *Ottoman Warfare 1500–1700* (London, 1999); G. Böreckçi, 'A Contribution to the Military Revolution Debate: The Janissaries' Use of Volley Fire during the long Ottoman-Habsburg War of 1593–1606 and the Problem of Origins,' *Acta Orientalia Academiae Scientiarum Hungaricae*, 59 (2006), pp. 407–38; G. Dávid and P. Fodor (eds), *Ottomans, Hungarians, and Habsburgs in Central Europe: The Military Confines in the Era of Ottoman Conquest* (Leiden, 2000).
9. M. Arfaioli, *The Black Bands of Giovanni: Infantry and Diplomacy during the Italian Wars, 1526–1528* (Pisa, 2005).
10. N. Barr, *Flodden 1513* (Stroud, 2001).
11. G. Phillips, *The Anglo-Scots War 1513–1550: A Military History* (Woodbridge, 1999).
12. G.J. Miller, *Tudor Mercenaries and Auxiliaries, 1485–1547* (Charlottesville, Va, 1980).
13. J. Raymond, 'Henry VIII and the English Military Establishment,' *Archives*, 28 (2003), p. 112.
14. F.N. Ardelean, *On the Borderlands of Great Empires: Transylvanian Armies, 1541–1613* (Warwick, 2022).
15. Ardelean, 'Frontiers and Military Organization in Transylvania: The Guardsman (Drabant/Darabont) during the Second Half of the Sixteenth Century,' in Ardelean, L. Cimpeanu, G. Fodor and L. Magina (eds), *From Medieval Frontiers to Early Modern Borders in Central and South-Eastern Europe* (Berlin, 2022), pp. 177–93.
16. J. O'Neill, 'Firearms and Fieldworks: Military Transformation and the End of Gaelic Ireland,' in M.C. Fissel (ed.), *The Military Revolution and Revolutions in Military Affairs* (Berlin, 2023), pp. 200–1.
17. W.E.D. Allen, *Problems of Turkish Power in the Sixteenth Century* (London, 1963), p. 38.
18. G. Parker, *The Army of Flanders and the Spanish Road, 1567–1659: The Logistics of Spanish Victory and Defeat in the Low Countries' Wars* (2nd edn, Cambridge, 2004); F. Gonzáles de Léon, *The Road to Rocroi: Class, Culture, and Command in the Spanish Army of Flanders, 1567–1659* (Leiden, 2009).
19. Parker, 'The Limits to Revolutions in Military Affairs: Maurice of Nassau, the Battle of Nieuwport, and the Legacy,' *JMH*, 71 (2007), pp. 331–72.

Chapter 5

1. S. Gordon, *Marathas, Marauders and State Formation in Eighteenth-Century India* (Oxford, 1994), p. 188.
2. B. Mugnai, *Wars and Soldiers in the Early Reign of Louis XIV. Vol. 7 – Armies of the German States 1655–1690, Part 1* (Warwick, 2024), p. 70.

3. D.P. Marston, *Phoenix from the Ashes: The Indian Army in the Burma Campaign* (Westport, Conn., 2004).
4. A. Lopes Pires Nunes, 'Les guerres hollandaises au Bresil,' in *Atti del XVIII Congresso internazionale di Storia Militaire* (Rome, 1993), pp. 459–60.
5. M. Pittock, *Scotland; the Global History* (London, 2022), pp. 38–46.
6. W. Louth, *The Arte Militaire: The Application of 17th Century Military Manuals to Conflict Archaeology* (Solihull, 2016); D. Yun, 'The "Push of Pike" in Seventeenth Century English Infantry Combat,' *JMH*, 86 (2022), pp. 837–57.
7. G. Satterfield, *Princes, Posts and Partisans: The Army of Louis XIV and Partisan Warfare in the Netherlands, 1673–1678* (Leiden, 2003).
8. P.M. Malone, *The Skulking Way of War: Technology and Tactics among the New England Indians* (Lanham, Md, 1991).
9. R.A. Kea, 'Firearms and Warfare on the Gold and Slave Coasts,' *Journal of African History*, 12 (1971), pp. 185–213; J. Thornton, *Warfare in Atlantic Africa, 1500–1800* (London, 1999).
10. NA. SP. 97/20.
11. A. Balisch, 'Infantry Battlefield Tactics in the Seventeenth and Eighteenth Centuries on the European and Turkish Theatres of War: the Austrian Response to Different Conditions', *Studies in History and Politics*, 3 (1983–4), p. 44.
12. Anon., *The New Exercise of Flintlocks and Bayonets; appointed by the Duke of Marlborough* (London, 1708), p. 6.
13. J.A. Lynn, 'Forging the Western army in seventeenth-century France,' in M. Knox and W. Murray (eds), *The Dynamic of Military Revolution 1300–2050* (Cambridge, 2001), pp. 39–40.
14. D. Lupton, *A Warre-Like Treatise of the Pike, or, Some Experimental Resolves, for lessening the number, and disabling the use of the pike in warre* (London, 1642), pp. 99–100.
15. G. Ágoston, 'The Ottoman Wars and the Changing Balance of Power along the Danube in the Early Eighteenth Century,' in C. Ingrao, N. Samardžić and J. Pešalj (eds), *The Peace of Passarowitz, 1718* (West Lafayette, Ind., 2011), pp. 95–6.
16. J.A. Lynn, *Giant of the Grand Siècle: The French Army, 1610–1715* (Cambridge, 1997), p. 476.
17. J. Douglass, *Schola Martis, or the Arte of War ... as Practised in Flanders*, BL. Add. 27892 f. 213–17; J. Childs, *The British Army of William III, 1689–1702* (Manchester, 1987).
18. H. Kleinschmidt, 'Using the Gun: Manual Drill and the Proliferation of Portable Firearms,' *JMH*, 63 (1999), pp. 601–29; C. Duffy, *The Military Experience in the Age of Reason* (2nd edn, London, 1998).

Chapter 6

1. Stuart, orders, BL. Add. 29198 f. 120–3.
2. M. Axworthy, 'The Army of Nader Shah,' *Iranian Studies*, 40 (2007), pp. 635–46.
3. G.T. Kulkarni and M.R. Kantak, *Battle of Kharda: Challenges and Responses* (Pune, 1980).
4. S. Gordon, *The Marathas, 1600–1818* (Cambridge, 1993).
5. S. Gordon, 'The Limited Adoption of European-style Military Forces by Eighteenth Century Rulers in India,' *Indian Economic and Social History Review*, 35 (1998), pp. 229–45,' and 'Symbolic and Structural Constraints on the Adoption of European-

style Military Technologies in the Eighteenth Century,' in R.B. Barnett (ed.), *Rethinking Early Modern India* (New Delhi, 2002), pp. 155–78.

6. J.N. Sarkar, *Sindhia as Regent of Delhi* (Bombay, 1953).
7. D. Sweet, 'Native Resistance in eighteenth-century Amazonia: The "abominable Mura" in war and peace,' *Radical History Review*, 53 (1992), pp. 49–80.
8. J. Henning, *Red Gold: The Conquest of the Brazilian Indians, 1500–1760* (2nd edn, London, 1995); G.D. Jones, *The Conquest of the Last Maya Kingdom* (Stanford, Calif., 1998), pp. 300–35.
9. L.Y. Andaya, 'Interactions with the outside world and adaptation in southeast Asian society, 1500–1800,' in N. Tarling (ed.), *The Cambridge History of Southeast Asia* (Cambridge, 1992), pp. 380–95.
10. R.S. Smith, *Warfare and Diplomacy in pre-colonial West Africa* (London, 1976); R.A. Kea, *Settlements, Trade, and Politics in the Seventeenth-Century Gold Coast* (Baltimore, Md., 1982), pp. 130–64; J.F. Searing, *West African Slavery and Atlantic Commerce. The Senegal River Valley, 1700–1860* (Cambridge, 1993).
11. J. Thornton, 'Warfare, Slave Trade and European Influence: Atlantic Africa 1450–1800,' in J. Black (ed.), *War in the Early Modern World* (London, 1999), pp. 129–46.
12. M. Edwardes (ed.), *Major John Corneille, Journal of my Service in India* (London, 1966), p. 35.
13. M.W. Aregay, 'A Reappraisal of the Impact of Firearms in the History of Warfare in Ethiopia, *c.*1500–1800,' *Journal of Ethiopian Studies*, 14 (1976–9), pp. 87–122.
14. D. Showalter, 'Tactics and recruitment in eighteenth-century Prussia,' *Studies in History and Politics*, 3 (1983–4), pp. 15–41.
15. D. Blakemore, *Destructive and Formidable: British Infantry Firepower, 1642–1765* (London, 2014).
16. Hill to his mother, 10 Aug. -, Hill papers. I am grateful to Enid Case for granting access to the Hill papers.
17. P. Levrau, 'Crippled by a Musket Shot and a Sabre Slash,' in D. Money (ed.), *1708: Oudenarde and Lille* (Cambridge, 2008), p. 70.
18. S.L. Kling (ed.), *The Great Northern War Compendium* (St Louis, Miss., 2015).
19. NA. WO. 34/125 f. 10.
20. G.S. García, 'La Nueva Infantéria española en acción,' *Revista de Historia Militar*, 102 (2007), pp. 245–84.
21. Cornwallis to Sir John Shore, 15 Oct., 27 Sept. 1787, NA. PRO. 30/11/165 f. 56, 42.
22. Journal, possibly by Henry Fletcher, Providence, Rhode Island, Brown University, John Carter Brown Library, Codex Eng. 41.
23. P. Mackesy, *The Coward of Minden: The Affair of Lord George Sackville* (London, 1979); Sackville to Holdernesse, 2 Aug. 1759, BL. Eg. 3443 f. 235.
24. J.A. Lynn, 'The Battle Culture of Forbearance, 1660–1789,' in W. Lee (ed.), *Warfare and Culture in World History* (New York, 2011), p. 94.
25. Conway to Charles Townshend, Secretary at War, 15 July 1761, 15 Aug., 20 Sept. 1762, NA. WO. 1/165, pp. 95–6, 141–2, 183.
26. Observer's account, BL. Add. 61669 f. 17.
27. C. Dalrymple, *Military Essay* (London, 1761), p. 56. See also P.J. Speelman (ed.), *War, Society, and the Enlightenment: The Works of General Lloyd* (Leiden, 2005).
28. Burgoyne, *State of the Expedition* (London, 1780), p. 121.
29. Beinecke, Osborn Shelves, pc. 224, 24 Sept. 1708.
30. Library of Congress, Washington, Greene Letter Book, 6 Dec. 1780.

31. A. Konstam, *Peter the Great's Army* (London, 1993).
32. Guy Dickens to Horatio Walpole, 18 Sept. 1736, NA. SP. 90/41.
33. L. Vergez, *Rocoux 1746: Bataille et combats pendant la guerre en dentelles* (Le Coudray-Macouard, 2017).
34. Dering to Egmont, 25 Oct. 1715, BL. Add. 47028 f. 91.
35. Lady to Lord Anson, 27 June 1758, Stafford CRO D 1615/P(S) 1/2/6.
36. Memoranda of *c.*1758, papers of St Paul, Ashington, Northumbria CRO. ZBU B2/3/1.
37. ZBU, B2/3/29.
38. K.and S. Möbius, *Prussian Army Soldiers and the Seven Years' War, The Psychology of Honour* (London, 2019), pp.122–3. On pressganging,Charles Whitworth, , British envoy in Berlin, to James, Viscount Stanhope, Secretary of State, 3 Feb. 1720, NA. SP. 90/11.
39. Nottingham, University Library, Mellish papers 172/111/4.
40. Evelyn to Sir Frederick Evelyn, 23 Ap. 1775, BL. Evelyn papers, LEI. See also *Memoir and Letters of Captain W. Glanville Evelyn ... from North America, 1774–1776* (2021).
41. Congreve to Reverend Richard Congreve, 4 Sept. 1776, Stafford, CRO. D 1057/M/F/30.
42. Jeffrey Amherst, Commander-in-Chief North America, to William, 2nd Viscount Barrington, Secretary at War, 8 Mar. 1760, NA. WO. 1/5 f. 100.
43. Gage to Barrington, 3 Oct. 1774, BL. Add. 73550.
44. M.H. Spring, *With Zeal and With Bayonets Only: The British Army on Campaign in North Aemrica, 1775–1783* (Norman, Ok., 2008).
45. NAS. GD. 26/9/513/8.
46. P. Russell, 'Redcoats in the wilderness: British officers and irregular warfare in Europe, 1740 to 1766,' *William and Mary Quarterly*, 3rd ser. 35 (1978), pp. 629–52.
47. C. Storrs, 'Philip V and the Revival of Spain, 1713–48,' in T.J. Dadson and J.H. Elliott (eds), *Britain, Spain and the Treaty of Utrecht, 1713–2013* (London, 2014), p. 84; G. Ágoston, 'Firearms and Military Adaptation: The Ottomans and the European Military Revolution, 1450–1800,' *Journal of World History*, 25 (2014), p. 123.
48. Stewart to John, 2nd Earl of Stair, 10 Sept. 1741, Beinecke, Osborn Shelves, Stair Letters, no. 70.
49. NA. WO. 1/57.
50. Bull to Amherst, 15 Ap. 1761, NA. CO. 5/61 f. 277.
51. M. McConnell, *Army and Empire. British Soldiers on the American Frontier, 1758–1775* (Lincoln, Neb., 2004).
52. J.F. Winkler, *Wabash 1791: St Clair's Defeat* (Oxford, 2011).
53. A. Starkey, *European and Native American Warfare 1675–1815* (London, 1998), pp. 159–63.
54. R.L. Tignor (ed.), *Napoleon in Egypt: Al-Jabarti's Chronicle of the French Occupation, 1798* (Princeton, NJ., 1993), p. 37.
55. A. Balisch, 'Infantry battlefield tactics in the seventeenth and eighteenth centuries,' *Studies in History and Politics*, 3 (1983–4), pp. 52–9.
56. J.R. Gibson, *Otter Skins, Boston Ships, and China Goods: the Maritime Fur Trade of the Northwest Coast, 1785–1841* (Montreal, 1992), pp. 220–4.

57. J.A. Lynn, *The Bayonets of the Republic: Motivation and Tactics in the Army of Revolutionary France* (Urbana, Ill., 1984).
58. On the flexibility of columns, J. Chagniot, *Le Chevalier de Folard, la stratégie de l'incertitude* (Paris, 1997).
59. Colonel Richard Grenville to George III, 13 Sept. 1782, Captain John Barker to Keith, 9 June, Colonel Gordon to Keith, 8 Sept. 1787, BL. Add. 70956, 35539.
60. Dundas, *Principles*, BL. Add. 27600 f. 44.
61. W. Cobbett (ed.), *Parliamentary History of England* 33 (London, 1818), cols 226–7.
62. F.C. Schneid (ed.), *European Armies of the French Revolution, 1789–1802* (Norman, Ok., 2015).
63. R. Muir, *Tactics and the Experience of Battle in the Age of Napoleon* (New Haven, Conn., 1998).
64. Jenkinson to his father, Charles, Lord Hawkesbury, 25 July 1792, Bod., Bland Burges papers, vol. 37 f. 62; Chauvelin to Lebrun, Foreign Minister, 9 Oct. 1792, AE. CP. Ang. 582 f. 318.
65. BL. Add. 13579 f. 7–8.
66. R.G.S. Cooper, *The Anglo-Maratha Campaigns and the Contest for India* (Cambridge, 2005).
67. Martin to Charles, 2nd Duke of Richmond, 19 Aug. 1748, Goodwood, Mss. 107 no. 685. I am most grateful to the Duke of Richmond for permission to use these papers.
68. Hatton to Robert, 4th Earl of Holdernesse, Secretary of State, 18 July 1758, BL. Eg. 3443 f. 34, 42. On Hatton, H.M. Little, *The Treasury, the Commissariat and the Supply of the Combined Army in Germany during the Seven Years War, 1756–1763* (DPhil, London, 1981).
69. HL. Loudoun papers, no. 10125.
70. W. Cobbett (ed), *Parliamentary History of England*, XX, col. 794; *The Papers of George Washington. Revolutionary War Series*, X, 230.
71. Cheshire, Chester Record Office, DCH/X/9A, no. 48.
72. Moore diary, BL. Add. 57326 f. 11.
73. A. Corvisier, *LArmée francaise de la fin du XVIIe siècle au ministère de Choiseul* (2 vols, Paris, 1964), I, 220–1, 229.
74. Arbuthnot to Sir Robert Murray Keith, envoy in Vienna, 28 Dec. 1789, BL. Add. 35541 f. 307.
75. M. Traugott, *The Insurgent Barricade* (Berkeley, Cal., 2010).

Chapter 7

1. Stanhope to Frederick, Duke of York, 19 June 1815, BL. Add. 34703 f. 22.
2. S. Brown, *By Fire and Bayonet: Grey's West Indies Campaign of 1794* (Solihull, 2018).
3. NAM. 2002-02-729-1.
4. Garland to William Siborne, 4 Dec. 1834, BL. Add. 34704 f. 1.Garland was badly wounded.
5. Moore to his father, 25 Mar. 1801, BL. Add. 59281 f. 74–5.
6. Lowe to father, 29 Mar. 1801, BL. Add. 36297C f. 12–13. See also Brigadier-General Hildebrand Oates, BL. Add. 36747C f. 44–5.
7. Wellington to General Beresford, 2 July 1815, *Despatches* XII, p. 529.
8. D. Walter, 'Reluctant Reformers, Observant Disciples. The Prussian Military Reforms, 1807–1814,' in R. Chickering and S. Förster (eds), *War in an Age of Revolution, 1775–1815* (Cambridge, 2010), p. 97.

9. Wellington, *Supplementary Despatches*, X, p. 513.
10. Anon., 'A French Infantry Officer's Account of Waterloo,' *United Services Journal* (Jan. 1879), p. 67; R. Muir, *Tactics and the Experience of Battle in the Age of Napoleon* (New Haven, Conn., 1998), p. 103.
11. M. Greig, *Dead Men Telling Tales: Napoleonic War Veterans and the Military Memoir Industry, 1808–1914* (Oxford, 2021).
12. F. Houghton, *The Veterans' Tale: British Military Memoirs of the Second World War* (Cambridge, 2019).
13. BL. Add. 56088 f. 5.
14. W. Reid, 'Tracing the Biscuit: The Commissariat in the Peninsular War,' *Militaria*, 7 (1995), pp. 101–8.
15. Memorandum of 17 Dec. 1808, Exeter, Devon CRO., Guard's letterbook 49/33 f. 10; I. Robertson, *A Commanding Presence: Wellington in the Peninsula, 1808–1814* (Stroud, 2008).
16. Lowe to Colonel Bunbury, 19 Oct. 1813, BL. Add. 37051 f. 162.
17. I. Gordon, *Soldier of the Raj* (Barnsley, 2001), pp. 92–3.
18. M. Broers, *Napoleon's Other War. Bandits, Rebels and their Pursuers in the Age of Revolutions* (Oxford, 2010).
19. Letter by an unidentified officer of Bengal 30th Native Infantry, 26 Jan. 1849, BL. IO. MSS. Eur. C. 605 f. 1–2.
20. London, National Army Museum, Archives, 1968-07-213-1, pp. 63–5.
21. J. Belich, *The New Zealand Wars and the Victorian Interpretation of Racial Conflict* (Auckland, 1986) has been criticised by some subsequent writers.
22. A. Roberts, 'Firearms in north-eastern Zambia before 1900,' *Transafrican Journal of History*, 1, 2 (1972), pp. 3–21.
23. J. Connor, *The Australian Frontier Wars, 1788–1838* (Sydney, 2002).
24. R. Smith, 'Yoruba Armament,' *Journal of African History*, 8 (1967), pp. 87–106.
25. Lister to Secretary to Governor of Bengal, 2 Feb. 1850, BL. Add. 49016 f. 88; J. Knetsch, J. Missall and M.L. Missall, *History of the Third Seminole War, 1849–1858* (Havertown, Penn., 2018).
26. Napier to Lord Dalhousie, 27 June 1849, BL. Add. 49106 f. 1–4.
27. J.S. Curtis, 'The army of Nicholas I: Its Role and Character,' *American Historical Review*, 63 (1958), p. 886.
28. S. Ross, *From Flintlock to Rifle. Infantry Tactics, 1740–1866* (2nd edn, London, 1996).
29. BL. Add. 49106 f. 7–26.
30. J. Lamphear, 'The Evolution of Ateker "New Model" Armies: Jie and Turkana,' in K. Fukui and J. Markakis (eds), *Ethnicity and Conflict in the Horn of Africa* (London, 1994), p. 89.
31. E.J. Hess, *The Rifle Musket in Civil War Combat: Realities and Myth* (Lawrence, KS, 2008) and *Civil War Infantry Tactics: Training, Combat, and Small-Unit Effectiveness* (Baton Rouge, La., 2015).
32. R.J. Spiller (ed.), *Battle Studies: Ardant du Picq* (Lawrence, KS, 2017).
33. NA. WO. 32/2819, p. 12.
34. J. Dunn, '"For God, Emperor, and Country!" The Evolution of Ethiopia's Nineteenth-century Army,' *War in History*, 1 (1994), pp. 278–99.
35. F. Yeşil, 'Drill and Discipline as a Civilising Process: The Genesis of the Modern Soldier in the Ottoman Empire, 1789–1826,' in S. Faroqhi (ed.), *Ottoman War and Peace – Studies in Honour of Virginia Aksan* (Leiden, 2020), pp. 101–23.

36. V. Aksan, *The Ottomans 1700–1923. An Empire Besieged* (2nd ed., London, 2022).
37. P.S. Thompson, *The Natal Native Contingent in the Anglo-Zulu War* (Scotsville, 2003); I.F.W. Beckett, *Rorke's Drift and Isandlwana* (Oxford, 2019). For the Russian case, A. Morrison, *The Russian Conquest of Central Asia: A Study in Imperial Expansion, 1814–1914* (Cambridge, 2020).
38. B. Robson (ed.), 'The Kandahar Letters of the Reverend Alfred Cane,' *Journal of the Society for Army Historical Research*, 69 (1991), p. 215.
39. D. Porch, *The Conquest of Morocco* (New York, 1983), pp. 184–8.
40. D. O'Connor, 'The Political Uses of Lawlessness: Kruger, Warren and the Bechuanaland Field Force, 1885,' *RUSI*, 150, no. 3 (June 2005), p. 71.
41. S.W. Baker, 'Experience in Savage Warfare,' *RUSI*, 17 (1873–4), pp. 904–21; H.C. Gawler, 'British Troops and Savage Warfare,' *Ibid.*, 922–39; C. Callwell, 'Notes on the Tactics of Our Small Wars,' *Proceedings of the Royal Artillery Institution*, 12 (1884), pp. 531–52, and 'Notes on the Strategy of Our Small Wars,' *Ibid.*, 13 (1885), pp 403–20; Callwell, 'Lessons to Be Learnt from the Campaigns in which British Forces Have Been Employed since the Year 1865,' *RUSI*, 31 (1887–8), pp. 357–411; A.C. Yate, 'North West Frontier Warfare,' *Ibid.*, 42 (1898), pp. 117–93; T. Moreman, 'The British and Indian Armies and North-West Frontier Warfare, 1849–1914,' *Journal of Imperial and Commonwealth History*, 20 (1992), pp. 35–64.
42. LH. Hamilton 1/2/7/2.
43. H.C.B. Cook (ed.), 'Letters from South Africa 1899–1902,' *Journal of the Society for Army Historical Research*, 69 (1991), pp. 240–1.
44. NA. WO. 33/2822, p. 10.
45. NA. PRO. 30/40/13, p. 62.
46. LH. Hamilton, 4/2/3, p. 17.
47. LH. Hamilton, 4/2/9.
48. B. Kruszyński, *The German 10th Infantry Division Tactical Combat Operations on the Western Front in August 1914* (Göttingen, 2021), p. 355.
49. BL. Add. 50344, p. 131.
50. BL. Add. 50344 pp. 131–2.
51. S. Manning, *Evelyn Wood. Pillar of Empire* (Barnsley, 2007), p. 229.
52. E.M. Spiers, 'Reforming the Infantry of the Line, 1900–1914,' *Journal of the Society for Army Historical Research*, 59 (1981), pp. 91, 94; S. Jones, *From Boer War to World War: Tactical Reform of the British Army, 1902–1914* (Norman, Ok., 2012).
53. V. Kolev and C. Koulouri (eds), *The Balkan Wars* (Thessaloniki, 2005), p. 68.
54. J. Lyon, *Serbia and the Balkan Front, 1914: The Outbreak of the Great War* (London, 2015).
55. NA. WO. 33/2822, p. 93, re 1900.
56. B. Menning, *Bayonets Before Bullets: The Imperial Russian Army, 1861–1914* (Bloomington, 1992), p. 64.
57. Z. Waters, *A Wilderness of Destruction: Confederate Guerrillas in East and South Florida, 1861–1865* (Macon, GA, 2023).
58. P. Beattie, *The Tribute of Blood: Army, Honor, Race and the Nation in Brazil, 1864–1945* (Durham, NC, 2001).
59. P.B. Miller, *From Revolutionaries to Citizens: Antimilitarism in France, 1870–1914* (Durham, NC, 2002).
60. F.P. Prucha, 'An Army Private and Old Fort Snelling in 1849,' *Minnesota History*, 36 (1958), pp. 15–16.

61. R.L. Nicholas, 'The Black Hawk War in Retrospect,' *Wisconsin Magazine of History*, 65 (1982), p. 239.
62. G. Linderman, *Embattled Courage: The Experience of Combat in the American Civil War* (New York, 1987).
63. J.M. Steplyk, *Fighting Means Killing: Civil War Soldiers and the Nature of Combat* (Lawrence, KS, 2018).
64. K. Hagemann, *Revisiting Prussia's Wars Against Napoleon: History, Culture, and Memory* (Cambridge, 2015); E.H. Bonekemper, *The Myth of the Lost Cause* (Washington, 2015).

Chapter 8

1. Exeter, Devon CRO. 5277 M/F3/29.
2. Devon CRO. 5277 M/F3/26.
3. M.O. Humphries, *A Weary Road: Shell Shock in the Canadian Expeditionary Force, 1914–1918* (Toronto, 2018).
4. B. Shephard, *A War of Nerves: Soldiers and Psychiatrists, 1914–1994* (London, 2000); G. Thomas, *Treating Trauma of the Great War: Soldiers, Civilians and Psychiatry in France, 1914–1940* (Baton Rouge, La., 2009).
5. LMA. CLC/521/MS 24718, pp. 2–3, 6–7, 22.
6. Arthur Child-Villiers to his father, Victor, 7th Earl of Jersey, 14 Nov. 1914, LMA. ACc/2839/D/002.
7. Alan to Edith Thomson, 1 Oct. 1915, Thomson papers.
8. Tameside, Manchester Regiment Archives, MB2/25/21, undated; B. Lamin, *Letters from the Trenches* (London, 2009), p.120.
9. Garvin to his mother, Christina, 18 Aug. 1915, M. Pottle and J. Ledingham (eds), *We Hope To Get Word Tomorrow. The Garvin Family Letters* (London, 2009).
10. T. Ashworth, *Trench Warfare 1914–1918: the live and let live system* (London, 1980).
11. LMA. GL. MS. 9400.
12. E. Mayhew, *Wounded: A New History of the Western Front in World War I* (Oxford, 2014).
13. Devon CRO. 413M add F1.
14. R. Duffett, *The Stomach for Fighting: Food and the Soldiers of the Great War* (Manchester, 2012).
15. R. Service, *Blood on the Snow. The Russian Revolution 1914–1924* (London, 2023), pp. 31–2.
16. LMA. CLC/521/MS 24718, p. 13.
17. G.D. Robert to Earl Fortescue, 9 Nov. 1915, Devon CRO. 126 M/FC60.
18. BL. Add. 49703 f. 42.
19. Smith-Dorrien to Robertson, 27 Ap. 1915, Devon CRO. 1262 M/FH 94.
20. Reproduced by permission of his grandson.
21. Birdwood to General Sir Charles Callwell, 15 May 1915, 8 June 19815, AWM, 3 DRL/3376, 11/4.
22. LMA. GL. MS. 9400.
23. LMA. MS9400; Devon CRO. 5277M/F130, 28 Sept. 1918.
24. LH. Benson A 3/7, pp. 1–2, 5.
25. LMA. CLC/521/MS 24718, pp. 124–6.
26. Devon CRO. 5277 M/F3/30.

27. Commander of 33rd Infantry Brigade to Colonel Alan Thomson, 12 Nov. 1918, Thomson papers.
28. G. Martin, 'German Strategy and Military Assessments of the American Expeditionary Force (AEF), 1918–18,' *War in History*, 1 (1994), pp. 190–1. See also M Grotelueschen, *The AEF Way of War: The American Army and Combat in World War I* (Cambridge, 2007).
29. D. Blair, *The Battle of Bellicourt Tunnel* (London, 2011).
30. D. Clayton, *Decisive Victory: The Battle of the Sambre, 4 November 1918* (Barnsley, 2018).
31. P.E. Hodgkinson, *British Infantry Commanders in the First World War* (Farnham, 2015).
32. Devon CRO. 5277 M/F3/30.
33. AWM. 3 DRL/6643, 5/27.
34. A. Nordlund, '"Done My Bit": British Soldiers, the 1918 Armistice, and Understanding the First World War,' *JMH*, 81 (2017), pp. 445–6; E. Gutiérrez, *Doughboys on the Great War: How American Soldiers Viewed Their Military Experience* (Lawrence, KS, 2014).
35. J.E. Kitchen, *The British Imperial Army in the Middle East: Morale and Military Identity in the Sinai and Palestine Campaigns, 1916–1918* (London, 2014).
36. P. Griffith, *Battle Tactics of the Western Front: The British Army's Art of Attack, 1916–1918* (New Haven, Conn., 1994), p. 193.
37. G. Sheffield, 'British High Command in the First World War: an overview,' in Sheffield and G. Till (eds), *Challenges of High Command in the Twentieth Century* (Camberley, 1999), p. 23.
38. D. Brock, *General Jan Smuts and His First World War in Africa, 1914–1917* (Brimingham, 2022).
39. LH. Liddell Hart Papers, 7/1920/167.
40. LH. Kennedy papers, 2/2.
41. NA. WO. 106/6238, p. 19.
42. Sayyid Muhammad 'Abd Allah al-Hasan, known to the British as the Mad Mullah.
43. LH. Ismay 3/1/1–83, quotes pp. 55, 58. See, more generally, R.L. Hess, 'The "Mad Mullah" and Northern Somalia,' *Journal of African History*, 5 (1964), pp. 415–33.
44. J. Sweet, *Iron Arm: The Mechanisation of Mussolini's Army, 1920–1940* (Westport, Conn., 1980).
45. L.A. Humphreys, *The Way of the Heavenly Sword: The Japanese Army in the 1920s* (Stanford, Calif., 1995).
46. E. Drea, 'The Imperial Japanese Army, 1868–1945,' J. Black (ed.), *War in the Modern World Since 1815* (London, 2003), p 97, 111.
47. M. Strohn, *The German Army and the Defence of the Reich: Military Doctrine and the Conduct of the Defensive Battle 1918–1939* (Cambridge, 2011).
48. R.W. Harrison, *The Russian Way of War: Operational Art, 1904–1940* (Lawrence, KS, 2001).
49. Montgomery-Massingberd to Edward, Viscount Halifax, Secretary of State for War, 17 Aug. 1935, LH. Montgomery-Massingberd papers, M 10/4/1.
50. NA. CAB. 16/109 f. 15.
51. P.S. Khoury, *Syria and the French Mandate: the Politics of Arab Nationalism, 1920–1945* (Princeton, NJ, 1987).

52. T. Rettig, 'French Military Policies in the Aftermath of the Yên Bay Mutiny, 1930: Old Security Dilemmas Return to the Surface,' *South East Asia Research*, 10 (2002), pp. 309–31.
53. *Times*, 28 Oct. 1933.
54. N. Smart, 'Living in the Past: British Generals and the Second World War,' *Archives*, 28 (2003), pp. 163–82, esp. p. 171.
55. R. Forczyk, *Case White. The Invasion of Poland, 1939* (Oxford, 2019), pp. 137–8, 213–14, 331.
56. P. Caddick-Adams, *Sand and Steel. A New History of D-Day* (London, 2019), pp. 704–6.
57. N. Revelli, *Mussolini's Death March: Eyewitness Accounts of Italian Soldiers on the Eastern Front* (Lawrence, KS, 2013).
58. J. Crang, *The British Army and the People's War* (Oxford, 2000); A. Allport, *Browned Off and Bloody-Minded: The British Soldier Goes to War, 1939–1945* (New Haven, Conn., 2015).
59. A.D. Harvey, 'The Bayonet on the Battlefield,' *RUSI Journal*, 150, No. 2 (Ap. 2005), pp. 62–3.
60. NA. PREM 3/328/5, pp. 24–6.
61. J. Kiszely, *Anatomy of a Campaign: The British Fiasco in Norway, 1940* (Cambridge, 2017).
62. J. Fennel, *Combat and Morale in the North African Campaign: The Eighth Army and the Path to El Alamein* (Cambridge, 2011).
63. G. Harper, *The Battle for North Africa: El Alamein and the Turning Point for World War II* (Bloomington, Ind., 2017).
64. C. D'Amours, 'Canadian Military Culture and Tactical Training, 1940–1944: The Making of Infantry Junior NCOs,' *JMH*, 82 (2018), pp. 1197–8.
65. S.T. Barry, *Battalion Commanders at War: US Army Tactical Leadership in the Mediterranean Theater, 1942–1943* (Lawrence, KS, 2013).
66. M. Milner, *Stopping the Panzers: The Untold Story of D-Day* (Lawrence, KS, 2014); L.P. Devine, *The British Way of War in Northwest Europe, 1944–5. A Study of Two Infantry Divisions* (London, 2016); A. Holborn, *The D-Day Landing on Gold Beach* (London, 2015).
67. Wyche Papers, East Carolina University. I am most grateful to Simon Trew for providing a copy of this document.
68. Blamey to John Curtin, Australian Prime Minister, 4 Dec. 1942, AWM. 3 DRL/6643, 2/11
69. V.J. Cirillo, *Bullets and Bacilli: The Spanish-American War and Military Medicine* (New Brunswick, NJ, 2004).
70. AWM. 3 DRL/6643, 3/10.
71. AWM. 3 DRL/6643, 3/12.
72. Blamey to Curtin, 4 Dec. 1942, AWM 3 DRL/6643, 2/11.
73. W.J. Slim, *Defeat Into Victory* (London, 1956), pp. 28–30.
74. Pownall to Ismay, 26 Ap. 1944, LH. Ismay 4/26/2. See also I.L. Grant and K. Tamayama, *Burma 1942: The Japanese Invasion: Both Sides Tell the Story of a Savage Jungle War* (Chichester, 1999).
75. D.P. Marston, *Phoenix from the Ashes: The Indian Army in the Burma Campaign* (London, 2003); T. Moreman, *The Jungle, Japanese and the British Commonwealth*

Armies at War, 1914–45: Fighting Methods, Doctrine and Training for Jungle Warfare (London, 2005).
76. K. Roy, 'Military Loyalty in the Colonial Context: A Case Study of the Indian Army during World War II,' *JMH*, 73 (2009), pp. 497–529, esp. 519.
77. D. Nash, 'Army Boots on Volcanic Sands: The 147th Infantry Regiment at Iwo Jima,' *Army History*, 105 (Fall, 2017), p. 10.
78. Caddick-Adams, *Monte Cassino: Ten Armies in Hell* (Oxford, 2013).
79. F. Römer, *Comrades: The Wehrmacht from Within* (Oxford, 2019).
80. W.B. Haworth, *The Bradley and How It Got That Way: Technology, Institutions, and the Problem of Mechanized Infantry in the United States Army* (Westport, Conn., 1999); D.M. Glantz, *Soviet Military Operational Art: In Pursuit of Deep Battle* (Totowa, NJ, 1991); J.A. English, *Marching Through Chaos: The Descent of Armies in Theory and Practice* (Westport, Conn., 1996), p. 154.
81. S. Daly, *A History of the Republic of Biafra: Law, Crime, and the Nigerian Civil War* (Cambridge, 2020), esp. 78–110.
82. A. Clayton, *Factions, Foreigners and Fantasies: The Civil War in Liberia* (Sandhurst, 1995).
83. A.G. Horowitz, *PTSD: A Short History* (Baltimore, Md., 2018).
84. J.S. Brown, *Kevlar Legions: The Transformation of the U.S. Army, 1989–2005* (Washington, 2011); P. Proctor, *Lessons Unlearned: The U.S. Army's Role in Creating the Forever Wars in Afghanistan and Iraq* (Columbia, Miss., 2020).

Chapter 9

1. Sean Langan, 'Life as a Russian soldier in Ukraine – what the British insider saw,' *Sunday Times*, 18 Feb. 2024, News section.
2. *Times*, 27 March 2004.
3. R.L. Brownlee and W.J. Mullen, *Changing an Army: An Oral History of General William E. DePuy, USA retired* (Carlisle Barracks, Penn., 2015).
4. S. Biddle, 'Back in the Trenches. Why New Technology Hasn't Revolutionized Warfare in Ukraine,' *Foreign Affairs*, 102, 5 (Sept/Oct 2023), pp. 153–64.
5. J. Watling, *The Arms of the Future: Technology and Close Combat in the 21st Century* (London, 2023).
6. G. Gatzemeyer, *Bodies for Battle: U.S. Army Physical Culture and Systematic Training, 1885–1957* (Lawrence, KS, 2021).
7. Y. Dai, *The White Lotus War: Rebellion and Suppression in Late Imperial China* (Seattle, Wa., 2019).
8. Dill to Montgomery-Massingberd, former Chief of the Imperial General Staff, 25 Sept., 18 Nov. 1939, LH. Montgomery-Massingberd papers, M 10/14.
9. Trelawny to Thomas, Duke of Newcastle, Secretary of State for the Southern Department, 4 Dec. 1738, NA. CO. 137/56.
10. Cavan to Maurice, 6 Feb. 1924, LH. Maurice papers, 3/5/150.
11. A. King, *Urban Warfare in the Twenty-First Century* (Cambridge, 2021).
12. General Staff, 'The Situation in Turkey, 15th March 1920,' NA. CAB. 24/101 f. 315.
13. R. Durán, *Milicias Indígenas en La América Hispana* (Madrid, 2023).
14. *Times*, 30 Mar. 2024.
15. AWM. 3 DRL/6643 3/9, p. 1.
16. C. Philp, *Times*, 17 Mar. 2024.

17. A. Bacevich, *Breach of Trust: How Americans Failed Their Soldiers and Their Country* (New York, 2013).
18. D. Kennedy (ed.), *The Modern American Military* (New York, 2013); A.J. Bacevich, 'The Revisionist Imperative: Rethinking Twentieth-Century Wars,' *JMH*, 76 (2012), pp. 333–42.
19. M. Dunigan and U. Petersohn (eds), *The Markets for Force: Privatization of Security across World Regions* (Philadelphia, Penn., 2015); B.E. Stanley, *Outsourcing Security: Private Military Contractors and U.S. Foreign Policy* (Lincoln, NB, 2015).
20. J. Holland, *Normandy '44. D-Day and the Battle for France* (London, 2019), p. 278.
21. M. Bonura, *Under the Shadow of Napoleon: French Influence on the American Way of Warfare from the War of 1812 to the Outbreak of WWII* (New York, 2012).

Chapter 10

1. Two similar accounts by Worrall, one dated April 1918, the other October 1931, Exeter, CRO. 5277/M/F3/29.
2. P. Hart, *The Heat of Battle: The 16th Battalion Durham Light Infantry – The Italian Campaign, 1943–1945* (London, 1999), pp. 201–2.
3. See, for example, E. Gutiérrez, 'Stephen Crane, *The Red Badge of Courage* (1895)', https://www.hoover.org/research/stephen-crane-red-badge-courage-1895.
4. R. Wooster, *The United States Army and the Making of America. From Confederation to Empire, 1775–1903* (Lawrence, KS, 2021).
5. T, Cook, *Vimy: The Battle and the Legend* (London, 2017); M. Uyar and S. Güvenç, 'One Battle and Two Accounts: The Turkish Brigade at Kunu-ri in November 1950,' *JMH*, 80 (2016), pp. 1117–47.
6. A. Smith, *Inquiry into the Nature and Causes of the Wealth of Nations* (London, 1776), pp. 699, 708.
7. R.M. Smuts, *Political Culture, the State, and the Problem of Religious War in Britain and Ireland, 1578–1625* (Oxford, 2023); F. Carvalho, *Natives, Iberians, and Imperial Loyalties in the South American Borderlands, 1750–1800* (London, 2022).
8. T.E. Rodgers, 'Billy Yank and G.I. Joe: An Exploratory Essay on the Socio-political Dimensions of Soldier Motivation,' *JMH*, 69 (2005), pp. 93–121.
9. R. Herrera, *For Liberty and the Republic: The American Citizen as Soldier, 1775–1861* (New York, 2015).
10. D.A. Carter, *Forging the Shield: The U.S. Army in Europe, 1951–1962* (Washington, 2015).
11. BL. Add. 50101 f. 8, 16, 19–21.
12. NA. WO. 33/2819, p. 26.
13. Monash to his wife, Hannah, 30 May 1915, AWM. 3 DRL/2316 1/1, p. 72.
14. M.P. O'Connor, 'The vision of soldiers: Britain, France, Germany and the United States observe the Russo-Turkish War,' *War in History*, 4 (1997), pp. 257–75.
15. Hely-Hutchinson, 22 Nov. 1806, 59282; Graham to Fitzroy, Lord Raglan, commander of British land forces sent to Black Sea, 8 May 1854, BL. Add. 59282 f. 76–81, 79696 f. 129; George Frederick Koehler, after visiting Turkish empire, to James Bland Burges, Under Secretary in Foreign Office, Bod. Bland Burges papers, 36 f. 99–100; Koehler to Burges, 10 Jan. 1793, NA. FO. 78/14 f. 7.
16. *Notes on the Turkish Army* (London, 1915), pp. 3, 5; E.J. Erickson, *Ottoman Army Effectiveness in World War I* (London, 2007).
17. NA. WO. 33/1493, p. 3.

18. V. Shirogorov, 'Quo Vadis? The Military Revolution in Eastern Europe,' in J. Black (ed.), *Global Military Transformations: Change and Continuity, 1450–1800* (Rome, 2023), p. 385.
19. BL. Add. 49964 f. 10, 34.
20. J.M. McCaffrey, *American Soldiers' Lives; The Army in Transformation, 1790–1860* (Westport, Conn., 2006). See also, I. Germani, *Dying for France: Experiencing and Representing the Soldier's Death, 1500–2000* (Montreal, 2023).
21. NAS. GD. 26/9/513/16.
22. J.S. Reed, 'The Infantry's "Problem of Quality": Classification and Assignment to MOS 745, Rifleman, 1942–1945,' *JMH*, 88 (2024), pp. 83–116.
23. *Times*, 19 April 1945.